BULLS, BEARS & GOLDEN CALVES

Applying Christian Ethics in Economics

JOHN E. STAPLEFORD

Foreword by
Francis X. Tannian

InterVarsity Press
Downers Grove, Illinois

InterVarsity Press
P.O. Box 1400, Downers Grove, IL 60515-1426
World Wide Web: www.ivpress.com
E-mail: mail@ivpress.com

InterVarsity Press® is the book-publishing division of InterVarsity Christian Fellowship/USA®, a student movement active on campus at hundreds of universities, colleges and schools of nursing in the United States of America, and a member movement of the International Fellowship of Evangelical Students. For information about local and regional activities, write Public Relations Dept., InterVarsity Christian Fellowship/USA, 6400 Schroeder Rd., P.O. Box 7895, Madison, WI 53707-7895, or visit the IVCF website at <www.ivcf.org>.

Cover illustration: Chigmaroff/Davison/Superstock

ISBN 0-8308-2680-7

Printed in the United States of America ∞

Library of Congress Cataloging-in-Publication Data

Stapleford, John E., 1946-
  Bulls, bears & golden calves: applying Christian ethics in economics / John E.
Stapleford; foreword by Francis X. Tannian.
      p. cm.
  Includes bibliographical references.
  ISBN 0-8308-2680-7 (pbk.)
    1. Economics—Religious aspects—Christianity. 2. Christian ethics. I. Title: Bulls,
bears, and golden calves. II. Title

BR115.E3 S82 2002
241'.64—dc21

                                                                    2001051796

| P | 19 | 18 | 17 | 16 | 15 | 14 | 13 | 12 | 11 | 10 | 9 | 8 | 7 | 6 | 5 | 4 |
| Y | 17 | 16 | 15 | 14 | 13 | 12 | 11 | 10 | 09 | 08 | 07 | 06 | 05 | | | |

Contents

SECTION I – Laying the Foundation

SECTION II – Reflections on the Basic Assumptions of Economics

SECTION III – Macroeconomic Issues

SECTION IV – Microeconomic Issues

SECTION V – International Issues

Foreword

What will you do with your life? That question and your answers are important. Evidence suggests that what you do with your own life and how well you perform will be influenced greatly by how well you can think.

Ethics and economics are the ground-level topics of this book. Both ethics and economics emerged over hundreds of years as branches of philosophy. Each is a complex system of thinking, and over time barriers have been put in place to keep these two fields of thought separated. Increasingly in the past fifty years economists, along with thinkers in other disciplines, felt they could improve their analytical reliability by cutting out many of the complications raised by ethics, but in fact, ethics and economics treat the same basic subject matter: how human beings make choices.

Most economists play down or omit altogether any evaluation of whether choices are good or bad for persons or for nations. In fact, words like *good, bad, right* and *wrong* are seldom found in economic analysis. For example, when time, money and other resources are combined to produce a service like healthcare, economists usually are little concerned about whether this "ought to" have happened, whether such a service is good or bad. Instead, economists determine whether the preferences of the people who wind up paying for the health services (benefits) match the value of the resources used up (costs) to produce these services. Economic thinking looks at healthcare as one among many costly services. To say that healthcare is somehow a "better" service is not within the range of economics. But such questions are central to the field of ethics.

The influence and popularity of economics as a way to think about the choices people make have been expanding. The nightly news will rarely come to a close without some discussion of job markets, unemployment, oil price shifts or some agency's proposal to spend more tax resources on the environment. The president of the United States is charged by law to make an annual economic report. No such charge is made that she or he provide an annual report on the ethical state of the union.

Ethics, specifically Christian ethics, remains largely hidden from public view and discussion. Ethics attempts to create a coherent and systematic exposition of values intended to guide personal conduct and character. What are the *objective* values we must live by? What are standards of good and bad personal behavior? Are these standards of good and bad behavior merely *subjective,* up to each one of us to select? These questions are the basic stuff of ethics.

Greek philosophers tackled these questions over two thousand years ago. They thought that a knowledge of the self was central to an excellent life. By contrast, an unexamined life was simply not worth living. The Greeks held that certain qualities of personal behavior—prominent among them temperance, courage and wisdom—lead to a harmonious life. These qualities became their standards of "good" behavior. Intemperance, cowardice and thoughtlessness broke down families and communities, and were thus objectively "bad."

Aristotle took this thinking a bit further. Among all creatures human beings are special. They have a life force called a soul and the ability to reason. People seek to gain honor, pleasure and wealth, and make mistakes of excess—taking their desires too far in some actions—or deficiency—not doing enough to achieve harmony. Virtue—the habits of the will—helps us to seek a "golden mean." The virtue ranked ahead of all others is wisdom, the joint exercise of our will and our highest human quality, reason.

In the same relative corner of the world and at the same time the people of Israel introduced the Decalogue, or Ten Commandments, a set of standards given by God through them to all humankind. We are to honor God. We are not to steal our neighbor's goods or spouse. Not to tell the truth is "bad" behavior, while giving support to parents is "good." Most violations of these Ten Commandments have been branded improper by cultures throughout the world. Many students of ethics also have reasoned that the norms of the Ten Commandments are embedded in human nature, so much so that these norms can be considered a natural law.

Jesus Christ came into a world where both Greek ethical thought and the divinely revealed Ten Commandments were present. And some of what Christ said was a jolt to both Greek and Jewish thinking. Saint Paul wrote that Christ's views would be considered "foolishness" by the Greek mind, and his actions and words would be shocking and offensive to the people of Israel. Christianity was (and is) a radical turn of spiritual and ethical outlook; according to Jesus neither the rules of the Decalogue nor the highest human thoughts are complete or adequate for salvation, which comes instead by God's grace through Jesus. To the question asked by the Greeks—"What is the greatest good?"—the Christian responds "spiritual regeneration": a redirection of our wills and the redemption of individual persons of all ranks.

This outlook is different from secular perfection and rational enlightenment. Over and above the science, knowledge and virtuous conduct prized by the classical Greeks or the standards of any time stand the virtues of

☐ faith in and dependence on God,

☐ hope in his promises and mercy,

☐ and above all else love for him and for each other person.

These are the norms of Christian ethics.

Historians such as Paul Johnson in his book *Modern Times* have noted the inhumane record of human actions of the twentieth century. Persons with decidedly anti-Judeo-Christian ethics like Adolf Hitler, Joseph Stalin, Pol Pot and Mao Zedong murdered millions of people. No prior century can match the "bad" behavior—the unsurpassed brutality— of the twentieth.

Strangely enough, this same time period was one of unparalleled inventiveness. From the standpoint of economic analysis, where trends in the material well-being of persons are points of reference, this murderous century probably set high performance records. New and expanded products, the fruits of investments made in agriculture, engineering and science, and exchange between many regions and nations have improved personal health and longevity in most parts of the world.

That record levels of economic performance have attended to such extensive human atrocities raises questions. Have we possibly paid too little attention to ethics? Would it be wise now in this new century to consider the relationships between economic analysis and our value (ethics) systems? The content of this book moves in that direction.

This book presents ideas and values expressed in the Bible and by Christian thinkers, and then uses these values or standards to interpret topics regularly addressed by economic analysis. A few examples of such topics are (1) economic growth, (2) the payment of interest to lenders and (3) the supply and demand for pornography. Readers are urged and invited to expand their understanding of both Judeo-Christian ethical principles and economic analysis, to consider the what and the why in the choices they make.

Francis X. Tannian
professor emeritus of urban economics, University of Delaware

Acknowledgments

First and foremost, this book could not have been produced had I not been employed at Eastern College. Eastern encourages its faculty to examine their disciplines, and all of life, from a Christian perspective. The integration of faith with scholarship is encouraged and respected.

William Pollard, CEO of ServiceMaster Corporation, provided a grant that helped to underwrite many of the initial research expenses. The U.S. Association of Christian Economists and the Christian Business Faculty Association helped to advance the work through their publication of both my papers and book reviews. Thanks go to the U.K. Association of Christian Economists for the invitation to present at Oxford University the paper that became the basis of my book proposal.

At Eastern College I am particularly indebted to Dr. Eloise Meneses for her insights and her belief in the project and to Dr. David Fraser for opening the gate that initiated my exploratory efforts with respect to the relationship between Christian ethics and economics. Dr. Jack Bower and all my other colleagues in the Department of Business have been supportive and enthusiastic throughout.

Dr. Douglas Vickers, professor emeritus of economics, University of Massachusetts, Amherst, was extremely generous with his time, reading drafts of early papers and sharing his thoughts on spiritual issues. A number of his books helped to frame and develop the contents of this text. Dr. Francis X. Tannian, professor emeritus of urban economics, University of Delaware, read through early drafts of the text and gave detailed comments and suggestions. His combination of spiritual depth and grasp of economics were most valuable. Dr. Bertram Levin, professor emeritus of economics, University of Delaware, also read through an early draft of the text and helped to focus its economic content.

Randy Peterson edited the entire text and immensely improved its readability. He brought a wonderful writing talent and solid Christian perspective to the project.

Persons who should be singled out at InterVarsity Press include Dr. Gary Deddo.

Special thanks go to the sharing group to which my wife and I have belonged for over two decades for their prayers and enthusiasm. Finally, hugs to my wife Linda and to my children—Tom, Liza and Cathy—for their love and prayers over the years.

Introduction

The objective of this book is to help the reader to apply Christian thinking to economic issues. Issues addressed range from the most fundamental assumptions underlying modern economics to society's placid acceptance of the legitimization and growth of immoral and spiritually destructive activities such as pornography.

The book assumes that ethics are inexorably intertwined with economic life and analysis. Ethics, whether transmitted through culture, religion or simply habit, influence the behavior of consumers and producers. Public policies, and their associated objectives, are almost always linked to ethical viewpoints. Lack of ethics such as honesty and trustworthiness can drive transactions' costs so high as to choke off exchange and economic growth.

The book is written from the perspective of Christian ethics—Christian standards of behavior as found in Scripture. God makes it quite clear that we are to know his Word and apply it in our lives (Deut 6:5-9). The greatest commandment, Jesus instructs, is to love the Lord our God with all our heart, soul and mind (Mt 22:36-37). As responsible disciples, we are to apply our minds to all aspects of life, including the economic. We are to wrestle as Christians with the many economic issues that play such a prominent role in the lives of billions of persons.

The book is arranged in five sections. The first section presents a framework of Christian ethics relevant to economics, thus laying the foundation for the Christian analysis in the following sections. Section two outlines Christian reflections on three of the most basic assumptions of market economics: the importance of self-interest, the goal of economic efficiency and the significance of private property rights. Sections three, four and five apply the Christian ethics framework to a series of macroeconomic, microeconomic and international issues.

While the book may be read by persons with little background in economics, it is primarily intended to be a supplemental text to students studying introductory economics. The chapter topics were selected after a thorough examination of the leading textbooks used in teaching principles of economics. Chapters two and three, for example, parallel *McConnell and Brue* chapters one and two, and chapter three (private property rights) accompanies *McConnell and Brue* chapter four. Appendix one shows how the chapters in this book tie into the chapters of many of the leading introductory economics textbooks.

Learning the conceptual frameworks of economics is not easy. Applying Christian ethics to these frameworks adds to the workload. Yet it is a challenge we are obligated to undertake if we have chosen to seek first the kingdom of God. As we toil, let us remember:

Instead of destroying the world,
as he did with Noah,
He destroyed the Old Adam in you.
Instead of drowning a false god,
    as he did with Pharaoh,
He drowned the idolatry within you.
Instead of taking you out of the land of darkness,
    as he did for the people of Israel,
He blotted out the darkness in your own heart
    and provides the light,
        the light of the Spirit of God,
            the light of Jesus Christ,
                the light of the world.

—Pastor Richard Ross[1]

1

GRID WORK
A Theological &
Ethical Framework

Economic life in all its ramifications is of profound ethical significance.
This is so because of scarcity which gives rise to conflict, because of interdependence
which creates mutual obligations, because of the wide range of
values sought through economic activity, and because of the significance for
human life of the economic process itself.

HOWARD BOWEN

Where do economists get their ethical systems?
My answer is: wherever they can find them.

GEORGE STIGLER

It's not the parts of the Bible I don't understand that bother me, but those I do.

MARK TWAIN

SYNOPSIS

Beginning with creation and the Fall, proceeding through the Old and New Covenants, this chapter summarizes what God has to say about our economic lives. In addition to the mandate to care for the poor, God provides directives on everything from private property rights to the accumulation of wealth. As Christians, we are to consider these ethical guidelines as we engage in economic affairs.

What does God have to do with economics? As Christians, should we conduct our economic lives in a particular way?

God has provided many avenues for exploring these questions. Through the death and resurrection of Christ we know we have the indwelling and guidance of the Holy Spirit. Through prayer we have access to God where we can ask him to open our minds to his will and to a greater fullness of life in Christ. We have encouragement and insights from our fellowship with believers. And we have church doctrine, which arose from prayer, study and meditation over the centuries.

Finally, and most important, we have Scripture, which brings us the words "spoken . . . by the holy prophets and the command given by our Lord and Savior through [the] apostles, [with] its origin [not] in the will of man, but by men [speaking] from God as they were carried along by the Holy Spirit" (2 Pet 3:2; 1:21). In quoting from the Psalms, Jesus tells us that David was "speaking by the Holy Spirit" (Mk 12:36). Paul tells us that the "God-breathed" Scripture is "useful for teaching, rebuking, correcting and training in righteousness, so that the people of God may be thoroughly equipped for every good work" (2 Tim 3:16-17). That includes *economic* works.

God makes it quite clear that we are to know his Word and apply it in our lives. In the Old Testament God continually warns the people of Israel of the terrible consequences of not observing his commandments. "But if you do not listen to me and carry out all these commands, and if you reject my decrees . . . I will . . . bring upon you sudden terror, wasting diseases and fever that shall destroy your sight and drain away your life. You will plant seed in vain, because your enemies will eat it. I will set my face against you, so that you will be defeated by your enemies; those who hate you will rule over you, and you will flee even when no one is pursuing you" (Lev 26:14-17). If we forsake the Lord, he will forsake us, leaving us exposed and ever fearful. And while he brings us grace, Jesus did not come to destroy the Law or the Prophets, but to fulfill. He warns that whomever breaks even one of the least of the commandments shall be called least in the kingdom of heaven (Mt 5:17-19). "If you love me," Jesus states, "you will obey what I command" (Jn 14:15).

But we have promises as well as warnings. Jesus says that "everyone who hears these words of mine and puts them into practice is like a wise man who built his house on the rock. The rain came down, the streams rose, and the winds blew and beat against that house; yet it did not fall, for it had its foundation on the rock" (Mt 7:24-25). Throughout Scripture, the emphasis is not just on revering God's Word, but obeying it. James calls us to be doers of the word and not hearers only (Jas 1:22).

Thus it is clear that Christians should live biblical lives, obeying the teachings of God's Word. Does this apply only to religious activities? Of course not. The Bible encompasses a broad range of human activities, including economic matters. We are called to seek out and conform to God's prescriptions on these matters as well.

That is what this book attempts to do: to explore biblical teaching on a variety of economic issues. Later chapters will discuss specific issues, but this chapter presents a broad framework. Obviously the Bible doesn't mention microwaves or micromanagement, downsizing, stock options or TV commercials. But it does offer a grid for Christian behavior that can help us evaluate and organize our actions in a host of modern situations that the biblical writers never imagined, including the economic decisions we make daily.

As we put together this grid, we'll be able to understand economic theory in a new way. And we'll be able to apply our framework of Christian ethics to any economic issue we encounter. It won't take the place of sound economic analysis, but it will contribute a biblical element to the decisions we make, whether those decisions are for personal conduct, management of a business enterprise or the formulation of government policy.

Ethics is the study of standards of conduct and moral judgement. While it is helpful to apply Christian ethics to particular economic issues where the Bible speaks clearly, our ultimate objective is to develop the capacity to puzzle through the Christian ethical perspective on any economic issue that might arise. This ethical framework becomes a toolkit that we can carry into the workplace, the town council meeting and the church finance committee's deliberations.

As we construct our grid of biblical economic ethics, we'll follow a theological outline. Christian ethics are grounded in Christian theology, the study of God (*theos,* God; *logos,* discourse). Since our Christian behavior is inspired by and rooted in our relationship with God, we should be able to determine some elements of Christian ethics from the nature of God, as revealed in Scripture. Even when the Bible doesn't prescribe specific behavior, we can still model our lives after the God it describes. So let's consider the biblical record of God's major revelations of himself to us, from creation through the Fall to the Old and New Covenants, and see what we can learn.[1]

One God

"Hear, O Israel: the LORD our God, the LORD is one!" (Deut 6:4). Men and women are to worship God, and God alone. Idols are forbidden. We are to obey his commandments. The New Testament confirms this commitment. Christians are invited into a personal relationship with God, acknowledging, worshiping, praising, communicating with and submitting to him. No one can serve two masters, Jesus said. We should rely on God rather than on material possessions; to do otherwise is idolatry. If we seek first the kingdom of God, "all these things" (Jesus was talking about food, drink and clothing) "will be given to [us] as well" (Mt 6:33).

The basic monotheism of the Judeo-Christian tradition has broader implications. Modern humanistic thinking, derived from the Age of Reason and the

Enlightenment, holds that all truth is relative, changing with the situation and the culture. But if there's one God, then there are absolute, transcendent values, rooted in his character. There is moral truth. Moreover, God conducts a theocracy, not a democracy. He doesn't survey public opinion to determine the nature of things. What he says, goes. When we truly hear that "the LORD is one," we commit ourselves to learn, understand and, within the limitations of our sinful natures, conduct ourselves according to his absolute values. This encompasses all areas of our lives, including the economic.

Creation and Stewardship

"From him and through him and to him are all things" (Rom 11:36). God breathed life into Adam and gave us free will. Men and women are allowed to make choices and are held accountable for those choices. They are given the intellectual capacity for understanding the order and facts of creation. Men and women are created in the image of God (Gen 1:27). The immense value and dignity of each person is to be upheld and respected in the political, social, cultural and economic spheres, and persons are never to be treated as a means to an end.[2] Money is not to be made from the degradation of people (such as child pornography) nor from the devaluation of human life (such as abortion, infanticide or euthanasia).

Likewise, God created the earth, saw all that he had made, declared that "it was very good" (Gen 1:31) and gave this creation to the people he had made. Adam and Eve (and presumably their descendants) were "to work [the earth] and take care of it" (Gen 2:15). So we have an ethical responsibility to care for the earth even as we use its resources to meet our needs.

Everything belongs to God. "God is the Creator and Sustainer of all life. He has made all things and he intends them to be used to His glory" notes John Sleeman.[3] While we are given dominion over the created order (Gen 1:28), we must never forget that we are "middle managers." We are tenants on this property, ultimately accountable to our Landlord. Scripture makes it clear that individual ownership of property is acceptable and generally encourages effective stewardship (see chapter four). Yet because everything ultimately belongs to God, there are no perpetual rights to property for individuals or institutions.

Through the creation of woman, God recognized humanity's deep need for community: "It is not good for the man to be alone," God said (Gen 2:18). This basic call to community indicates that our stewardship of creation should benefit the family, the community and future generations, not just individuals. And we can also see our stewardship responsibility as both individual and collective (e.g., institutions, government). That is, while we can't assume that our neighbors, bosses or government officials share our view of creation, we believe God holds *them* accountable too, and so we should do all we can to influence them to act with proper stewardship.

The Fall and the Judgment

Even when most of our needs are met, we humans are restless and subject to temptations, the most basic of which is a desire to be like God—to exist forever and to have complete knowledge. That is what got Adam and Eve into trouble. As a result of their free choice to sin in the Garden of Eden, all men and women now live in a fallen world filled with self-centeredness, greed, lust, fear, injustice, disease and natural disasters. The Bible tells us that "all have sinned and fall short of the glory of God" (Rom 3:23). We find that sin poisons our relationships with others and our fellowship with God. We tend to search for security in material possessions, control of nature and power over others.

But not only do we struggle with our own sinful tendencies, we also have to deal with a fallen world. Adam worked in the Garden, so work itself is not bad. Since the Fall, however, human work "now involves an element of struggle and domination."[4] As a result we should look for and expect sin in economic relationships. Some businesses will try to charge the highest price possible regardless of production costs or the ability of people to pay. The desire for money will lead some politicians to sell regulatory advantages for bribes. Special interest groups may feather their own nests while disadvantaging the majority of the public. Some employees will shirk responsibilities and still accept a complete paycheck. Wise Christians will seek to structure their lives and their institutions in ways that recognize and minimize the impact of that sin.

How do we understand the lessons of creation in light of the Fall? While we are responsible to care for the resources of God's creation, we also know we have to use those resources to survive. We are accountable to God for the stewardship of those resources—but also for the stewardship of the individual talents and ingenuity he has given us. People need to be "inventive, prudent, farseeing, hardworking—in order to realize by their obedience to God's call the building up and perfecting of God's kingdom on earth . . . to labor for human progress."[5]

Technological progress from human initiative can be used for both good and evil—and certainly it has in the last three hundred years. It has emancipated millions from the back-breaking toil that barely permitted the majority of humans to survive on a subsistence diet in minimal shelter with illness and death hovering ever at the threshold. Technology has also facilitated philanthropy, reduced physical suffering and allowed the gospel to be taken to more people more ways than ever imagined. On the other hand, technology has also abused the environment, broken down community, developed weapons of mass destruction and served as an instrument for social domination.

A fundamental assumption of economics is the existence of scarcity, the limited supply of resources in creation relative to our unlimited wants due to our fallen human natures. As David Colander states in his introductory text, "The goods available are too few to satisify individuals' desires," and we can not "eliminate scarcity entirely since new wants are constantly developing."[6] Nevertheless, if the righteousness of God is present, there is not scarcity. God promises that if his decrees are followed and his commands obeyed that there will be "rain in its season, and the ground will yield its crops and the trees of the field their fruit . . . and you will eat all the food you want and live in safety in your land" (Lev 26:3-5). Scarcity is not a supply-side problem. From the manna in the wilderness, to the feeding of the multitudes, to the sharing of the church immediately after Pentecost, Scripture shows that if people's hearts are right with the Lord through the Holy Spirit, then through hospitality, charity and the grace of God there will always be sufficiency.

Neither is scarcity intended to be a demand-side problem, a result of "unlimited wants." Consumerism and material envy is the sin of the rich and the poor, a potential ensnarement to both. Jesus calls us to set constraints on our human impulse for acquisition and its concomitant ceaseless striving (Mt 6:25-34). The market economy is not the cause of this ceaseless striving, rather: "Consumerism is a matter of the heart; not the market. . . . Markets by themselves can only create situations for the realization of virtue or vice."[7] "The market mechanism, *per se*, does not disclose anything concerning underlying human motivations, which may be good, bad, or neutral."[8]

The Covenants

As the flood waters receded, God promised Noah that, "though every inclination of [man's] heart is evil from childhood," still he would never again "destroy all living creatures" (Gen 8:21). Reflected here is the grace God ultimately offers to all men and women through the sacrifice of his Son. God's grace is extended to all humankind regardless of their spiritual standing before God. The dignity and the spiritual, emotional and economic condition of all persons is of consequence to God. No person, no group, is to be economically exploited or left in desperate economic deprivation.

God cares about all he has made. The covenant with Noah had implications for the whole earth as well. And, as the apostle Paul describes, God's ultimate plan is that "the creation itself will be liberated from its bondage to decay and brought into the glorious freedom of the children of God" (Rom. 8:21). However, creation, exclusive of man, does not have a soul and is not made in the image of God. Therefore, nature is not to be worshiped. Pantheism is rejected; living souls are of greater merit than nonhuman creation. Each person with a soul destined for everlasting life is by nature superior to nonhuman creation.

In his covenant with the people of Israel, God gave the Law, which provided detailed guidelines for the structure of society (including the family and the state), the division of land, the pattern of work, lending and borrowing, charity (including tithing), treatment of the poor and the administration of justice.[9] He promised the Israelites that obedience to the Law would bring spiritual and material prosperity and disobedience would bring punishment.

Through Jesus Christ and the sending of the Holy Spirit, God's covenant extends beyond the people of Israel to all persons, going beyond the Law to grace. It is made clear that all are intended to be God's people and to love one another. Based upon the ministry, death and resurrection of Jesus, the new covenant allows sinful people to reestablish fellowship with God through the free gift of grace from Christ and the communion of the Holy Spirit. Christ lived and died for all. The new covenant does not abolish the ethical Law, but through the revelation of God in Jesus it requires us to go beyond the Law both behaviorally and spiritually. Those who trust Christ are forgiven for their shortcomings and empowered by the Spirit. We don't trust our works to save us, but we do good works as an offering to God (Eph 2:8-10). While work, sacrifice and death are assured in this world, the Spirit offers love, joy and peace. Individual Christians are instructed to gather together in communities called churches (*ecclesia*) to worship, teach and support one another.

Woven through these covenants are a number of important ethical themes, including charity and community, work, and justice. Christians are to love God, their families and their neighbors. Believers who refuse to provide for their relatives are accused of denying the faith (1 Tim 5:8). And Christ calls us *beyond* our family obligations to show love to our neighbors and even our enemies. As one scholar notes, "Our economic life must recognize this common humanity, providing opportunities to serve God and to serve other human beings. . . . God's household becomes our household, and there are no longer any strangers among us."[10] Inhumanity to others, oppression and exploitation are cases of one brother or sister treating another brother or sister as a mere object, a convenience. Each human life is sacred. "Every person has a right to share in God's provision for mankind for their basic needs of food, clothing and shelter," observes Donald Hay. "These needs are to be met primarily by productive work."[11] Every person should have access to the resources necessary for life. But everyone should also have the opportunity to participate as an accepted member of the community and have access to productive resources for dignified participation in the economy. We must offer charity to those who are in need, particularly because of circumstances beyond their control. Christians are called to support the church and the needy, and should not neglect justice, mercy and faithfulness (Mt 23:23). Both rich and poor are to financially support the church (Ex 30:14; Lk 21:1-2) and that support is to be of the free will (Ex 35:20-29 and Lev 2—3). The church, in turn, is to announce the Good News of the Gospel.

Work

As clearly established through the creation and Fall, men and women have a right and an obligation to work. God's call to work preceded the Fall, but the Fall made work more difficult, and the consequences of *not* subduing and conquering became more dire. "I went past the field of the sluggard; . . . thorns had come up everywhere, the ground was covered with weeds, and the stone wall was in ruins. . . . A little sleep, a little slumber, a little folding of the hands to rest—and poverty will come on you like a bandit and scarcity like an armed man" (Prov 24:30-34). If people are able to work, they are to do so. If they choose not to work, they are to be held accountable. Says the apostle Paul, "If a man will not work, he shall not eat" (2 Thess 3:10).

Work not only satisfies basic needs, it can be a privilege from God. "A man can do nothing better than to eat and drink and find satisfaction in his work. This . . . is from the hand of God" (Eccles 2:24). Why should work bring enjoyment? The creation narrative shows God to be a worker, a diligent laborer. Made in his image, men and women find that it is natural and rewarding, in many cases dignifying, to be engaged in productive work. As a consequence, to deny or deprive others of work is an offense against the image of God in them. This carries various implications. For example, for the right to work to be exercised, the economy must be generating jobs (ideally with multiple possibilities of employment and reward, minimally with jobs that provide an adequate level of sustenance). Economic structures that inhibit employment growth, such as the concentration of economic power (e.g., monopoly or state ownership of the means of production), are to be challenged. Access of individuals to work should not be limited by discrimination (by race, gender, ethnicity, status), favoritism (e.g., political access to public jobs) or lack of competition (e.g., monopsonists or entrenched unions).

God has endowed individuals with differing talents and skills (1 Cor 12; Rom 12). As Douglas Vickers points out, it is then "a shallow myth, a misconception of humanist thought and in no sense a revelatory thought form of the Scriptures, to claim that all men are equal" with respect to economic resources and their standing in secular society.[12] All persons' status before God as sinners is equal. But God allows economic distinctions among persons. "Rich and poor have this in common: the LORD is the Maker of them all" (Prov 22:2). "The LORD sends poverty and wealth; he humbles and he exalts" (1 Sam 2:7). The evidence of God's disposition in this regard appears as early as Genesis 4 where one person is called to be a herder, another a tiller, another a metal crafter, and another a musician. Laborers should be free to organize in order to counterbalance the concentrated power of management, but they should not be jealous of the variations in talents and skills endowed by God.

The economic and ethical consequences are intriguing. Because of variations in supply and demand, different occupations command different levels of remuneration. Due to this (as well as inheritances and other such nonmarket advantages), within societies we find an unequal distribution of income. An unequal distribution of income, together with institutional structures, property rights and physical richness among regions, lead to the accumulation of wealth and the existence of poverty. Reduction in poverty therefore requires, among other things, voluntary charity and special stewardship responsibilities. This charity is to be exercised individually and through the church as a freewill choice. There are some references in Scripture to using the coercive powers of government to redistribute income from the wealthy to the poor (e.g., regulations on gleaning, Joseph's administration of grain in Egypt, the third-year tithe), but nowhere is the goal of an equal distribution of income mentioned. The teachings of the Old Testament and the apostle Paul, though, do make it clear that an important function of government is to ensure justice in the conduct of economic affairs, particularly for the poor and less powerful.

An unequal distribution of talents (and the natural variety of resources among regions) also means that specialization and trade ("trucking and bartering") will facilitate economic growth. Before the industrial revolution, specialization generally led to individualism; however, for modern organizations seeking technical efficiency, specialization makes most productive work a cooperative venture, where individuals join together in a common task. Based upon Scripture, markets and economic institutions should facilitate the exercise and development of individuals' talents and reward them appropriately ("the laborer deserves his wages" [Luke 10:7; Col 4:1]). It is then the individual's responsibility to develop his or her talents (2 Tim 1:6) and to use the talents and the subsequent fruits to the glory of God (1 Cor 10:31).

While sloth is a sin and Christians in whatever they do are to do it heartily, "for the Lord, not for men" (Col 3:23), this is not exhortation to workaholism. For we serve the Lord Christ (Col 3:24) and we are not to turn our work into idolatry. "Do not work for food that spoils, but for food that endures to eternal life, which the Son of Man will give you" (Jn 6:27). For what does it profit a man or a woman to gain the whole world only to lose their soul? Similarly, in the drive for success in the world of work, Christians are not to allow other laborers to be exploited (e.g., dangerous working conditions, the withholding of wages)[16] or tempt laborers to place work before God and his priorities. As established by the law of the sabbath (Ex 20: 8-11), the annual feasts of the Old Testament, and the behavior of Christ, for example, persons have both a right and an obligation to rest. This affords time to enjoy creation, serve others (starting with our families) and spend time in communion with and in corporate worship of God. The strain, therefore, between management and employees occurs in part from the denial of the distribution of talents that God has ordained and in part because many managers have denied the scriptural mandate to justice and equity.

This natural tension between employer and employees, and our Christian obligation to its resolution, is well expressed by the Evangelical Lutheran Church in America: "Employers need competent, committed workers, but this does not necessarily presume respect for the personal lives and needs of individual workers. Individual workers depend on the organization for employment as their means of livelihood, but this does not necessarily presume respect for the organization's interests or goals. Management and employees move toward justice as they seek cooperative ways of negotiating these interests when they conflict."[17]

Poverty and Wealth

Poverty is a part of God's creation until Christ returns. Throughout Scripture God expresses concern for justice toward the poor and we are admonished to act upon it. Christ instructs us, "Do not be afraid, little flock, for your Father has been pleased to give you the kingdom. Sell your possessions and give to the poor. Provide purses for yourselves that will not wear out, a treasure in heaven that will not be exhausted, where no thief comes near and no moth destroys" (Lk 12:32-33). Of particular concern is poverty that results from oppression and calamity, as opposed to poverty emanating from sinful personal choices (e.g., sloth, alcoholism, drug abuse). Benign neglect of poverty is not acceptable for Christians.

Given the unequal distribution of talents among persons and the differential endowment of wealth that results, it would be foolhardy to imagine that Scripture condemns wealth as such. Abraham, David and Solomon were very wealthy men. Job had his wealth restored as a reward for his faithfulness. Through investments wealth allows for the improvement in the material well-being of all persons by facilitating economic growth. Through charity, wealth allows for the relief of poverty.

Wealth, at the same time, is fraught with spiritual dangers. It can easily lead to idolatry, and can lead men and women into "many foolish and harmful desires that plunge [them] into ruin and destruction" (1 Tim 6:9). These desires include covetousness (greed), conspicuous consumption, and self-indulgent, pleasure-oriented hedonism. Most dangerous of all, as shown in Scripture, is that the blessing of wealth has led many people, including God's people, to credit their prosperity to themselves and turn from their worship of God. Pursuit of riches seduce men and women into forsaking their children, denying time to persons who are hurting, cutting ethical corners and denying the very God who is their ultimate purpose of living and salvation. "Command those who are rich in this present world not to be arrogant nor to put their hope in wealth, which is so uncertain, but to put their hope in God, who richly provides us with everything for our enjoyment. Command them to do good, to be rich in good deeds, and to be generous and willing to share. In this way they will lay up treasure for themselves as a firm foundation for the coming age, so that they may take hold of the life that is truly life" (1 Tim 6:17-19).

Wealth includes property, and while ultimately everything belongs to God, in the intermediate term Scripture sanctions individual and institutional property rights. God promised land to Abraham and his descendants. Abraham purchased a burial site for his beloved wife Sarah from the Hittite Ephron and received a deed evidencing his property rights (Gen 23). By forbidding stealing, the Eighth Commandment clearly establishes the right to property, while other Old Testament laws protect private property from damage and negligence. Removing the landmarks that establish property boundaries is clearly forbidden (Deut 19:14; 27:17; Job 24:2; Prov 22:28; Hos 5:10). And other than for delinquent taxes (Rom 13:7), kings may not force a subject to sell property nor can they take a property by force without payment (Ezek 46:18). Also, recall God's punishment of Ahab and Jezebel for stealing the vineyard of Naboth the Jezreelite. Both men and women can own and inherit property, as can communities such as tribes (Num 36:1-12). Gronbacher states: "Human nature requires private ownership for the successful navigation of the material world, for the care of family members and the weak, and for the acquisition of virtue through generosity and good stewardship."[18]

Justice

As God is on the side of the poor, the weak and the oppressed, clearly he wants his people to fight economic injustice. God desires us to recognize and protect the sanctity and rights of the individual. Persons are to be treated equitably. There is to be distributive justice: the universal application of rules without partiality or exception and access for all to economic opportunities and resources. Since final judgment is God's and we ourselves are steeped in sin, forgiveness and redemption are to characterize our personal and economic relationships. Christians are called to be agents of reconciliation.

Liberty is the freedom to do what is right. Our freedom must not impinge on the rights of others. "Any economic system that attempts to force acts of love, such as charitable giving, violates the true nature of love and so commits injustice," says Calvin Beisner. "Charitable giving cannot be compelled."[16] As Craig Blomberg notes, however, "It is one thing to generate income which is then channeled into Kingdom purposes (Lk 16:9; 19:11-27); it is quite another to accumulate and hoard resources which are likely to be destroyed or disappear before being put to good use (Lk 16:19-31; Jas 5:1-6)."[17] This bias against a growing inequality in the distribution of wealth is reflected in the Old Testament traditions of the Jubilee year where debts were forgiven, property was restored to the original owners, and persons who had sold themselves into servitude to satisfy debts were set free. In a democracy, citizens have the right to voluntarily redistribute wealth and provide charity personally as well as through elections and pressure applied to elected officials.

God desires commutative justice in economic affairs (e.g., prices are not just when there is fraud or coercion in the market). Weights and scales are to be honest (Lev 19:35-36; Deut 25:15); a full measure pressed down, shaken together and running over is to be given (Lk 6:38); and currency is not to be debased by inflationary monetary policy or other means (e.g., mixing lead with silver, Is 1:22). Lies and deceit are not to enter into economic transactions (Lev 25:14), nor are bribes (Ex 23:8). Procedural justice requires that contracts and commitments be honored (Lev 19:11-13). Neither consumers, nor borrowers, nor lenders, nor laborers, nor suppliers are to be exploited. Absence of commutative and procedural justice in an economy raises the costs and reduces the frequency of transactions, reducing overall economic well-being.

God also desires justice to restore what is lost when people are wronged economically. In cases of accidental loss the costs of restoration are to be borne partially or fully by the negligent party (Ex 21:33-36; 22:5-8, 10-15). In cases of crimes against property or persons, the perpetrator's punishment may include confession, multiple financial restitution and even death. False accusations generally result in the accuser being made to suffer the penalty associated with the alleged crime (Deut 19:16-19).

Because humans are steeped in sin, we need the state to administer justice, to protect against aggression and to provide for public works (1 Kings 10:9). For the same reason, concentration of civil (and economic) power should be kept limited, with appropriate checks and balances; complete freedom in economic affairs is rejected. As one observer commented, "We are sinners, and our economic life always shows it." The judiciously constrained coercive powers of government are to be used to encourage economic competition and minimize exploitation in product and resource markets (e.g., enforcing antitrust legislation, limiting barriers to entry, guaranteeing the right to collective bargaining).

Christians have the same civic responsibilities as all citizens, and as citizens of the kingdom of God are to bring God's transcendent standards of righteousness and justice into the public square. Christians are to pay their taxes (Rom 13:6-7; Mt 22:15-21). Civil authorities are to be obeyed until they set themselves in opposition to divine law. From a kingdom perspective the individual (and family) takes precedence over the state and the social order.

The End-Time Perspective
With the final victory over Satan following the second coming of Christ, the human struggle for physical survival and wealth will cease. Babylon, the epitome of commerce, whose merchants were the envy of the world, where trade even included the "bodies and souls of men," will be thrown down (Rev 18). The city that wanted a tower that would reach to the heavens, so they could "make a name for themselves" (Gen 11), will be no more. This will mark the defeat of *cosmos*, the world with its systemic evil.

This is not to trivialize the importance of the application of Christian ethics in our daily economic affairs. We all will appear before the judgment throne to answer for our behavior and decisions. Even now, though, our economic behavior and choices today bring direct relief to those who are suffering (Mt 25:35-40), and our witness may be used by the Holy Spirit "to shine light on those living in darkness and in the shadow of death, to guide [their] feet into the path of peace" (Lk 1:79).

Conclusion
We have briefly outlined Christian ethics in economics, guidelines from Scripture for Christian conduct in economic life. Keep in mind that these ethical principles

generally do not describe what is, rather what should be. We have gleaned broad principles from Scripture rather than specific prescriptions for modern issues. Every age has its own understanding of what's acceptable in economic matters, but we always need to weight those temporal notions against God's values. As Timothy Gorringe says, "Where moral systems are relative, [Christian] ethics are valid in every situation and age because they are rooted in the . . . sacred, as absolute."[18]

If Christ is Lord of all of life, then we cannot compartmentalize economics apart from Christian thought. As economists, Christians are to work to bring societal structures into "closer conformity with the scripturally articulated preceptive will of God."[19] We are called by God to stand against injustice, to be concerned for the poor, to preserve the dignity of the individual, to be stewards of God's creation, to avoid the idolatry of materialism, to work to our capabilities and to commit to community through loving our neighbors.

Now that we've developed a minimal outline of a system of biblical ethics for the conduct of Christians in economic activity, the remainder of this text focuses on the application of these ethics. These applications are made first to some of the major underlying assumptions of market economics, then to microeconomic, macroeconomic and international issues. Before we proceed, however, two caveats are in order.

First, while it has its imperfections, the technical structure of mainstream market economics as presented in your principles textbook has unquestionably proven its worth as a body of knowledge. All the jokes about economists aside, increasingly over the past decades applications of mainstream market economics on both the macro and the micro levels have substantially improved economic conditions within the United States and around the world, and for persons from all levels of society. The ethical principles presented here are, in the main, intended to supplement, not substitute for, economic theory. John C. Bennett and others say it well: "Those who represent Christian ethics must recognize the limits of any distinctively Christian guidance for economic institutions. There is no 'Christian economics'; though there are Christian motives and Christian goals and Christian insights into human nature, which should guide Christian thinking about economic life."[20] To ignore or gloss over the existence of serious ethical issues, however, leaves economics disabled at the very core. And this includes Christian challenges to the assumptions that underlie current mainstream economics.

Second, Christian economic ethics establishes some clear objectives and boundaries, but specific policy choices require additional hard reasoning, research and practical application by trial and error. As we struggle with the application of Christian ethics to economic policy let us do so humbly, remembering that in this fallen world we see but a poor reflection and we know only in part (1 Cor 13:12). Our knowledge is limited by our fragmented lives, the imperfection of our faith and our relative cultural experience. This does not discourage us, because we accept our relativities with "faith in the infinite Absolute to whom [they] are subject. With the little faith we have in the faithfulness of God, we can make the decisions of little faith with some confidence, and with reliance on the forgiveness of the sin that is involved in our action."[21] We thus choose involvement in economic affairs with reasoning faith, doing our partial, relative work, speaking the truth with love (Eph 4:15), grateful for the grace that accompanies our limited efforts.

Discussion Questions

1. The first responsibility given to men and women was to care for God's creation. What position should Christians take on environmental issues?

2. God has given each person different gifts and talents. What are the economic implications of this?

3. Because we live in a fallen world, what actions might we expect to characterize economic life? As Christians, what are the most effective ways we can counter the consequences of sin in economic life?

4. What are God's intentions for men and women with respect to work?

5. What are the various types of justice God calls Christians to through the Bible?

2

ME, MYSELF & WHY?

Pursuit of Self-Interest
Promotes What Exactly?

Perhaps Christians have too easily bought into secular ways of thinking about
work and business practices without stopping to ask whether
these practices are really consistent with the morals of their tradition.

SCOTT RAE AND KENMAN WONG

It is false to think that a market economy, if freed from
all government interference, would create what the Bible means by justice.

RON SIDER

SYNOPSIS

*Adam Smith recognized the power of self-interest to contribute to the common good and
also acknowledged the need for it to be constrained through competition, the law and individual morality. Because economic activity occurs in community, it is impossible to discuss
economic theory and policies without some reference to values. Jesus' position on self-
interest is quite clear: whoever desires to come after him must "deny himself and take up
his cross…for whoever desires his life will lose it, but whoever loses his life for [Jesus']
sake will find it" (Mt 16:24-25).*

You were in it to make money?" queries the reporter.

"What the hell is wrong with that?" replies Jeffrey Wigand.

Wigand had been corporate vice president of research for Brown and
Williamson, a major tobacco company. As depicted in the gripping docudrama film
The Insider, Wigand ultimately blew the whistle on the tobacco industry because
simply making money was not enough to ease his conscience. Despite death threats
and a smear campaign, Wigand went public in court testimony and a *60 Minutes*
interview, charging that the tobacco industry is not only in the "nicotine delivery

business," it also uses ammonia and other chemicals to enhance the effects of the nicotine on the central nervous system. What a way to retain customers!

For perjuring themselves and knowingly addicting people to a product that endangers their health and lives, the tobacco industry is settling suits with all fifty states in a payout that may exceed $300 billion.

We learn a lesson here in economics and morality. As represented in the leading textbooks, the classic position of market economics has been understood to go something like this: *the unconstrained pursuit of self-interest will promote the general welfare of society.* Isn't that the basic idea of Adam Smith, architect of capitalism? But the misdeeds of Big Tobacco illustrate what some Christians have long been saying: that we *cannot* trust unconstrained self-interest to help society. According to Wigand, the tobacco companies' craving for money led them to devise ingenious ways to enslave more customers, thereby hurting the welfare of society. From this and other examples, many observers hold that "the unconstrained pursuit of self-interest" actually promotes only self-centeredness, greed, hedonism, materialism and a disregard for others.

Certainly there is some truth in this observation, but that's not the whole story. Before we discard the most powerful known system for the material betterment of humankind, let us take time to be more discerning about its fundamental assumption.

More careful consideration unveils a number of interesting facts. First, Adam Smith himself might have a problem with the notion that unconstrained pursuit of self-interest *always* promotes the general welfare of society. Most economists would agree that this idea needs some tinkering before we make it a fundamental principle. Second, we find that the market economy functions better when it follows what the Bible says, especially what Christ said, about self-interest and kingdom values. Finally, Christians can participate in the market economy, but it requires spiritual discipline and honesty about our own weaknesses if we're going to withstand the many temptations to sinfulness (such as self-centeredness, envy, materialism and hedonism).

The True View of Adam Smith

Of the one million introductory economics textbooks sold each year in the United States, most include the following original "invisible hand" quote from Adam Smith's classic work, *Wealth of Nations.*

> Every individual is continually exerting himself to find out the most advantageous employment of whatever capital he can command. It is his own advantage, indeed, and not that of the society, which he has in view. But the study of his own advantage

naturally, or rather necessarily, leads him to prefer that employment which is most advantageous to the society. . . . He intends only his own gain, and he is in this, as in many other cases, led by an invisible hand to promote an end which has no part of his intention. Nor is it always the worse for the society that it was no part of it. By pursuing his own interest he frequently promotes that of society more effectually than when he really intends to promote it.[1]

This quotation is typically used in introductory textbooks to establish two important economic principles. First, that people can be expected to act out of self-interest. Second, that individual pursuit of self-interest advances rather than diminishes the well-being of society.

However, a careful reading of this paragraph is instructive. One quickly realizes that Smith is referring to an individual's search for the most "advantageous" use of his or her capital, rather than self-interested spending on *all* goods and services. In fact, Smith was discussing specifically the individual's allocation of capital investment in domestic industry as opposed to foreign trade (although he does add the phrase "as in many other cases").

Moreover, Smith was contrasting this mode of individual investment to the specific alternative system whereby policymakers or lawgivers "direct private people in what manner they ought to employ their capitals."[2] Following the famous quote above, Smith adds, "I have never known much good done by those who affected to trade for the public good." In other words, officials who try to manipulate the economy for the benefit of society typically do little to increase the general welfare, especially compared to individual citizens who just try to succeed in business (not an unusual sentiment for a Scotsman who grew up under the arbitrary and often rapacious rule of the British).

But notice the qualifications Smith used. When self-interested individuals seek their own gain in the employment of their capital, Smith says, they unintentionally promote an end that is not "always the worse for the society . . . [but in fact] *frequently* promote [it]." This qualified recognition that social benefits *may* accrue from the self-interested investment of capital is a far cry from the typical claim that unconstrained pursuit of self-interest in all areas of economic activity *always* promotes the general welfare. Nor can the above famous quote be considered a summary of Smith's overall position, because it is the only time in *Wealth of Nations* where he uses the term "invisible hand."[3] (And it should be noted that the term *laissez faire*, denoting a lack of government intrusion into economic affairs, never appears in *Wealth of Nations*.)

Why didn't Smith offer an unqualified blessing of the unconstrained pursuit of self-interest? Because he recognized that human nature may lead persons to act in a manner that is, in fact, to the economic disadvantage of society. In talking about the conduct of ordinary commerce, Smith comments, "People of the same trade seldom meet together, even for merriment or diversion, but the conversation ends in *a conspiracy against the public* or in *some contrivance to raise prices*"[4] (emphasis added). With regard to the compensation of workers, Smith observes, "Masters are always and every where in sort of tacit, but constant and uniform combination, not to raise wages of labour above their actual rate."[5] Smith notes that British manufacturers have used high duties or absolute prohibitions (quotas) to restrain the importation of foreign goods and obtain "either altogether, or very nearly a monopoly against their countrymen."[6] When prices for a particular commodity are rising, he adds, suppliers are "generally careful to conceal this," lest the great profits attract entry and cause prices to be reduced "to the natural price or even below it."[7] "The affluence of the rich," says Smith, "excites the indignation of the poor, who are often both driven by want, and prompted by envy, to invade his possessions."[8]

In the original edition of his first book, *The Theory of Moral Sentiments*, Smith clearly expresses his doubts about the natural virtue of humanity: "Man when about to appear before a being of infinite perfection can feel but little confidence in his own merit or in the imperfect propriety of his own conduct. . . . Repentance, sorrow, humiliation, contrition at the thought of his past conduct, are upon this account, the sentiments which become him. . . . Some other intercession, some other sacrifice, some other atonement, he imagines, must be made for him beyond what he himself is capable of making, before the purity of the Divine justice can be reconciled to his manifold offences."[9] Although himself a Deist (a believer in an external "impartial spectator," "the Author of nature," "the Deity"), Smith's view is in keeping with the Christian position that we are born sinful and that sin is a reality of the human condition. The fruits of the Fall are evidenced by the frequent incidence of greed, selfishness, rapacity, dishonesty and exploitation in the conduct of economic affairs.

Yet Smith rejects the brutish view of humankind advocated by Thomas Hobbes and Bernard Mandeville, stating in Part I of *The Theory of Moral Sentiments* that

> how selfish soever man may be supposed, there are evidently some principles in his nature, which interest him in the fortune of others, and render their happiness necessary to him, though he derives nothing from it except the pleasure of seeing it.[10]

This pity and compassion for the sorrow of others, the joy and gratitude for their deliverance and success, Smith terms "sympathy." While not universal among all persons, generally this sympathy results in humankind being community oriented. Smith observes:

> All the members of human society stand in need of each other's assistance, and are
> likewise exposed to mutual injuries. Where the necessary assistance is reciprocally
> afforded from love, from gratitude, from friendship, and esteem, the society flourishes and is happy. All the different members of it are bound together by the agreeable bands of love and affection, and are, as it were, drawn to one common center of
> mutual good offices.[11]

Yet should this mutual love and affection not flourish, society will still subsist
due to individual self-love (self-interest).

Comparing the theory of human behavior put forward by Smith in *The Theory
of Moral Sentiments* to that in *Wealth of Nations*, economic historian Jeffrey
Young concludes: "The frugal, self-interested man of *Wealth of Nations* is also
the prudent man of *Theory of Moral Sentiments*, and self-interest in both is to be
understood as 'proper regard for self'—that degree of self-love which elicits the
approval of the impartial spectator because it does no harm to others."[12]

That "approval" is a key ingredient of Smith's vision. People care what others
think of them, and it is this desire for the good opinion of others that constrains
people in their pursuit of self-interest. In fact, it is a necessary condition for the
conduct of commerce. Such social reciprocity promotes virtuous conduct, curbing what many feared would be the amoral individualism of a commercial society. This constraint, according to Smith, is reinforced by competition and by the
jurisprudence system, which Smith was writing about at the time of his death.

For Smith competition serves as a major curb on the excesses of self-interest.
The market prices charged by a supplier of commodities and goods are constrained by his or her competition, and the wages paid to laborers are bid up by
competition among buyers. Consequently, Smith was a strong opponent of the
use of the powers of the sovereign to limit entry to markets, including the granting of monopolies to an individual or a trading company and the application of
duties and restrictions on imports. Smith opposed "the exclusive privileges of
corporations, statutes of apprenticeship, and all those laws which restrain, in particular employments, the competition to a smaller number than might otherwise
go into them."[13] Because of the tendency to collusion, Smith even opposed any
regulations such as taxes "to provide for their poor, their sick, their widows and
orphans" that necessitated the assembling of merchants of the same trade.[14]

When the system of natural liberty and free markets prevails, Smith believed,
the sovereign must attend to only three duties: protection of society from foreign

invasion, the erection and maintenance of certain public works, and "duty of protecting, as far as possible, every member of society from the injustice or oppression of every other member of it, or the duty of establishing an exact administration of justice."[15] (We will examine the role of government in more detail in chapter six.) These duties of jurisprudence encompass *remedial* justice, including redress for injury to persons (physical and reputation) and property, and *commutative* justice, centered primarily around laws that protect property rights and encourage equilibrium between the market and the "natural" price (the Scholastic tradition of the "just" price). Smith makes no definitive statement on *distributive* justice; however, after reviewing his various isolated remarks, Jeffrey Young concludes, "Distributive justice emerges as an important concern in his political economy. Smith finds the existing patterns of wealth and income shares far from optimal because of the continuance of mercantilist regulation, certain taxes, and remnants of feudalism in the agricultural sector."[16] Although not a clarion call for a welfare state, Smith's position on jurisprudence and justice reflects an other-regardedness that goes unrecognized by many theologians and Christian critics.

The Current Economic Presentation

Most of the bestselling economics texts, using the "positive-normative" disclaimer (positive economics explains "what is," normative economics "what ought to be"), purport to be value-free, presenting a positive intellectual framework that simply describes how self-interested economic agents act. For example, in their introductory economics textbook, Mansfield and Behravesh state, "Positive economics is science in the ordinary sense of the word. . . . We can, in principle, test propositions in positive economics by an appeal to the facts."[17]

But as we have seen with Adam Smith's work, a value-free interpretation leads to all sorts of abuses. The majority of introductory economics textbooks include Smith's famous "invisible hand" quote, but also defensively state that the pursuit of self-interest does not equate directly to greedy materialism and the unbridled accumulation of wealth.[18] Yet without an understanding of Smith's moral values, they're at a loss to explain why selfishness and greed aren't rampant. While Smith clearly wanted the government to let economic forces do their stuff, he was also assuming that responsible people would "constrain" *themselves* in "the pursuit of self-interest." Smith is building upon a groundwork of values, which we must understand if we're to read him properly.

Economics is obviously about value—the relative worth of this coin to that loaf of bread—but it's also about *values*, and it always has been. What values, traditions, beliefs determine how people interact in economic community? While some might selfishly pursue wealth and hoard it, others use their earnings to support social causes, such as providing prenatal care to poor women. Some executives turn down promotions with high salaries and extreme time commitments in order to spend more time with their families. And certainly not all income goes to consumption and personal savings; in 1998 individual Americans gave an estimated $129 billion to charities and churches. Economic decisions are intertwined with moral decisions.

Because economic activity occurs in community, it is futile to try writing a value-free book on economics. Economist Roger Miller comments:

> Do not get the impression that a textbook author will be able to keep all personal values out of the book. They will slip through. In fact, the very choice of which topics to include in an introductory textbook involves normative economics. There is not a value-free, or objective, way to decide which topics to use in a textbook. The author's values ultimately make a difference when choices have to be made.[19]

In fact, as a matter of course, introductory textbooks cover a wide range of ethical issues. Most introductory textbooks, for example, recognize and briefly discuss such topics as the distribution of income within society, discrimination in the labor market, the fairness of inheritance, air and water pollution, market concentration and the exploitation of consumers and suppliers, the distribution of resources between the private and public sectors, the limitations of Gross Domestic Product as a measure of societal well-being, decision making in the absence of perfect information, and the rights and wrongs of private property rights. Many of these (such as pollution) are readily acknowledged and accepted as failures in the market system, requiring some form of redress.

Economics is commonly defined as the study of the allocation of scarce resources among competing demands. This is a sterile understatement. It presumes that individuals simply weigh the marginal utility (satisfaction) per dollar cost among alternative goods or services, and buy accordingly. It also assumes that firms buy inputs until the last bit of revenue produced just equals the cost of the input and then stop overall production at the point where marginal revenue and marginal costs equate, thus maximizing profit. That definition gets the mechanics right, but not the real stuff behind decision making.

If we want to understand and anticipate the economic behavior of individuals, firms, institutions and government, in order to develop effective economic policy, as economist John Neville Keynes stated a century ago, we need to engage in the "art of economics." The art of economics is the application of the knowledge learned in *positive economics* to the achievement of the goals determined in *normative economics*. It recognizes that in analyzing economic behavior one must take into account historical precedent and social, cultural, legal and political forces.[20]

In most Hispanic neighborhoods in the United States, for example, there is little demand for nursing homes because of a cultural commitment to the extended family and, consequently, care of one's elders. Matzo sales rise during the Jewish Passover. Parents don't charge children for their food (unless they move back home after college). Churches and temples don't restrict their soup kitchens or food banks to persons who are only Christians or Methodists or Baptists or Muslims. Most societies find the selling and buying of body organs repulsive. Fewer divorces occur in areas of the United States and in nations that are predominantly Catholic.

Economist Richard Titmuss discovered a similar moral element in his research on the markets for human blood.[21] In the private blood market of the United States, he found the commercialization of blood and donor relationships repress the expression of altruism, erode the sense of community, lower scientific standards, limit both personal and professional freedoms, legalize hostility between doctor and patient, increase the danger of unethical behavior in various sectors of medical science and practice, and redistribute blood from the poor to the rich as proportionately more blood is supplied by the poor, the unskilled and the unemployed. Compared to the voluntary blood donor market in Great Britain, the commercialized market comes up short in four economic areas: it's wasteful, administratively inefficient, higher priced and lower quality. Titmuss concludes that a proper understanding of how these markets function requires an appreciation for the moral commitment of the individuals who give blood. In other words, not only prices and quantity determine market outcomes, values do also.

Values—such as altruism, community and social cohesion—can play a significant role in the operation of a market, as we see in this smattering of examples. To achieve economically efficient outcomes, one must consider the values of the people involved.

Within mainstream economics today, only *qualified* support is given to the assumption that unconstrained pursuit of self-interest promotes the general welfare of society. An economy is not a machine that hums along, following fixed patterns; there are people involved. Still, with those qualifications, we can affirm Adam Smith's general idea. Voluntary exchange among self-interested individuals within a price system *is* a powerful mechanism for producing wealth and promoting economic well-being, but it is important to recognize its limitations and dangers.

Let us now consider what the Bible has to say about the pursuit of self-interest and the general welfare.

A Biblical Perspective

From the Garden of Eden onward, we see people driven by self-interest. What does the Old Testament have to say about a regard for others? After the commitment to one's spouse(s) and family, the Old Testament makes it clear that God's people have a special responsibility for others, specifically the widow, the orphan, the poor, the oppressed and the stranger. Other than for idolatry, no other sin so frequently kindles God's wrath and prompts his punishment as the neglect of the needy. Still, the accumulation of wealth is not condemned; in fact, it is frequently taken as evidence of God's special blessing for the individual, family or tribe. But God does require generosity, especially from the wealthy. (This is covered in more detail in chapter nine.)

In the New Testament the position of Jesus is quite clear as well. When asked to name the greatest commandment in the Law, Jesus replies, "'Love the Lord your God with all your heart and with all your soul and with all your mind.' This is the first and greatest commandment. And the second is like it: 'Love your neighbor as yourself.' All the Law and the Prophets hang on these two commandments" (Mt 22:36-40). Jesus consistently calls us to fulfill the Old Testament Law and go beyond it. Who is our neighbor? Not just the special persons identified by God to the people of Israel, but everyone with whom God may bring us into contact, including the outcast (the leper, the Samaritan) and even our enemies!

Jesus states that if anyone desires to come after him he must "deny himself and take up his cross. . . . For whoever wants to save his life will lose it, but whoever loses his life for me will find it. What good will it be for a man if he gains the whole world, yet loses his soul? Or what can a man give in exchange for his soul?" (Mt 16:24-26). This business of dying to self is serious: a trade-off between the things of the world (e.g., material goods, power, prominence and achievement) and our very souls.

Does this mean that Jesus is unaware of our basic physical needs? No, he just wants us to get our priorities straight.

> Do not worry about your life, what you will eat or drink; or about your body, what you will wear. Is not life more important than food, and the body more important than clothes? Look at the birds of the air, they do not sow or reap or store away in barns, and yet your heavenly Father feeds them. Are you not much more valuable than they? Which of you by worrying can add a single hour to his life? And why do you worry about clothes? See how the lilies of the field grow. They do not labor or

spin. Yet I tell you that not even Solomon in all his splendor was dressed like one of these. If that is how God clothes the grass of the field, which is here today and tomorrow is thrown into the fire, will he not much more clothe you, O you of little faith? So do not worry, saying, "What shall we eat?" or "What shall we drink?" or "What shall we wear?" For the pagans run after all these things, and your heavenly Father knows that you need them. But seek ye first his kingdom and his righteousness, and all these things will be given to you as well. (Mt 6:25-33)

Jesus is calling us to an "enlightened" self-interest. He does not mean the "enlightened" self-interest where restraining from evil impulses and performing external deeds of righteousness brings the utilitarian praise of our peers.[22] Rather, he calls us to a genuine refocusing of our internal and external lives to his kingdom. Don't store your treasures on earth where moth and rust destroy; store your treasures in heaven (Mt 6:19-20). Jesus realizes we are concerned about our own well-being and we are certainly instructed to provide for the needs of our families (1 Tim 5:8), but he wants us to direct our energies to the best, the most secure and permanent ends. Jesus doesn't ask us to set aside our self-interest; he just wants to keep us from making a poor investment. "Jesus is not asking us to give up the idea of abundance and quality of life. He is rather calling upon us to relocate the sphere in which we search for it."[23] Jesus tells us, "Do not be afraid, little flock, for your Father has been pleased to give you the kingdom. Sell your possessions and give to the poor. Provide purses for yourselves that will not wear out, a treasure in heaven that will not be exhausted, where no thief comes near and no moth destroys" (Lk 12:32-33).

What is this kingdom of God (also called the kingdom of heaven)? Simply put, God's kingdom is "righteousness, peace and joy in the Holy Spirit" (Rom 14:17). It was made available to us through Christ's incarnation, death and resurrection. We have occasional fleeting experiences of the kingdom within us during those times when we truly allow God to reign in our lives, and it will be established for eternity in the new heaven and the new earth following Christ's return. In the Lord's Prayer we pray for the final coming of God's kingdom; and, urged on and led by the Holy Spirit, we continue to work daily to actuate the kingdom on this earth.

The prophet Isaiah tells us that in this new heaven and new earth we will "be glad and rejoice forever. . . . Jerusalem [will] be a delight and its people a joy. . . . The sound of weeping and of crying will be heard . . . no more. Never again will there be . . . an infant who lives but a few days, or an old man who does not live out his years. . . . Before [my people] call I will answer; while they are still speaking I will hear" (Is 65:17-25). According to the prophet Micah, "Nation will not take up sword against nation, nor will they train for war anymore. Every man will sit under his own vine and under his own fig tree, and no one will make them afraid" (Mic 4:3-4).

The kingdom of God sets us free from bondage to the gods of our sinful desires in this life. Through the Spirit we are released from the lusts of the flesh and made alive with Christ. We are no longer enslaved by the notion that certain things belong to us and that our survival is linked to maintaining these possessions or securing the benefits that the world provides.[24] It is for freedom that Christ has set us free.

How does this work? How can we practice this freedom from possessions in our daily lives? In Mark 10:29-30 Jesus assures us that anyone who has left house or land or family or friends for the gospel will receive a hundredfold of the same *now in this time*. Is that possible? We get some insight from a Mennonite pastor named Virgil Vogt, whose family is committed to the practice of simple living as a means of bearing witness to their faith. He relates how his family, despite the lack of a car or a vacation home, through their brothers and sisters in Christ always had a car available to them and homes open to them throughout the country. Vogt explains:

> Within [the] covenant circle there are a whole new set of relationships. Other believers become our brothers and sisters, and our lives are linked with them in a profound way. Their houses become ours and our houses theirs. Thus through the love and sharing of believers, we experience the reality of this promise—we have houses and lands a hundredfold. As sons and daughters of the Kingdom we have access to all the resources of the Kingdom's citizens. The hundredfold houses and lands spoken of by Jesus are received as a gift from God given to those who are not seeking houses and lands. They are seeking the Kingdom. Furthermore, the abundance of the Kingdom is maintained without our clinging to it or trying to protect it.[25]

It seems clear that the manifestation of the kingdom of God in this world requires active community. (In fact, because love of neighbor is inseparable from the love of God, the Catholic church's official doctrine states that the Christian life requires living in community.) For Christians to exchange with others, mutual service and dialogue are not an extraneous addition but a requirement. As the apostle Paul instructs, "Each of you should look not only to your own interests, but also to the interests of others. Your attitude should be the same as that Christ Jesus" (Phil 2:4-5).

Despite the superiority of the market system of economy in generating wealth, many Christian pastors, theologians and leaders express discomfort with it; its emphasis on individualism and self-interest seems to take the focus off community and perhaps even renders community more difficult. Relationships in markets are viewed as coldly calculating ("What's in this for me?"), transient, and superficial, where humans even prey on each other. Governments and other associations are simply voluntary contracts among atomistic individuals who join together because it is in their self-interest to do so. Institutions are collections of self-interested individuals who, when the institution no longer generates for them benefits greater than costs, will quickly cast it aside and move on. There is no commitment to the common good.

Can the kingdom of God be reconciled to the market economy? Of course, if we are willing to live with imperfection. As Michael Novak says, "At the heart of Judaism and Christianity is the recognition of sin, as at the heart of democratic capitalism is a differentiation of systems designed to squeeze some good from sinful tendencies."[26] To move forward constructively we must take into account both the sin in ourselves and the weaknesses, irrationalities and evil forces pervasive in the world, and disbelieve any promises that "the world now or ever will be transformed into the City of God."[27] There will be a New Jerusalem, but our earthly Babylon will first be destroyed.

Consequently, the market system is most productive when it is undergirded by moral values such as trust, honesty, obligation and cooperation, and as Adam Smith recognized, it may in fact break down (together with society) if it is not. These, we should note, are historically biblical values. Property rights, for example, would be impossible to enforce unless people have some respect for the rights of others or an appreciation of the golden rule (Mt 7:12).[28] Ethics and moral consensus are key factors in generating economic value. Without moral consensus, transaction costs would be so high that market exchange and economic growth would be seriously impeded, perhaps even impossible. In commenting on Max Weber's Protestant work ethic, James Buchanan observes that "a society whose members share the Puritan virtues, no matter what the source or for what reason, will be economically more successful than the society in which these virtues are absent or are less widely shared."[29] Those "Puritan virtues" aren't just about hard work, as some might think, but generosity, honesty and teamwork as well.

What's more, our legal system is built on an understanding of human sin. We count on the government to curb and remediate the excesses of human nature in economic affairs. Fines and prison sentences are levied for price fixing and false representation of products. Antitrust action is taken to prevent or ameliorate the accumulation of market power by firms. Inheritance laws and taxes limit the intergenerational accumulation of wealth by individuals or within families. ("Woe to you," says Isaiah, "who add house to house and join field to field till no space is left" [Is 5:8].) We have three branches of government (executive, legislative and judicial) because we are a government of fallen people, not angels. All of this underscores the connection between a successful free-market economy and values, especially Bible-inspired values . . . that are held by individuals and the community at large.

Conclusion

The notion that unconstrained pursuit of self-interest promotes the general welfare of society has never been an unqualified basic assumption of market economics. Markets fail, people can behave disreputably and even cruelly, and extramarket factors such as historical precedent and social, cultural, religious, legal and political forces frequently influence economic decisions. Nevertheless, pursuit of self-interest can have a healthy effect on society, within the confines of competition, a jurisprudence system that maintains remedial and commutative justice, a government system that ensures every person access to the resources necessary for life and access to the productive resources for dignified participation in the economy, and general consensus on transcendent values.

Until a more productive and democratic economic arrangement is identified, Christians can and should participate in the market economy. However, our pursuit of self-interest is to be "enlightened," as we seek first the kingdom of God. The universality of human sinfulness is to be taken seriously and anticipated through the structuring of institutions and government, the legal system and even personal accountability groups. But there is no reason to throw the baby out with the bath water. Nash observes: "Competition can lead individuals and organizations to act in ways that are dishonorable or dishonest. But these problems are simply another manifestation of original sin. They do not demonstrate that there is anything wrong with competition itself. Competition often has beneficial social consequences by affording people ways of resolving conflicts over some scarce goods in a nonviolent way...providing better goods and services at the lowest possible price."[30] When it comes to improving the economic human condition, nothing has proven superior to the market economy.

Like Jeffrey Wigand of the movie *The Insider*, we often struggle with the freedoms afforded in our market economy. While the profit motive and relative prices can help an economy produce goods and allocate resources efficiently (meeting human needs, providing jobs, etc.), we also see that these advantages can be offset by the all-too-apparent weaknesses of our human natures: jealousy, selfish ambition, greed, arrogance, envy, stealing and lying. Sometimes it seems that the market *encourages* these vices. But Christ is at work within us through the Holy Spirit, transforming us, and helping us put aside these self-destructive weaknesses of our flesh. We're not perfect, but we can strive to act righteously within a system that accommodates both vice and virtue.

Christians are called to be the salt of the earth, the light of the world, the leaven that spreads through the whole lump of dough. This applies to our economic lives as well as to other areas. Christians are not free to ransack the environment, exploit customers or suppliers, work in markets selling pleasure-oriented hedonism or put profit before the health of employees. This discipline is not easy. When we are in our daily routines, we can become immersed in our institutions or occupations, and we often forget to step back and question whether our goals and actions are in accord with our ultimate goal of the establishment of God's kingdom. To do this requires time in prayer, communion with God through the Holy Spirit, meditation on Scripture and participation in Christian community. But the rewards are love, joy, goodness and peace now and for eternity. That is "enlightened" self-interest, which benefits us as individuals, as well as our families and society.

Discussion Questions

1. What is the difference between self-interest and selfishness? Why is this distinction important when considering the competitive market economy as appropriate for a society?

2. Does your textbook present only positive economics and avoid any normative economics? If not, give some examples of normative issues covered in your textbook.

3. According to Adam Smith, what serves to curb self-interest in an economy?

4. What does it mean to seek the kingdom of God in a democratic capitalist economy? How can it be done?

3

WASTE NOT?

Reappraising the Goal
of Economic Efficiency

Economists have seldom spent much time exhorting individuals
to higher motives or more exemplary conduct. . . . Day in and day out for the
economist the society's problems are usually problems of efficiency.

GEORGE STIGLER

Economists need to pay much closer attention to the social and
cultural fabric of a system than they often do.

JAMES HALTEMAN

SYNOPSIS

Economic efficiency, where society achieves the maximum output (wealth) and the combination of goods and services buyers prefer, is a goal of most Western nations. Some other nations and cultures, however, put their primary emphasis on other goals, including justice, particularly in the distribution of resources and benefits; social relationships of all types; and the pursuit of spirituality. Ultimately, for a Christian the only true priority is humility, our recognition of our ultimate dependence upon God. Giving first place to anything else would be idolatry.

In *The Graduate*, Dustin Hoffman appears as a young man who's unsure about his future. In one classic scene an older man, a guest at his college graduation party, whispers in his ear: "One word: *plastics*."

Considering that the movie was made in the 1960s, the comment was fairly prophetic. The young man would have done well if he had gone into plastics manufacturing. But of course he was looking for more than a paycheck. In the story, he was on a deeply personal journey of self-discovery, and that's why the "one word" is so funny in that movie. "Plastics" represents everything he *doesn't* want out of life.

Every decade or so there's a new phrase whispered in the ears of enterprising young men and women. "Silicon chips." "Stock market." Now it's "Internet." There is always a brand new frontier to roam, with seemingly endless possibilities.[1]

Among students of economics, the whispered words are a bit more obscure, for example, "efficiency." Every basic textbook lists efficiency as one of the major goals of economic policy—achieving the maximum output with the available resources and technology. That's the ideal. No dormant factories. No wasted resources. No workers sitting around playing cards. The economy hums like a well-oiled machine. Whether you're making plans for the whole society or for particular industries or companies, it is assumed that economic efficiency is the pathway to the pot of gold at the end of the rainbow.

However, it may not be all it is supposed to be. While textbooks focus on efficiency, they spend much less space on *consumption,* or *economic, efficiency* and even less on issues of social justice. *Consumption* or *economic efficiency* assume the existence of technical efficiency, entail maximum output and regard the allocation of goods and services. Will people have access to what they want, when they want it and at a price they can afford? Is the economy producing the mix of goods and services people prefer given their incomes? Certainly a quest for economic efficiency is more people-centered than simply maximization of output *(technical efficiency),* but even that does not ensure social justice. How can we make sure that people have fair access to jobs, wages, resources, training and products? For the economics student with a deeper sense of calling, hearing the steady whisper of "economic efficiency" is unsatisfying.

Introductory economics textbooks, such as by N. Gregory Mankiw of Harvard, recognize this dilemma. "Efficiency," says Mankiw, "is the property of a resource allocation of maximizing the total surplus received by all members of society." Efficiency, however, does not insure equity, "the fairness of the distribution among the members of society."[2]

Christians live in many different cultures and thus encounter many different economic choices. All choices involve tradeoffs, and cultures are not neutral on what should be traded for what. Cultures prioritize values and socialize their members to neglect some areas of life for others. In many cultures, Christians can recognize that the priorities being pushed are essentially false gods.

Although it is not always acknowledged, the selection of economic efficiency as a major policy goal is a value choice. Textbooks claim to be neutral, and the possible tradeoff between efficiency and equity (the "fair" distribution of resources within society) may be acknowledged. Nonethelesss, the vast majority of the economic theory presented is focused upon maximizing wealth and consumption in society. You don't need to buy it. That might be a core value of Western culture, but it's not a Christian one. We serve a different God.

The assumption of economic efficiency as a primary objective for economic policy can, therefore, be criticized for at least two reasons. First, it is a culturally narrow view that has limited applicability outside the developed Western world. Materialism, particularly, is not universally accepted; many non-Christians as well as Christians reject it. It is inappropriate to apply the Western assumptions concerning personal consumption and accumulation of material things to the economies of other cultures.

Second, Christians understand that, just like many other cultural objectives, the drive for economic efficiency can lead to idolatry.

Somewhere in the guts of your TV set, there are probably several knobs that change the quality of the picture you see: color, tint, contrast, brightness. Each of these has a different effect on the total picture, and you can toy with the settings, depending on what you want to see. The same sort of thing occurs with different cultures as they balance several different spheres of life. Here are the four variables they can tinker with:

1. the factor of *wealth*, and therefore of work and productive activity in general
2. the concern for *justice*, particularly in the distribution of resources and benefits
3. *social relations* of all types, including family and community
4. the willingness to put aside material and other concerns in the pursuit of *spirituality*

The dangers inherent with a singular focus on any of these factors should be obvious. Just as a TV set will provide an awful picture with just one of the knobs turned way up, so historically we have observed problems when cultures pursue only one of those four goals. For example, overvaluation of wealth has brought us Western materialism, while a blind pursuit of distributive justice led to the brutalities of Marxism. At the extreme, we see a concentrated emphasis on family and community in peasant conservatism and a myopic focus on spirituality in Eastern (and now Western) self-absorbed ritualism. True humility remembers the contingent nature of all of these spheres of our lives and is able to put them in proper perspective. The well-lived Christian life has none other than Jesus at its center.

There's nothing inherently evil about any of these aspects of life. As Christians, we believe that God initially created our human condition to be good. But we have a long history of allowing the good things of life to replace our ultimate dependence upon our Creator. Lewis Smedes comments, "It is simple to make an idol: slice one piece of created reality off the whole and expect miracles from it."[3] We begin to look to wealth, or family, or government or to our religious practices to meet all of our needs, something only God can do. Consequently, we find ourselves getting out of balance in the various aspects of our lives and sliding away from full dependence upon the Center, who is Christ.

Let us look at each of these spheres in turn, seeking ways to balance them with the others, and to submit them all to our ultimate Lord.

Wealth

It is human nature to pursue material security. Wealth provides a certain independence, perceived security, and in many cultures, power. Cultures vary in the importance they place on wealth, but in many societies the wealthy are respected and admired. Whatever the character of the individuals involved, those with the most material assets often have the most prestige. People seek out their opinion, company and approval. Sometimes they're thought of as divinely favored. Details might differ, but certainly there is more emphasis upon the accumulation of wealth in the market economies of the Western nations than in any other culture.

God does not scorn wealth. In fact, there are many instances in Scripture where God blesses his people with riches (e.g., Abraham, Job, the people of Israel coming into the Promised Land). Yet the Bible warns again and again about the dangers of wealth and admonishes us to place wealth in its appropriate place. We are to seek first the kingdom of God (Mt 6:33), to be servants (Mt 23:11-12) and to give to the poor (Lk 12:32-33; 18:22). We are not to "trust in wealth, which is so uncertain, but to put [our] hope in God, who provides us with everything for our enjoyment" (1 Tim 6:17-19). As we learn from Jesus' parable of the rich man and Lazarus, the wealth secured in this world is fleeting; so we must keep our focus on our eternal home. Wealth is not evil, but our sinful natures may lead us into evil when driven by our lust for wealth. Theologian Ron Sider comments:

> An abundance of possessions can easily lead us to forget that God is the source of all good. We trust in ourselves rather than the Almighty. . . . Not only do possessions tempt us to forsake God, but the pursuit of wealth often results in war and neglect of the poor. . . . Scripture is full of instances in which rich persons are unconcerned about the poor at their doorstep.[4]

We are reminded of God's warning to the Israelites as they were about to enter the Promised Land:

> "Lest when you have eaten and are full and have built beautiful houses and dwell in them; and when your herds and your flocks multiply, and your silver and your gold

are multiplied, and all that you have is multiplied . . . you forget the Lord your God. . . . Then you say in your heart, 'My power and the might of my hand have gained me this wealth.' " (Deut 8:12-17 NKJV).

Justice

How well do the political and social systems of a culture uphold what is right? That's the question of justice. All cultures recognize the need for justice, but each defines it differently. Some, for instance, stress egalitarian objectives, while others affirm hierarchy in nature and society. Furthermore, the difficulty encountered today, particularly in the developed nations, is a breakdown in consensus with regard to what is moral. Christians, thankfully, can turn to Scripture for guidance—and we must.

As used in the Old Testament, the word *justice* most frequently refers to the act of deciding what is right, to rectitude and to restoration. "But let justice roll on like a river, righteousness like a never-failing stream" (Amos 5:24). Calvin Beisner[5] identifies three categories of justice in Scripture. First is *remedial justice*, where reparation is made for malicious injury to life, liberty or property. "If a man steals an ox or a sheep, and slaughters it or sells it, he shall restore five oxen for an ox and four sheep for a sheep" (Ex 22:1 NKJV). *Restore* in this instance goes beyond recompense and means to make peace with, make whole, reestablish *shalom*. Second is *commutative justice,* which has to do with truthfulness in transactions. And third is *distributive justice,* which focuses on equality of treatment, though not necessarily equality of outcome.[6]

Jesus does not reject the justice traditions of the Old Testament, nor does he get bogged down in equality of economic outcome. Jesus' focus is on the spirit and on action. Are we actively concerned about economic justice? Do we feed the hungry, give drink to the thirsty, clothe the naked and take in the stranger? God's call to compassion and justice for the poor throughout the Old and New Testaments is clear. "He will judge your people in righteousness, and your afflicted ones with justice. . . . He will defend the afflicted among the people and save the children of the needy; he will crush the oppressor" (Ps 72:2, 4).

In a Western culture that gives supreme importance to wealth, justice takes on a narrow focus. As long as no laws are broken, we can justify all sorts of greedy behavior that hurts others. Moreover, as we increasingly legalize the immoral, society assumes that since something is legal it must also be moral (see chapters twelve and thirteen). We assume that the rich must get richer and the poor will struggle—that is just the way society is. However, the situation is different in many parts of the world, especially among egalitarian tribal cultures.

Egalitarian tribal cultures are those in which the primary means of subsistence is foraging, pastoralism or horticulture, and in which no form of centralized power has developed. Social and political functions are according to lineage, with kinship networks providing for nearly all of society's needs. At one time, all of humanity lived in such cultures—you might be familiar with this pattern from the stories of Abraham, Isaac and Jacob. But now, egalitarian tribal groups are heavily marginalized by peasant and urban peoples. In particular, the past century has seen the rapid decimation of tribal peoples through the annexation of their land, using the authority of government.[7] However, many such groups remain, such as the Australian Aborigines, Native Americans, Central African forest dwellers ("Pygmies"), North African and Central Asian pastoralists, Inuit ("Eskimo") and others. Some estimate that 200 million indigenous people of tribal background live in various parts of the world.[8]

Tribal societies are egalitarian in political ideology, with a strong emphasis placed on the dignity and worth of every adult.[9] Especially in pastoral societies, personal honor is highly valued, and affronts to such honor lead quickly to quarrels or even wars. Leaders must campaign and cajole people into following them because authority, i.e. the power of office, is nonexistent. Thus, mechanisms are in place to prevent any from usurping excessive power over others, and the distribution of wealth via reciprocity is relatively even. Sharing comes easily with those who are in need, but those perceived to be lazy receive their share of criticism, gossip and verbal beatings. In extreme circumstances, unrepentant disrupters are ostracized, but for the most part, the community holds itself accountable for each member.

Egalitarian tribal cultures can be said to do well with the handling of justice issues centering around inequality.[10] While they still place value on wealth, it is balanced by their concern that each member of the community be fairly provided for. This balance might keep them from achieving absolute economic efficiency, but they have other priorities.

Certainly the United States is not an egalitarian tribal culture, nor will it ever be. The same is true for most other Western nations. Their size and diversity keep these societies from functioning like pastoral nomads. But we might still learn something from the balance of wealth and justice (and social relations) in such tribes. Economic efficiency is not the be-all and end-all of public life.

At the same time, we should learn another lesson from failed social experiments that have prized economic equality above all else. Karl Marx's quest was absolute egalitarian justice, and the bulk of the twentieth century showed us that it doesn't work. Not only does it make the economy grossly inefficient, but more importantly, it doesn't create justice! Society needs a balance of these four concerns: wealth, justice, social relations and spirituality.

Social Relations

Many cultures place a higher value on social relationships than on self-interest and maximization of economic output. Anthropologists explain that those relationships are formed by reciprocity, the exchange of goods and services. Marcel Mauss, in a classic work, *The Gift*,[11] demonstrated that all relationships must be established and maintained through material exchange.[12] This is most clear in "feudal peasant" agrarian societies (found throughout the Third World) where enormous amounts of surplus food are raised for gift giving. In extreme cases gift inflation occurs as leaders compete with one another to give the biggest gifts, and significant proportions of food crops rot each year from a lack of consumers. Hence, where economists expect people to establish relationships for self-interested utilitarian reasons, anthropologists expect people in certain cultures to produce material goods that will be used in the establishment of relationships. At the deepest level, the question is whether the culture sees relationships as being in service of the production of goods, or goods as being in service of the production of relationships.[13]

The Old Testament depicts God's justice as producing a community of love, bound together by mutual obligation (e.g., Deut 19—26). Infractions of the social law, especially against the poor and the stranger, will be punished. "You trample on the poor and force him to give you grain. Therefore, though you have built stone mansions, you will not live in them; though you have planted lush vineyards, you will not drink their wine. For I know how many are your offenses and how great your sins. You oppress the righteous and take bribes and you deprive the poor of justice in the courts" (Amos 5:11-12).

Jesus spoke clearly of the need for self-sacrifice in relationships. In the parable of the Good Samaritan, the Samaritan not only sacrifices money and time, but risks his own life (presumably there were still bandits about) in order to save the life of another. Jesus demonstrated a lifestyle of sacrifice for his disciples, leading up to his final sacrifice of himself for all of humanity.

In Western culture, we don't ignore the value of relationships, but they often take a back seat to the pursuit of wealth. Witness the many overworked employees who merely have time to wave hello and goodbye to their families each day, if that. In many families with young children, it is assumed that both parents will work full-time, leaving their impressionable youngsters in the guiding hands of day-care workers. Businesses transfer workers without much thought to the uprooting of relationships that a relocation entails. In workplace decisions, personal or community loyalties are expected to be discarded in favor of the bottom line.

And yet, history has seen some examples of the overvaluation of relationships as well. This usually takes the form of a dedication to one's own clan, race or community, with discrimination against all others. It might sound good to put relationships above everything else, but this can become idolatry when the community itself becomes a god (as it did in Nazi Germany). Strong communities can sacrifice God himself to their own survival. Remember what the chief priest said about Jesus: "You do not realize that it is better for you that one man die for the people than that the whole nation perish" (Jn 11:50). From a Christian perspective, we recognize that our love for our neighbors should spring from our love of God and not vice versa (Mt 22:37-40).

Spirituality

How much time and effort does a culture put into religious practice? The Bible tells us that ever "since the creation of the world, God's invisible qualities—his eternal power and his divine nature—have been clearly seen, being understood from what has been made" (Rom 1:20). And so all cultures, as they "clearly see" God's "invisible qualities," must come to terms with religion. Religions recognize the dual existence of a seen and an unseen world, and expect the latter to give significance to the former. All religions wrestle with the tension between our commitments to these two worlds. At one extreme, adherents of some world religions, such as Hinduism, resolve this tension by declaring the seen world illusory and collapsing it into an epiphenomenon of the unseen. At the other extreme, secularists (and some Buddhists) deny the unseen and are left with an exclusively material world. Most religions, though, attempt to interrelate the two spheres of existence in some meaningful way, while giving primacy to the unseen world.

Our immediate experience of the seen world can easily make us neglect the unseen, that is, material wealth can crowd out the spiritual life. Hence most religions devalue material wealth in some way: requiring wealth redistribution, "disarming" the wealthy by allowing them to purchase spiritual merit, or morally chastising the wealthy in stories, proverbs, sermons or songs. Religions instead value time and effort invested in the unseen (spiritual) world. Some require enormous sacrifices and mortifications to appease gods and receive blessings. Others regulate the minutest details of life in the quest for personal enlightenment. Humanity's attempt to find God has often been characterized by two paradoxically intertwined efforts: (a) self-immolation and (b) selfish demands.

God taught the Israelites two important things about our spiritual relationship with him: (a) that he loves us and does not need to be manipulated or persuaded to bless us ("But you, O Lord, are a compassionate and gracious God, slow to anger, abounding in love and faithfulness" [Ps 86:15]), and (b) that he nonetheless is a jealous God and requires our complete faithfulness ("Do not worship any other god, for the LORD, whose name is Jealous, is a jealous God" [Ex 34:14]). To depart from faithfulness is to commit the most serious sin, that of idolatry. There is no need for self-immolation and no place for selfishness in our relationship to God.

Jesus moved spirituality from outward form to inward practice. His teachings on prayer, his willingness to break Pharisaical law for higher purposes (Mt 12:1-8; Mk 3:1-6) and most importantly the intimate communion he had with the Father, all reflected a deep inner life with God that produced an outer life of love. In the garden of Gethsemane, his earnestness and effort reached full pitch, as he shed blood-like drops of sweat in his passion for the will of God (Lk 22:44). Hence, our commitment to inner communion with God will be reflected in all the outward aspects of our lives, including the economic.

Today many people think it doesn't matter which religion you choose, as long as you're religious. As Christians, we can't buy that. Some religions, such as ascetic Hinduism, promote spirituality for entirely selfish reasons, the salvation of the individual soul. Others, such as Islam, promote an aggressive reform of the seen world to satisfy a less than fully compassionate God. And others, such as most traditional religions, advocate the manipulation of the unseen for evil—as well as good—personal and tribal purposes. Many peasant religions mirror the social hierarchy in the supernatural one, thus legitimizing differences in human worth. Despite what Scripture teaches, Christians too have at times used religion for selfish purposes, to justify the quest for worldly influence, and to defend social inequalities. Spirituality based on deception or turned toward evil is more dangerous, perhaps, than no spirituality at all.

Democratic Capitalism: The Zenith of Economic Efficiency

The economically efficient, wealth-generating performance of the Western market exchange economies is nothing short of astounding. Using World Bank classifications,[14] the Gross Domestic Product (GDP) per capita in the market exchange countries is more than 5 times the average GDP throughout the world, almost 14 times the average GDP per capita in middle-income nations and 73 times greater than the average for the low-income countries. It is almost 11 times the GDP per capita in Colombia, 30 times that of China and 234 times that of Ethiopia. Ron Sider, upon a detailed comparison of national economies, concludes: "The different scales and comparisons all tell the same story. The rich one-fifth are incredibly wealthy and the poorest one-fifth are desperately poor."[15]

The West is doing fine in the wealth category. But what about those other factors: justice, relationships and spirituality? Let's give ourselves a report card.

First, let's consider justice. How fairly is this extraordinary income distributed? Available data show that market exchange economies have a much larger middle class than other nations have, and there's less divergence between the bottom and top of the income distribution.[16] But before we go patting ourselves on the back, let's consider some other statistics. Time series data for the United States indicate since the late 1960s a growing *inequality* in the distribution of income. Families and individuals at the bottom of the income distribution have experienced a decline in their share of total income while those at the top gained.[17] Not surprisingly, during the mid-1970s the U.S. poverty rate stopped falling, started rising in the late 1970s, and with some business cycle fluctuations has remained well above its 1973 low (about one-fourth higher).

Does this mean that distributive justice is on the wane in market exchange economies, such as the United States? It depends upon how rigid this new income structure is. If there were little mobility within the income structure, the charge of unequal treatment would be stronger. But research shows extraordinarily high individual mobility in the market exchange economies, especially the United States. That is, many people move into and out of poverty. More than three-quarters of all poverty spells are shorter than two years, and only 7 percent of the spells last seven years or more. (If discontinuous but repeated spells are considered, the percentage of spells lasting seven years or more rises to 20 percent, but the remainder of spells stay short-lived.) The same pattern is found among welfare recipients, where only about 30 percent of the cases are chronic.[18] And, of course, there is mobility within the income distribution. Over a decade or more, 86-95 percent of all persons in the bottom quintile of the U.S. income distribution move to a higher quintile, the majority becoming middle class.[19]

As Bradley Schiller comments, "If people can change places in the [income] distribution, then the inequality that exists at any moment may not be so critical."[20] Certainly such movement demonstrates an abundance of opportunity. But before declaring the triumph of justice, we should get to know the characteristics of the chronically poor. While the data show the majority of poor people aren't "trapped" in poverty, some are. In the United States the chronically poor tend to be persons with less than a high school education, unwed mothers, nonwhites and persons who grew up in impoverished households and communities. Scripture clearly calls Christians to address poverty caused by oppression, discrimination, calamity and even by sinful choices so long as further irresponsibility is not encouraged (see chapter nine).

In market exchange cultures there is a danger that social relationships may be sacrificed to self-interest. The primary exchange system is not driven by benevolence but by appealing to the self-interest of the buyer and seller. Generally, social relationships are a spin-off, a derivative of economic activity. Individuals establish acquaintances, yet most of these fade quickly away when the main basis for contact—exchange—disappears.

When combined with the tremendous wealth generated by the market exchange economies, this tendency toward self-interest has led to a general breakdown in community. Increasingly, we live to ourselves. Increasingly, we drive to work alone, spend more and more hours watching television or videos, and have fewer interactions with folks in our residential communities. This anomie is evidenced in the United States through various cultural indicators.[21] Over the past three decades we have seen the divorce rate more than double, single parent families rise from 9 percent to 29 percent of all families with children, births to unmarried women rise from 5 percent to 28 percent of all births, the percentage of children living with both biological parents drop from 78 percent to 57 percent, and both the juvenile violent crime arrest rate and the teenage suicide rate more than triple. Social security, Medicare and Medicaid, private pension funds and growth in assets (particularly the value of the primary residence) have discouraged the continuation of the extended family. Compared to the egalitarian tribal cultures and the feudal peasant cultures, the market exchange culture does little to encourage and facilitate meaningful social relations.

There is no question that over the last three decades spirituality has increasingly been excluded from the public domain in the United States, including everything from prayer in public schools to references to transcendent values in decisions of the Supreme Court. This appears to be a reflection of a larger trend among individuals and families. In the United States and among most Western European nations the time and effort put into religious practice has waned. Only 27 percent of western Europeans say religion is "very important" to them, and on an average Sunday only 2.2 percent of persons in Great Britain attend the Church of England.[22] In the United States, despite a rise in demand for Christian literature and music and a stated regard for God, weekly church attendance has fallen to a national average of less than 27 percent of all adults, and only 19 percent regularly practice their religion.[23] After examining survey data, pollster George Gallup referred to Americans as "a nation of biblical illiterates."[24] And polls consistently show that those Americans with more education and more money find religion less important and are less likely to attend church.

It appears that Western capitalist cultures place the least emphasis upon religion. Certainly the wealth of the capitalist cultures and the self-interest underlying the generation of that wealth are contributing causes to the decline in spiritual commitment. We find cases in Scripture where, in response to their obedience to his law, God blesses his peoples with wealth (Deut 8:1-14). And it is not wealth, *per se*, that God condemns, but oppressive practices in the earning of wealth. We're also warned of the danger that wealth will displace our love for the Lord. The story of the rich young ruler ("How hard it is for the rich to enter the kingdom of God" [Lk 18:24]) and the rich man and Lazarus (Lk 16:19-31) show how easily we can be blinded to the transitory nature of wealth in regard to eternity. For "what good is it for a man to gain the whole world, and yet lose or forfeit his very self?" (Lk 9:25). The apostle Paul warns: "People who want to get rich fall into temptation and a trap and into many foolish and harmful desires that plunge men in ruin and destruction. For the love of money is a root of all kinds of evil. Some people, eager for money, have wandered from the faith and pierced themselves with many griefs" (1 Tim 6:9-10).

Conclusion

Although capitalist cultures produce extraordinary wealth and provide considerable opportunities for the redistribution of income through the market process (although chronic poverty exists), they have experienced a rapid breakdown in community (particularly within the family) and have seen an erosion in religious activity. Of the various spheres of culture—economic, political, social and religious—in the West, it is the economic sphere upon which the other spheres are built. Obviously in such an environment economic success and individualism have become gods. In capitalist cultures it is hard for anyone, including Christians, to avoid falling into the competition for wealth and the false security, power and respect which accompany it. Ample proof is provided by the long lines winding out of convenience stores selling the latest high payoff lottery tickets.

How should a Christian deal with life in such a culture? Fight against the pull toward materialism, follow biblical priorities and principles with respect to worship, family, work and charity, and participate in Christian community where the emotional and material needs of others are met. In the following account, a capitalist convert to Christianity describes his life before and after conversion:

[Before my conversion] the drive for success was on. I'd prove to the world I was important. My work took me about Wall Street and little by little I became interested in the market. Many people lost money—but some became very rich. Why not I?

[After alcoholism and failure] I humbly offered myself to God, as I then understood Him, to do with me as He would. I placed myself unreservedly under His care and direction. I admitted for the first time that of myself I was nothing; that without Him I was lost. I ruthlessly faced my sins and became willing to have my new-found Friend take them away, root and branch. I have not had a drink since.[25]

Certainly, from Genesis onward Scripture makes it clear that God favors good stewardship of the resources he has given us. Profligacy is condemned in both the Old and New Testaments (Deut 21:20; Lk 15:13). Jesus criticizes the slothful servant in the parable of the talents (Mt 25:14-30) and after the feeding of the five thousand instructs his disciples to "Gather the pieces that are left over. Let nothing be wasted" (Jn 6:12). We see a kind of economic efficiency here, though not the idol set up by modern economists.

This chapter has demonstrated that various culture types give priority to various factors, often trading off one for another. Despite all the attention paid to it by textbooks, economic efficiency is but one among many priorities. Egalitarian tribal cultures often sacrifice wealth for kin-based relations; feudal peasant cultures may give primacy to lines of hierarchy and authority with religious life being subordinated to the power structure; and productively efficient capitalist cultures can achieve enormous wealth at the expense of social relationships and spirituality. Kin-based relations, submission to authority, and wealth are all—in moderation—declared "good" in the Bible. But, due to the fallen state of humanity, we often place one factor or another on a pedestal and begin to worship it, throwing our lives (and societies) out of balance. No culture is without its idols. For a Christian, the only true priority is humility, our recognition of our ultimate dependence on God for all of our needs and balance in our lives.

Discussion Questions

1. What are the pitfalls facing a society that pursues justice at the expense of all other objectives?

2. What should characterize Christian social relations? Does this run counter to maximizing economic output?

3. Does economic success in a society tend to crowd out spiritual life and development?

4

IT'S MINE!

Private Property
Rights

When property is insecure, so are all our other rights.

TOM BETHELL

**The property which every man has in his own labour,
as it is the original foundation of all other property,
so it is the most sacred and inviolable.**

ADAM SMITH

SYNOPSIS

It has been recognized since the time of Aristotle that communal property rights encourage overuse while private property rights encourage good stewardship. Beginning in Genesis, Scripture makes it clear that everything in this world belongs to God. Men and women, however, are given responsibility for the stewardship of the earth's resources, and private property rights are acknowledged in the Old and New Testaments.

How important are secure private property rights? In the last century we saw a graphic experiment. It was called the Berlin Wall. A city was partitioned and half of it was ruled by communism, depriving people of private property rights. The other half continued to allow private property. When the wall came down, nearly fifty years later, it was startlingly clear that the communist side was impoverished while West Berlin had flourished. It was the same story in the other nations that had been ruled by Iron Curtain communism. The lack of private property choked off economic development, and when the curtain fell, these nations had some major catching up to do.

Aristotle articulated the connection between economic growth and private property rights more than 2,300 years ago, attributing it to human nature. Under a communal property system, he said, "those who do more work and get less recompense will be bound to raise complaints against those who get a larger recompense and do little work. . . . What is common to the greatest number gets the least amount of care. Men pay most attention to what is their own; they care less for what is common. . . . It is a fact of observation that those who own common property, and share in its management, are far more often at variance with one another than those who own property in severality."[1] Communal property rights encourage overuse and abuse of property and reward shirking one's obligations. Private property rights encourage property to be treated as a long-term asset and provide a direct link between individual effort and economic return.

Wanna Buy an Elephant?

Because of the high value of ivory it is estimated that poachers kill more than 200 elephants every day in Africa. In reaction, most countries, like Kenya, have enacted regulations that place limitations on the export of ivory and ban the killing of elephants. Despite these regulations, combined with government patrols allowed to shoot poachers on sight, over a decade Kenya's elephant population plummeted from 140,000 to 20,000. Overall, in central Africa where elephants are basically communal property, the population has declined 57%.

Several countries in southern Africa have implemented an alternative, private property approach. Permits to hunt elephants are now issued to villages, and these permits can be bought and sold. Villages now consider elephant herds an important economic asset for the long run. Consequently, herd sizes in the countries that have established property rights (Botswana, Namibia, South Africa and Zimbabwe) have risen. In Botswana alone the elephant population jumped from about 20,000 to 50,000 over a decade.

Source: *The Margin,* January/February 1990, pp. 2-3.

For a variety of reasons—greed, hubris, social engineering and paternalism—Aristotle's simple warning has been ignored repeatedly throughout history with disastrous results. For centuries monarchs owned land through "divine law." Peasants farmed the land, but had little incentive to increase productivity. Police states and insecure property rights turned formerly verdant land in the Middle East into vast deserts through overgrazing and lack of cultivation. Insecure property rights in Ireland encouraged English nobles to rape the land, getting a quick return before the property was passed on to another member of the nobility.

Improvements to property by Irish tenants were not compensated (and thereby discouraged). Both these conditions contributed significantly to the great Irish potato famine. Similar situations continue today in the razing of the Brazilian rain forest, the allocation of water in California and the decimation of elephant herds in parts of Africa.[2]

Apart from the abuse of communal property (the "tragedy of the commons") and the dilemma of "free riders" (persons or organizations who benefit from a good without paying for the costs of its supply), secure private property is essential to an efficient system of voluntary economic exchange. As we know from Adam Smith, voluntary economic exchange is at the heart of the "wealth of nations." Private property is a precondition for free enterprise markets and limits government's intervention into the private lives of individuals, firms and organizations. Campbell McConnell and Stanley Brue state, "Property rights are significant because they encourage investment, innovation, exchange, and economic growth. Why would anyone stock a store, construct a factory, or clear land for farming if someone else, including government, could take that property?"[3] Similarly, Gwartney, Stroup and Sobel observe, "When the property rights of all citizens—including the vitally important property right to their labor—are clearly defined and securely enforced, production and trade replace plunder as the means of acquiring wealth. When property ownership rights are well defined and enforced, people get ahead by helping and cooperating with others."[4]

Government plays a number of important roles in the maintenance of private property rights. First, government prevents the taking of property through force, fraud or theft. Second, through the enforcement of contracts, government ensures the fair exchange of property (physical and intellectual). Third, government enforces legal limits on how property may be used. Finally, government itself is not to engage in "unjust taking" of property. When property is taken by government on constitutional grounds (the exercise of eminent domain), fair compensation is to be rendered to the owners.

Why the Bias?

Given the evidence of the past 2,300 years, it's hard to argue with Aristotle's observations regarding human nature and property. Why then, particularly in the last three centuries, has there been such a bias among liberals and socialists against private property? In part it has been blind faith stemming from the Enlightenment and the Age of Reason—faith in the continual improvement in the nature of humankind. As people become more educated and as more of their basic physical needs are met, it is argued, they will be more community minded and more likely to make decisions on the basis of what is best for society rather than for themselves and their families. For a Christian this hypothesis is untenable. Hearkening back to our theological framework (chapter one), we know that our sinful nature poisons relationships with others and with God. We relentlessly search for security through material possessions, control of nature and power over others. Human nature often tends to be ugly.

Part of the bias against private property may spring from the hope that as individuals are brought to common ground materially—as differences among us are reduced in the number of possessions, the size of our houses and the quality of our clothes—our relations will be more congenial, less marked by envy and conniving. People will supposedly turn from pursuit of the material to higher-order activities such as the arts and literature. Certainly, as Christians we are instructed not to covet. Yet, generally, this temptation is to be overcome through a life of prayer, devotion and dependence upon the Holy Spirit. Nothing in Scripture calls for equality of outcome or lifestyle as a means of dealing with covetousness.

Even the extreme sharing in the Jerusalem church described in Acts 2, 4 and 5 was voluntary. "All the believers were together and had everything in common, selling their possessions and goods, they gave to anyone as he had need. Every day they continued to meet together in the temple courts. They broke bread in their homes and ate together with glad and sincere hearts, praising God and enjoying the favor of all the people" (Acts 2:44-47). Does this mean that Christians renounced the idea of individual ownership? Is that, then, an ideal for Christians in every time and place? No. It's clear that the Holy Spirit called these early Christians to offer some radical financial aid to meet the burgeoning needs of the growing church. These needs were especially great because some of the new believers were travelers and disgruntled families would have disowned others. The church then became a new household for these essentially homeless converts. But in the midst of all this common sharing, we read of Ananias and Sapphira, who voluntarily sold property and donated part of the proceeds. Their mistake was lying about it, claiming they were donating the whole amount. Peter said to Ananias, "Didn't it belong to you before it was sold? And after it was sold, wasn't the money at your disposal?" (Acts 5:4). Apparently the church was not *requiring* complete commonality.

We see the same call to voluntary charity later from the apostle Paul: "Our desire is not that others might be relieved while you are hard pressed, but that there might be equality. At the present time your plenty will supply what they need, so that in turn their plenty will supply what you need. Then there will be equality, as it is written: 'He who gathered much did not have too much, and he who gathered little did not have too little'" (2 Cor 8:13-15). He was asking the Corinthian church to meet the needs of the Jerusalem church, but in a voluntary and even "cheerful" way.

Inheritance and the Bible

Economists debate whether more restrictive inheritance laws reduce the work effort of individuals. Certainly Proverbs reinforces the common view that "a good man leaves an inheritance for his children's children" (13:22). Yet today God's real concern, and Christians' real concern for their families and others, is that they receive "the promised eternal inheritance" from Christ who has died as a ransom to set them free from their sins. The result is an inheritance "that can never perish, spoil or fade—kept in heaven for you, who through faith are shielded by God's power until the coming of the salvation" (1 Pet 1:4-5).

This does not mean that God is unconcerned about justice in worldly inheritance. For example, the law of Israel required that men inherit property. In Numbers 27, however, we read how the daughters of Zelophehad came before Moses, Eleazar the priest, the leaders and the whole assembly in the Tent of Meeting to appeal for the property of their father who had died with no sons. So Moses brought their case before the Lord, who said to him "What Zelophehad's daughters are saying is right. You must certainly give them property as an inheritance...and turn their father's inheritance over to them. Say to the Israelites, 'If a man dies and leaves no son, turn his inheritance over to his daughter.' "

Up to that time inheritance had never been done that way, but justice and righteousness took precedence over comfort and tradition. Christians must look to God where issues of justice are involved and be receptive to adjusting their attitudes and actions.

Another major source of the bias against private property may stem from envy and resentment toward the rich. There can be much injustice in how property is distributed, and these injustices can be perpetuated through the system of inheritance. For centuries, due to the predominance of the agrarian economy, land was the major source of wealth throughout the world. In many instances, wealthy families acquired their land in dubious ways, involving fraud, violence, influence at court or coercion. Sometimes they exploited the original owners during times of misfortune such as death of a breadwinner, droughts or recessions. Resentment against such landowners was clearly evident in the attitude of Adam Smith and some other classical economists toward landlords and the rent they received, "reaping without sowing," "earning income from other people's labor." More recently, stringent inheritance laws in countries such as the United States and England, which are partly a reflection of this bias, have done much to reduce the ongoing disparities in wealth. In ancient Israel, the sabbatical year and especially the year of the Jubilee would minimize disparities in wealth resulting from accumulation of property within families over time. As theologian Ron Sider notes, the Jubilee year "does not point us in the direction of the communist model where the state owns all the land. God wants each family to have the resources to produce its own livelihood. Why? To strengthen the family."[5]

There is also some resentment over disparities in wages, though these feelings may not run as strong. As noted in chapter one, Scripture makes it clear that God has endowed individuals with differing talents and skills. Early in Genesis we find that Abel kept the flocks while Cain worked the soil, Jabal raised livestock, Jubal was a musician and Tubal-Cain a blacksmith and metalworker. On the positive side, these variations in talents help society by encouraging workers to specialize in their areas of ability, creating opportunities for exchange, interdependence and cooperative ventures. But less positively, certain talents have greater earning power than others. The result is an unequal distribution of income and property. We can accept that all people, no matter what their station in this life, stand equal before God as sinners. Still, in this world God has allowed a situation where our economic status is not equal. "Rich and poor have this in common: the LORD is the maker of them all" (Prov 22:2).[6]

For many, this has been a difficult pill to swallow. Certainly it has helped to fuel the intellectual fires of socialism and communism over time. It led Karl Marx to claim that the only legitimate property is the right of each person to his or her own labor—and yet Marx's social system would not allow individuals to retain the ultimate differential earnings from their labor.

It is tempting to try, in the name of economic justice, to wipe out inequality altogether. However, the stark reality is that the weakening of property rights for the rich or the talented also endangers the property rights of the remainder of society and undermines economic growth. As economist Jean-Baptiste Say noted, private property is "the most powerful encouragement to the multiplication of wealth" and the poor have as strong an interest as the rich in upholding its inviolability.[7] In fact, Leviticus 19:15 warns us against creating even more injustice in our attempts to help the poor: "You shall do no injustice in judgment. You shall not be partial to the poor, nor honor the person of the mighty. In righteousness you shall judge your neighbor" (NKJV). For Christians this means that land reform (the redistribution of land in developing countries from the few to the many) must include just or reasonable compensation to the current oligopolistic landowners, unless it can be clearly demonstrated that they acquired the property through theft. When law does not protect property rights, property investments decrease and transaction costs soar.

Gregory Mankiw notes that "market prices are the instrument with which the invisible hand of the marketplace brings supply and demand into balance. An important prerequisite for the price system to work is an economy-wide respect for property rights . . . the ability of people to exercise authority over the resources they own."[8]

Property Issues

Beginning in Genesis, Scripture makes it clear that everything in this world, human and nonhuman, was made by and belongs to God. "The earth is the LORD's," sings the Psalmist, "and everything in it, the world, and all who live in it" (Ps 24:1). While humans are given dominion over the created order to provide for our existence, we are also accountable to God for our stewardship of those resources and of our own individual talents. All resources are ultimately to be used for the purposes of the kingdom of God. We are to rely on God, not possessions.

Because everything belongs to God, there are no individual or institutional rights to property in perpetuity. In the intermediate term, however, Scripture approves of individual property rights. Abraham purchased a burial site for his beloved wife Sarah and received a deed proving his property rights (Gen 23). By forbidding stealing, the Eighth Commandment clearly establishes the right to property. Calvin Beisner writes, "And with the right to property comes the right to use it freely, short of violating the rights of others by damaging their lives, liberties, or properties."[9] According to Exodus 22, financial restitution must be made to property owners in cases of theft or negligence (e.g., the accidental setting of a fire, the loss or destruction of a borrowed item, one owner's animals grazing in another owner's pastures). Lost animals are to be returned, even when they belong to an enemy (Ex 23:4; Deut 22:1-4)! Force is permitted to protect private property, and if the thief should die there is no guilt for his bloodshed (Ex 22:2). Removing the landmarks that establish property boundaries is clearly forbidden (Deut 19:14; 27:17; Job 24:2; Prov 22:28; Hos 5:10). And kings may not force a subject to sell property nor can kings take a property by force without payment, other than for delinquent taxes (Rom 13:7). Recall God's punishment of Ahab and Jezebel for stealing the vineyard of Naboth (1 Kings 21). "The prince must not take any of the inheritance of the people driving them off their property" (Ezek 46:18).

"No one can serve two masters," Jesus tells us, "for either he will hate the one and love the other, or else he will be loyal to the one and despise the other. You cannot serve God and mammon [money]" (Mt 6:24). Jesus is not denouncing private property, but he is warning us that its lure can be a major challenge to our faith. "For everything in the world—the cravings of sinful man, the lust of his eyes and the boasting of what he has and does—comes not from the Father but from the world" (1 Jn 2:16). Yet free will choices are essential to a vital Christian life. As stated in chapter one, Christian ethics demands that every person should have access to the resources necessary for life. We all should be ensured the opportunity to participate in the economy. We are obligated to show charity to those who are in need, particularly when it's because of circumstances beyond their control. Giving under compulsion, particularly through the coercive powers of the state, is not charity. How can giving be considered charity, an act of free will, unless the givers first own the rights to the property sacrificed? The same can be said of God's mandate to financially support the church. Without private property rights, the choice between God and money is not as challenging.

Since Christians are both accountable to God for their stewardship of his resources and responsible to support the needy, it would seem sensible for Christians to advocate private property rights, because of the economic growth and economic well-being that results. This does not mean that Christians should turn a blind eye to those areas of market failure where private property rights produce outcomes that are less than efficient or just. An obvious area of potential failure is in the accumulation of wealth by individuals, families and institutions (corporations, oligopolies). Isaiah 5, for example, chastises the wealthy—but their right to "add house to house and field to field" is not condemned; it's the conceit, exploitation and perversion of justice that goes with it. The Bible makes it clear that God cares about distributive and commutative justice.

Throughout the world, especially the Third World, concentration of wealth often leads to exploitation by powerful people. Under such disparities in power, generally consumers pay higher than efficient prices, have access to fewer goods and services, and have less access to productive resources such as land. Suppliers of abundant resources, such as labor, usually receive compensation below what would prevail in competitive markets. Rather than being independent agents who enter transactions voluntarily, suppliers of resources (especially labor) are trapped in conditions of desperate servitude by the dominant parties. This injustice is unacceptable to God and to his people. To the extent that regulations, liberal inheritance laws and the threat of violence are used to maintain these positions of dominance, it is the responsibility of Christians and the church to work for change.

Another area of market failure with respect to private property rights, recognized in all introductory economics textbooks, has to do with externalities (for example, water pollution from a private factory that destroys water quality and aquatic life for miles downstream, or the noise from a busy interstate highway that makes conversation in a living room a struggle and depresses the value of nearby homes). Here the intervention of government through the law and regulations makes sense (see chapter ten). Of course there are difficulties in finding the most accurate ways to assess these damages and make amends (e.g., quotas, fines, effluent fees).

Another widely recognized instance of market failure in the area of property rights has to do with public goods. For goods and services where consumption by one person does not limit consumption by others and where the costs of excluding nonpaying consumers are high, the level of supply by the private sector will be deficient and government provision or control is warranted. Examples include national defense, expansive national and state parks, mosquito spraying, the airwaves and the ocean floor. And, although private property law covers many areas of intellectual property through patents, copyrights and trademarks, because the resale of information is so easy, government supply of some types of information, such as weather forecasting services, may also be warranted.

A more controversial area of government activity is in the taking of property through the right of eminent domain. The Fifth Amendment of the U.S. Constitution allows the federal government to take property, provided that the taking is for a public purpose and the owner is justly compensated. State constitutions are modeled similarly. Certainly there is some controversy over what constitutes just compensation (e.g., use value as opposed to exchange value),[10] yet the most heated debate concerns the definition of a "just" public purpose. No taking is painless and without its critics. Nevertheless, takings for public schools, hospitals, fire stations and highways generally stir up less of a storm than takings for the preservation of a wetland, a missile site or a landfill. Local governments have even taken land to provide sites for manufacturers!

Individual aversion to such takings should come as no surprise to Christians. Remember how God dealt with Ahab and Jezebel for using the sovereign power of the state for an unjust taking. When the Israelites first clamored to have a king, Samuel warned them of such takings: "He will take the best of your fields and vineyards and olive groves and give them to his attendants. He will take a-tenth of your grain and of your vintage and give it to his officials and attendants. Your manservants and maidservants and the best of your cattle and donkeys he will take for his own use. He will take a tenth of your flocks, and you yourselves will become his slaves" (1 Sam 8:14-18). Since Christians have a mandate to be stewards of God's creation, we don't need knee-jerk reactions against public takings for environmental purposes or social services. At the same time, we understand the constant possibility of corruption in the human heart, even in the hearts of public officials, and we have been warned about the possible consequences of unconstrained sovereign power with respect to the sanctity of private property.

Conclusion

For centuries in an agriculture dominated economy, ownership of land meant wealth and financial security. Even today, ownership of land can mean wealth, as does ownership of other forms of private property. Although all property ultimately belongs to God, he has entrusted it to us as good stewards. Whether private property becomes a snare or a blessing is ultimately up to us and our choice to use all we are given to further the kingdom of God.

Discussion Questions

1. What is to prevent various nations, such as Japan, from harvesting the oceans to exhaustion?

2. Should inheritance taxes be high or low? Support your position with Scripture.

3. Cite three instances where private property rights may lead to failure in free markets. What actions can be taken to ameliorate this failure?

4. Does Scripture support the right of eminent domain?

5

HOW DOES YOUR GARDEN GROW?

The Possibilities & Perils of Economic Growth

Man is a creature of desire and not a creature of need.

MARCEL AMUSES

Be content with what you have because God has said,
"Never will I leave you; never will I forsake you."

HEBREWS 13:5

SYNOPSIS

Sustained economic growth tends to improve the quality of life for all segments of a society. Christians are wary because economic growth can encourage greed, conspicuous consumption, reliance on wealth for security, and conflict among nations. For centuries economic growth came from one society or nation plundering another. Then, as explorers opened up new territories and transportation became more efficient, the wealth of most nations became a function of trade. While comparative advantage and trade are still important today, economic growth is increasingly dependent on the development of new technology and on innovation. For Christians, unlimited economic growth is not an acceptable goal in and of itself; rather, Christians desire economic growth that enables all people to better honor God.

People have always wanted to improve the quality of their lives. It's no fun to work twenty hours a day or to forage for food amid dwindling resources. We want easy access to basic supplies as well as a chance to enjoy "the good life." This basic desire for both necessities and luxuries drives us, individually and socially, into economic growth. We define economic growth as *the sustained increase in the output per person of a society or nation.*

Growth is a mixed blessing as Karl Case and Ray Fair observe: "It is through economic growth that living standards improve, but growth brings change. New things are produced, while others become obsolete. Some believe growth is the fundamental objective of a society, because it lifts people out of poverty and enhances the quality of their lives. Others say economic growth erodes traditional values and leads to exploitation, environmental destruction, and corruption."[1]

Economic growth is no modern invention. In Genesis 1 men and women are directed to "Be fruitful and increase in number; fill the earth and subdue it. Rule over the fish of the sea." Some see this verse as a mandate from God for society to strive continually for maximum productivity, to take the economy to its full potential and to pursue development relentlessly. Robert Nelson has identified this position as one of the major tenets of modern economic theology. According to this view, if we succeed in eliminating economic scarcity, we will curb avarice and the pursuit of self-interest. This in turn would reduce strife and conflict and generally transform the human condition. That is, if there is plenty for everyone, there is nothing to fight over.[2]

But judging from the moral and spiritual condition of the world's wealthiest nations, economic growth has done little to save souls and promote charity among all members of society. In fact, the pursuit of economic growth has often led to egregious abuse of individuals, families, communities, organizations and the environment. Yet, we want people to find meaningful employment, to have access to health care and "eat and drink to their full." In the view of the Talmud, the highest degree of charity is to assist a poor person with a business loan or help someone find employment because work restores self-respect and independence.[3] Economic growth and progress makes this more likely. As some Christian economists would argue, however, unlimited economic growth as an economic objective in itself is clearly objectionable for encouraging greed, conspicuous consumption, reliance on wealth for security and conflict among nations. A more theologically acceptable goal is to develop the world to enable humanity to honor God.[4]

In this chapter we will consider from a Christian perspective how the idea of economic growth has developed over the centuries, and what policies have evolved. We will also look at the benefits and costs of growth. Our challenge is to find a scriptural balance on this essential issue that directly touches the everyday well-being of so many billions of persons.

When Growth Comes from Plunder

There has been little overall economic growth throughout most of human history. Prior to the 1700s the common way for one community or nation to gain was through plundering the resources of another. God allowed the Israelites, after wandering in the desert for 40 years, to occupy the fertile lands of Canaan and east of the Jordan. In an agrarian economy, ownership of land was a great privilege, and the land the Lord God provided was a good land—"a land with streams and pools of water, with springs flowing in the valleys and hills; a land with wheat and barley, vines and fig trees, pomegranates, olive oil and honey; . . . where the rocks are iron and you can dig copper out of the hills" (Deut 8:7-9). While much of the land possessed by the twelve tribes of Israel was unoccupied, frequently God commanded towns and cities to be destroyed along with all their inhabitants, from fighting men to women and small infants (Josh 10:40). God wanted to prevent the infiltration of the idolatry of the Gentiles into the theocracy of Israel. Similar commands were often given by God with regard to the material plunder of the conquered people: it was to be destroyed rather than taken (Josh 7).

History records literally thousands of examples of this philosophy of economic growth through plunder. Beginning with Columbus in 1492, the development of maritime skills encouraged Spain and Portugal to launch expeditions westward in search of an ocean highway to the spices and other product markets of Asia. Jumping off from the Azores and Canary Islands into the westward-flowing north equatorial currents and the northeast trade winds (with the returning Gulf Stream current and westerly winds), the mercenaries soon stumbled on the islands of the Caribbean, Central and South America, and Florida. The passion among the Spanish was for gold.

In Española and the other islands, Columbus found friendly natives, aloes, cotton and spices, and a limited supply of gold ornaments, which the natives were more than willing to trade for useless trinkets. Leaving 39 colonists at La Navidad, Columbus returned a year later to find them all dead—killed by each other and by natives grown hostile. Shortly after Columbus's departure the men had begun indulging their lust for the Indian women, taking multiple partners. Simultaneously, they gave up bartering for gold and simply seized it from the natives, using violence as necessary. They then began killing one another over the gold. Columbus returned and immediately instituted an annual tribute of gold upon the natives. Natives who did not meet the tribute from the scant gold available were savagely punished. As the natives rebelled, they were forced to build forts and conscripted for other labor. If natives responded with violence, punishment was swift and harsh with the inhabitants of whole villages sentenced to execution or torture. Within two years 100,000 of the 300,000 native population of Española had perished, and within a decade only 20,000 were left.[5]

While it took a quarter-century of bouncing from island to island and shoreline to shoreline, eventually in early 1519 Hernando Cortés happened upon the

Aztec Empire in Mexico, a generally bloodthirsty society that used the terror of human sacrifice—including the slaughter of babies and day-long killing orgies—to maintain a tight autocracy. The Aztecs had substantial gold, and they were no match for the Spanish guns and cannon, steel swords and lancers on horse. The destruction of the Inca Empire, which included Peru and much of northern South America, took Francisco Pizarro a bit longer, but the result was the same. By the 1570s it was over. The gold was flowing back to Spain in quantities beyond the wildest expectations. The Spanish war machine, a well-administered and ruthlessly applied system of native slave labor, together with the introduction of a myriad of European diseases, resulted in an estimated decline in the Mexican native population of 90 percent (from 25 million to between 1 and 2 million) and about a 20 percent decline in the Peruvian native population. By early 1600 Spain was the greatest economic power in the world.[6]

Economically, however, Spain ran into two problems. First, economic growth sustained by plunder requires the flow and stock of plunder to continue. Competition from other European nations, particularly Britain, France and Denmark, made this impossible for Spain. Second, as Adam Smith would so clearly articulate a few centuries later, the wealth of nations and the consequent basis for economic growth is not gold. In the absence of productive capacity, more gold simply drives up prices, the result being high inflation and a constant or even falling standard of living. While Spain was plundering, it was not producing. The lack of productive capacity had been made worse by the Spanish Inquisition that had driven the majority of the most innovative and entrepreneurial individuals out of Spain for centuries following.

In the long run economic growth through plunder is technically ineffective. How should Christians view it? Certainly, with respect to the taking of the lands of Canaan, it is difficult to reconcile the God who evidences his love for us daily in acts of compassion with the God who ordered the killing of all breathing things, including infants. This presents theological issues which we cannot fully consider in these pages. But we do know three things. First, in the Old Testament, God was attempting to establish a covenant people, a nation set apart from the idolatrous societies around them through their love of and dedication to the one God and their devotion to his laws. Second, the instances where God directed the destruction of whole communities were few. Third, as we see again and again in Old Testament history, when Israel failed to drive the Gentiles completely out of their land, they adopted the heathen customs of their neighbors, typically within one generation following the death of a strong spiritual leader. Unity in government was lost, the guiding foundation of God's law was abandoned or compromised, and idol worship and human-instituted religion led the majority of Israelites away from faith in God.

What of the many instances of growth by violent and cruel plunder involving ostensibly Christian nations, the church and Christian persons? The Italian Christopher Columbus was a deeply religious Christian, a lay member of the Order of St. Francis. His name, Christopher, literally means "Christ-bearer." According to his journals, the primary inspiration for his voyage to the new world came from Isaiah 49: "I will also make you a light to the Gentiles, that you may bring my salvation to the end of the earth." Failing to secure financing from the kings of Portugal and England, he happened to solicit the Catholic Majesties of Spain at the very moment that the Moors were surrendering. Not having decided upon the appropriate expression of gratitude to God for their deliverance, their Majesties funded Columbus's expedition as a crusade to discover new lands for the glory of God and his church, and to spread the Gospel to the ends of the earth. Columbus christened his first island landfall San Salvador—"Holy Savior"—and upon his return to Spain the Majesties fell to their knees, singing the *Te Deum*. Pope Alexander VI, in a 1493 message of congratulations to the Spanish rulers Ferdinand and Isabella, rejoiced that they had undertaken this expedition "in order to induce the natives and inhabitants thereof to worship our Redeemer" and that the "name of our Lord and Savior Jesus Christ might . . . be introduced to the aforesaid lands and islands."

So we see that the violent plunder of the New World began, at least, with good intentions, even *Christian* intentions. Yet we also see here a danger underlying the individual and corporate drive for economic growth. Often what pushes growth is the desire to be like God: to have security, power, prestige or even to be worshiped. Ever since the Garden, Satan has stood ready to use these desires to destroy the soul. Near the end of his life, Columbus wrote in his diary: "Gold constitutes treasure, and he who possesses it may do what he will in the world, and may attain as to bring souls to Paradise."[7]

Growth Through Trade

As we noted in chapter one, God has chosen to endow individuals with differing talents and skills. This clearly establishes a basis and a need for trade, since those variously gifted people have to do business with one another. Thus, trade has been an aspect of life almost since Eden. Tubal-Cain, who forged all kinds of tools out of bronze and iron (Gen 4:22), certainly needed to trade his goods with his brethren for wheat and wine. Solomon provided food for the royal household of Hiram in exchange for the cedar and pine logs of Lebanon to be used in the construction of the temple (1 Kings 5:6-9).

Over the centuries individuals have attempted to gain ground economically through trade. Because there has been little overall economic growth throughout most of human history, merchants became very valuable to their nation-states. Savvy traders could enhance the power of one nation over another. This was a "zero-sum" game: one nation's growth could only come at the expense of the trade losses of other nations. In essence it was moderate plunder with a pleasant face. This approach to national economic growth, which first emerged in the early 1500s, became formally known in the seventeenth and eighteenth centuries as "mercantilism."

The major tenets of mercantilism are simple. The most important determinant of a nation's wealth is its trade balance. A nation will thus become wealthy only if it exports more than it imports. Increased wealth is considered synonymous with economic growth. Merchants (rather than the aristocracy) are the key players in such a system and should be provided every comparative advantage in world trade that the power and coercion of the state can provide. If military force allows a monopoly to be established in a distant foreign market, then merchants should charge the highest price possible. Restraint was to be exercised in the consumption of imports, but dumping in foreign markets was condoned as national policy. Domestic wages should be kept as low as possible in order to discourage the consumption of imports and assure a surplus for export. Export cartels were officially sanctioned, goods were to be shipped by national transport only and military force was acceptable as a means of maintaining foreign trade power and sovereignty. The importation of raw materials from trading partners was encouraged because domestic labor could then be used to capture the added value from finishing and processing. Exploitation in the pursuit of national economic advantage was not viewed as vice. It was a matter of national survival.[8]

Naturally, abuses occurred. One example is in the development of the sugar cane trade. The Arabs brought sugar cane from India to grow in the Mediterranean, using slave labor from East Africa. As a result of the Crusades, sugar was brought to Europe. Although slavery had long since given way to serfdom in Christian Europe, racism permitted the export of African slaves to sugar plantations in the Cape Verde Islands and later South America and the Caribbean. Inhumane working conditions and superprofits resulted in the estimated import of some 10 million African slaves over three centuries. Unspeakable shipboard conditions produced an average shipping loss of one in seven slaves, with losses of one in three not considered excessive. Caribbean slaves died faster than they reproduced.[9] Even in genteel England, any efforts to outlaw the shipping of African slaves were vigorously opposed by plantation owners and shipping interests. Because of the trade advantages from the sugar cane, they argued, such reforms would be detrimental to the national economic interests of Britain.

Then in 1787, a Christian member of Parliament wrote: "As soon as ever I had arrived thus far in my investigation of the slave trade, so enormous, so dreadful, so irremediable did its wickedness appear that my own mind was completely made up for the abolition. A trade founded in iniquity and carried on as this was, must be abolished." His name was William Wilberforce, and he became slavery's most influential foe. Year after year he introduced into Parliament a bill for the abolition of the slave trade. He organized a boycott of slave-grown sugar. He brought 519 petitions signed by thousands of British subjects to the House of Commons. The bill for abolition finally passed on February 22, 1807.[10]

While efforts by Christians such as Wilberforce brought the leaven of the Kingdom of God into the brutal world of trade advantage by coercion, the real waning of mercantilism came with the rise of the Industrial Revolution in England. At the time, philosophers John Locke and David Hume were emphasizing individual liberty, the rights of the individual to pursue ideas and engage in daily life with minimal interference from the state. If economic growth were to flourish, it was now argued, the functions of government should be limited to provision of law and order, the enforcement of contracts, and the maintenance of major public works. As the Magna Carta made the sovereign subject to God, the new democracy movement made government subject to the citizens. Democracy, together with the accumulation of capital, the division of labor, regional and international absolute advantages, and the facilitation of voluntary exchange among self-interested parties, was the true source of the economic growth and the wealth of nations, according to economic philosopher Adam Smith. These ideas coincided with the development of new technology, and the Industrial Revolution began to roll.

Technological Progress
Most economists today agree that the major determinants of the rate of economic growth include:

☐ comparative rather than absolute advantages
☐ a stable political and legal framework
☐ clear property rights, including protection of intellectual property rights (together with tax laws that encourage entrepreneurship)
☐ stable human rights
☐ free markets

☐ maximization of competition (freedom of exchange)

☐ investment in human capital (education)

☐ regulation of financial markets

☐ moderate government consumption, with low inflation

☐ increased capital per worker (capital accumulation)

☐ technological progress through innovation and investment in basic and applied research and development

The last factor listed has proven most important. When the contributions of all the major factors to long-term economic growth per person are examined, advances in knowledge, or innovation and continual technological progress, consistently account for more than half of the gains.

Economic growth through technological progress is the process termed "creative destruction" by economist Joseph Schumpeter. It is a dynamic process where equilibrium in markets is short-lived; in fact, markets for products and services now often come and go faster than grasshoppers on a hot tin roof, and those who hesitate to act are quickly left behind. The Enlightenment, with its emphasis on the scientific method and reason, certainly paved the way for an acceleration in technological change, the rise of the western Industrial Revolution, and a shift of emphasis to financial capital and democracy. The *laissez faire* capitalism of the Industrial Revolution encouraged self-initiative and self-improvement, the breaking down of class barriers and traditional community, and the rise of a chaotic world of ever-faster changing technologies, prices and economic identities.[11]

The pace of change was astounding and unprecedented. In the United States, for example, canals, turnpikes, steam power and railroads slashed transportation costs 95 percent between 1800 and 1859.[12] From 250 miles of track laid between Baltimore and West Virginia in 1828, total railroad mileage expanded to over 110,000 miles by 1900. From 75,000 jobs in 1810, manufacturing employment exploded to almost 5.9 million jobs by 1900.[13] The proportion of the population that was urban rose from 6 percent in 1800 to 40 percent by 1900[14] and inflation-adjusted output per capita rose 133 percent.[15]

Communities often sprang out of nowhere and disappeared as rapidly. In 1850 New England was 70 percent open farmland and 30 percent woods. Today the proportions are reverse. The invention of the McCormick reaper and the development of the railroads shifted the agricultural comparative advantage to the large, rock-free rolling fields of the Midwest. By 1860 nearly half of Vermont-born people (200,000 out of 450,000) had relocated.[16]

From 1860 to 1880 Chicago's lumber shipments rose from 220 million board feet to over a billion as growth in the railroads generated demand for wood for fuel, bridges and ties; demand for fence posts boomed as barbed wire spread across the West; and the innovation of the balloon frame house using mass-produced nails revolutionized the building industry.[17] In 1890, Henry Bagley, a railroad man from Cincinnati, gazed upon the stately virgin white pines and poplars of the Chattahoochee region of Georgia and saw a low-cost way to meet the seemingly insatiable demand for wood by the railroad industry and the growing housing and nonresidential construction industries. Besides the profits from the sale of the timber, Bagley earned revenue on the freight charges for hauling the timber to the various consumer markets. Within 30 years nearly all the hills of Northern Georgia were "turned into sunny groves of stumps."[18]

Edison invented the light bulb in 1879 and harnessed electricity. The turn of the century saw a burst of structural change with the arrival of the automobile, the telephone, airplanes, phonographs, radios and more. But few bursts of "creative destruction" rival the microprocessor miracle. The first integrated circuit on silicon in 1958 was followed 13 years later by the silicon-etching process and the microprocessors. In the next three decades processing power jumped 7,000-fold, single chip memory 250,000 times and transmission speeds by a factor of nearly 200,000. Chips sold for $7,600 per megahertz in 1970 and 17 cents today. Shipments of personal computers went from zero in 1970 to 43 million in 1999, with 53 percent of U.S. families owning PCs and 38 percent hooked to the Internet. The total supply of U.S. computer programmers, operators and scientists leaped from 284,271 in 1970 to an estimated 2.5 million today.

Microprocessors are used in everything from navigation systems, to medical diagnosis, to monitoring industrial waste, to genetic testing. Processing an Internet transaction costs a bank a penny compared with $1.14 with a pen, paper and teller. Microprocessor chips have reduced the costs of operating home appliances by one-third to two-thirds over the last 25 years. Wal-Mart cut as much as 20 percent off the cost of operating a delivery truck by installing computers, global positioning gear and cell phones in 4,300 vehicles.[19]

While the types of technology have changed, we still find that economic growth comes mostly from innovations and less from trade or plunder. So, from a Christian perspective, is this a better place to be? Yes . . . achieving economic growth through violence is certainly not a Christian ideal, and it's not much better to win a trade war at the expense of others. However, there are still some cautions, we must ask whether unlimited economic growth is theologically acceptable. To help answer this question, let us briefly consider the benefits and costs of economic growth.

The Benefits and Costs of Growth

A major benefit from economic growth is jobs, the opportunity for individuals to find a wide variety of employment at sustainable wages. While a rising tide does not lift all boats equally, during periods of sustained economic growth all segments of a nation's population appear to benefit through lower unemployment rates, higher labor force participation rates, greater income from wages and lower levels of poverty. In chapter one we saw that God's call to work preceded the Fall, and that men and women have a right and an obligation to work. Made in God's image, men and women find that it is natural and rewarding, and in many cases dignifying, to be engaged in productive work. To deny or deprive others of work is to offend against the image of God in them.

Other positive aspects of economic growth are obvious. Certainly, if we had to choose, most of us would prefer indoor plumbing to open outdoor latrines, penicillin to the application of leeches for the treatment of a fever, flying between London and New York to riding for a month on a leaky vessel in stormy seas, electric lights to candles for bedtime reading, and working in an air-conditioned office instead of an open field or shed when the thermometer hits 90 degrees. These examples just touch the surface with regard to the explosive rise in the standard of living in most industrialized countries over the past three centuries.

Food and drink are, for example, the most basic component of our standard of living. As reported by Fernand Braudel in sixteenth century Holland, meat was normally for nobles. "Poor townspeople rarely saw it: for them there were 'turnips, fried onions, dry if not mouldy bread' or sticky rye bread and 'small beer.' . . . The evening meal was often only gruel made from left-over bread soaked in milk."[20] Note the changes in the United States in the last century. About 1900, Americans spent 46 percent of their income on food, and today they spend 14 percent. Over this time the price of bread has fallen by 70 percent, the prices of milk and tomatoes by 82 percent, the price of chicken by 91 percent and the price of eggs by 94 percent.[21] This has been accomplished through extraordinary increases in agricultural productivity (three- to five-fold); improvements in shipping (e.g., containerization and refrigeration) and storage (e.g., flash freezing); modest improvements in processing; and significant changes in retailing. Since 1970 the average number of items per American supermarket have increased from 7,800 to more than 19,600; there are also more cash registers, operating hours and total floor space.[22] Together with the steady decline in food prices, price dispersion within categories of food products is at an all-time high as bar code scanners reduce the need for stock clerks and improve inventory management. As part of the free market's relentless drive to meet the specific desires of consumers, product variety at U.S. grocery stores has exploded. Over the past two decades the number of cereals has gone from 34 to 192, salad dressings from 79 to 260, cheeses from 65 to 300, laundry soaps and detergents from 12 to 48, and soft drinks from 26 to 252.[23] You want milk? Choose from whole milk, no-fat, 1 percent, 2 percent, 3 percent, lactose free, chocolate flavored, heavy cream, half and half, and synthetic creamer.

Economic growth has brought medical progress and concomitant reduction in physical suffering and increased life expectancy. Improved transportation and communication systems have facilitated social contact and the sharing of information. Individuals are more likely to be aware of both employment and consumption opportunities and thus far less likely to be exploited.

But, of course, there are costs to economic growth as well. The drive to maintain or increase the standard of living has caused the work week to rise steadily over the past 20 years and wives, including mothers with young children, to enter the labor force in droves (see chapter seven). This growing fixation with personal possessions and a rising standard of living has reduced time spent in family relationships and often made communities little more than a collection of well-appointed motels. For many people, time spent with God has been sacrificed for the idols of material gain and career, and the spiritual harm is reflected in a myriad of deteriorating social indicators.

The competitive market process of "creative destruction," as old goods and livelihoods are replaced by new ones, is painful. Workers find themselves displaced from occupations in which they have been employed for years, even decades. Certain groups such as older workers, minorities, the less educated and union members do not fare as well as the economy transitions from one industry to another. It takes these groups longer to find new jobs, and their post-displacement wages tend to be lower than what they had been earning.

Finally, there is the issue of environmental degradation (see chapter ten). In an increasingly global economy where competitive advantage requires either lower costs or higher productivity, producers are unlikely to voluntarily absorb the environmental costs that spill over from their activities. The record in the United States is clear. While there may be individual firms that are exceptions, industry has generally used every means possible to keep from assuming the costs of the environmental damage they generate. Companies are successful at this largely because they are a small, motivated, well-funded interest group. By contrast, the citizenry that suffers from environmental abuse has few financial resources, and the potential individual gains from winning are small relative to the costs of fighting.

For example, the U.S. Clean Water Act of 1972 had to be approved over a presidential veto. The Environmental Protection Agency's charge was simple:

establish technology-based uniform water standards and issue permits to individual businesses giving emission limits based upon those standards. Industries took EPA to court on procedural challenges over the standards, with the result that guidelines have been issued for only 51 industries. Enforcement, in many cases, has relied on telephone calls or letters. EPA infrequently brings civil or criminal charges, and even in cases of successful court action, fines and prison terms are not severe. With the mushrooming of new high-growth industries, challenges to EPA's performance will be even greater.[24] As detailed in chapter one, God has given men and women dominion over creation and they will be held accountable to God for their stewardship of those natural resources.

Conclusion

Christians certainly do not want to advocate policies that inhibit the improvement in the material and physical condition of our billions of brothers and sisters around the world. At the same time, for Christians unlimited economic growth as an economic objective in itself is clearly objectionable. A more theologically acceptable view is to develop the world to enable people to honor God. We want to encourage economic growth, but within the constraints of Christian ethics.

It would be near-sighted, for example, for Christians to stubbornly advocate protectionism in the long run for industries whose competitive advantages and customer base are clearly on the wane. The French weavers who fought the mechanization of the textile industry by sticking their wooden clogs into the gears of the water-powered looms simply saw their jobs lost to factories from England and American mills in New England. At the same time, however, job displacement is painful to individuals and their families. The research in the United States is clear. Beyond the negative impacts on self-esteem and self-worth, displaced workers generally make less money in their new jobs when they are older, less educated, less skilled, black, female, or union. And it takes these people longer to find new work. That's the dark side of progress: it can leave our neediest citizens behind. And those are the very people for whom Jesus urged us to care.

But progress will continue. Rather than stand against the inevitable restructuring of industries and markets, Christians should support policies to ease the painful impact of job displacement on individuals and their families. Federal law now requires companies to give notice well in advance of plans to close production sites. Federal and state programs and many individual companies provide displaced workers with a variety of services such as career planning, resume writing, practice in job interview, out-placement identification of new positions and retraining. If a worker's job is lost due to foreign competition, federal funds are available to finance the costs of retraining. Some states even allow displaced workers to take their unemployment insurance payments in a single lump sum to be used for education. These are examples of policies and programs that Christians can advocate. Simultaneously, churches and Christian organizations can provide support groups for the unemployed, job banks, and training in resume writing, and sponsor courses to retrain individuals in skills for which labor market demand is growing.

While economic growth has obvious costs, it has many more advantages. Christians can generally support sustainable economic growth, not in idolatry or greed, but in a sincere desire to please God.

Discussion Questions

1. Countries, individual companies and individual persons have become wealthy through the exploitation of other countries and individuals. Should, such as in the case of African Americans or former European colonies, reparation be made? If so, what form should the reparation take?

2. List five major benefits of economic growth. Now list five major costs.

3. Is it mercantilist thinking to want to have a positive trade balance? How can countries such as the United States have steady economic growth and a high standard of living with negative trade balances year after year?

6

RENDER
UNTO CAESAR
The Role of Government
in the Economy

In capitalism man exploits man; in socialism it's the other way 'round.

ABBA LERNER

Market capitalism can deliver goods and services in amazing quantities,
but it cannot guarantee caring communities that sustain body and spirit.

JAMES HALTEMAN

My kingdom is not of this world.

JESUS CHRIST (JOHN 18:36)

SYNOPSIS

*Despite the demise of most communist nations, there is still a broad variance in the size
and role of government among countries. In Italy, for example, government expenditures
account for 48 percent of Gross Domestic Product (GDP) compared to 22 percent in the
United States. Increasingly, however, government's control of resources is being shifted to
competitive markets as citizens are voting in favor of democratic capitalism and less government. Regardless of where a nation falls on the spectrum between socialism and capitalism, without transcendent values—the moral foundation provided by God—democratic
institutions do not function effectively. Christians need to be active in the public square.*

Meeting in a meadow called Runnymede, between Windsor and Staines,
King John of England, under duress from his nobles and church leaders, signed the Magna Carta on June 15, 1215. The Magna Carta
established the principle that neither citizens nor kings are above the rule of law,
and God endows the law. The Magna Carta was the first significant blow to absolute state despotism. It covered a laundry list of liberties that survive to this day,
such as the right to a fair trial by a jury and under the laws of the land, compensation for the confiscation of property by the state, the raising of taxes by common

consent and the freedom of the church from civil interference. Following the Magna Carta and the "Glorious" Revolution of 1688, came the 1689 English Bill of Rights and Act of Toleration (with respect to freedom of worship). Completing the transfer of sovereignty to the people, the 1689 Bill of Rights was the antecedent of the American Bill of Rights.

The concept of government "of the people, by the people and for the people" is steadily encroaching on nations in every continent. This does not mean, however, that there is consensus on how much government people want and need. Certainly communism, except in recalcitrant Cuba, North Korea and China, is dead. Nevertheless, socialism, where citizens through the expression of their collective will determine the allocation of resources and the resultant goods and services, is very much alive. While direct government ownership of the means of production is on the wane, central planning, substantial redistribution of income, and social engineering through regulations and the law all occur in the more socialist nations. A mixed capitalist economy such as the United States where central government expenditures account for 22 percent of GDP stands in sharp contrast to such nations as Israel and Italy (48 percent of GDP), France (47 percent), Sweden (44 percent), Hungary (43 percent), Denmark and Portugal (41 percent), and the United Kingdom (39 percent).[1] And environmental laws aside, the recent trend in the United States has been toward deregulation of economic activity (e.g., railroads, airlines, trucking, the Internet).

In this chapter we will consider two issues. First, what is the prevailing range of views among economists with respect to government's size and the extent of its involvement in daily affairs? We will briefly examine the position of those economists who favor reliance primarily on competitive markets and the beliefs of those who favor socialism. Second, do we find scriptural support for any one particular view? Should Christians favor socialism or capitalism? Is Christianity, as theologian Paul Tillich claimed, the religion of socialism, or the religion of capitalism, as claimed by Michael Novak?

The Perspectives of Economists

Adam Smith believed that, when the system of natural liberty and free markets prevails, government must attend to only three duties: protection of society from foreign invasion, the erection and maintenance of certain public works, and "duty of protecting, as far as possible, every member of society from the injustice or oppression of every other member of it, or the duty of establishing an exact administration of justice"[2] (see chapter two). These duties of jurisprudence encompass both *remedial* justice, including redress for injury to persons (physical and reputation) and property, and *commutative* justice, centered primarily on laws that protect property rights and encourage equilibrium between the market and the "natural" price (the Scholastic tradition of the "just" price). Smith makes no definitive statement on *distributive* justice, although various remarks in his writings show a recognition that markets can fail in their distributive function due to regulations, taxes and patterns of property ownership founded upon greed.

Adam Smith clearly saw human nature as fallen and believed that competition serves as a major curb on the excesses of self-interest. Smith was a strong proponent of the use of the state's powers to keep entry to markets open. Government should be very judicious in the granting of monopolies and tariffs, he said, and quotas should generally not be used to limit foreign competition. Smith opposed regulations that gave exclusive privileges to corporations, that limited entry into occupations through apprenticeships and that in any other way constrained the open operation of product and labor markets.

Today, economists who favor competitive markets as the primary means for determining the allocation of resources, output and income do not go far beyond Adam Smith's basic position. Such economists do recognize market failure and the consequent need for government action with respect to external effects such as air and water pollution (chapter ten) and the lack of perfect information (unavoidable ignorance) among consumers and employees. They acknowledge that the market produces an unequal distribution and wealth, and so they support various temporary economic "safety nets," but they oppose massive redistribution of income through government taxes and social programs (chapter nine). They also concede that the macroeconomy rarely comes to equilibrium at full employment with low inflation, but reject the neo-Keynesian fiscal adjustments to the economy. Instead, they support deliberate, transparent monetary policy to dampen the business cycle.

These economists tend to favor economic growth over social goals and see economic growth as coterminous with quality of life. They, therefore, are wary of any governmental actions that may intrude upon the free process of innovation and "creative destruction" that drives economic growth over the long haul (chapter five). This would include an aversion to over-regulation and to inheritance and anti-trust laws that may reduce individual and collective entrepreneurship and incentives to hard work and productivity. They see competitive markets as generally providing a level playing field for everyone willing to put forth reasonable and sustained effort, and although opposing discrimination, are not strong advocates of government regulations or actions that give special advantage to any one group. Individuals should be constrained primarily by their personal moral codes, they say, and the social processes and social order emerge spontaneously as an undirected consequence of chance interactions.

The views on government put forward by Gwartney, Stroup and Sobel are representative of this more conservative position. They make four assertions. First, higher taxes or additional borrowing will impose an increasing burden of dead-weight losses on the economy, as the size of government expands. Second, as government grows relative to the market sector, diminishing returns will reduce the rate of return derived from government. Third, the political process is much less dynamic than the market process and there is less incentive for increased productivity. Fourth, as government grows, it invariably becomes more heavily involved in the redistribution of income and regulatory activism—two activities that encourage wasteful rent-seeking, as individuals and firms seek returns that exceed opportunity costs.[3]

On the other hand, economists who favor socialism, or at least a greater presence of government in economic affairs, believe the selfishness of individuals requires the imposition of an ordered society based on reason and conscious design (i.e., planning). They would not necessarily cast Adam Smith aside, but would put greater emphasis on the need for distributive justice, government regulation and a trade-off between economic growth and quality of life orchestrated by government. Greater emphasis on distributive justice is exhibited in such countries as France, Sweden and Denmark through such actions as government-provided health care to all citizens, free child care, extensive housing subsidies, extended paid maternity leave, free college education, substantial subsidies to agriculture, and unemployment benefits that extend for a year or more. Government regulations are much stricter with respect to such issues as the environment, worker safety, land use and building codes. The government even mandates to employers the minimum amount of vacation that workers must receive (e.g., four weeks in Germany). While neo-Keynesian policies would appeal to economists favoring socialism, given the already substantial size of government, they would not necessarily favor full employment over social welfare. This is evidenced in part by the high, even double-digit, unemployment rates found in many of the socialist countries. Most of the industrialized socialist nations do adhere to stable monetary policies in order to keep inflation well under control.

Which group of economists is right? The trend over the past two decades has most definitely been toward more reliance on competitive markets. This includes the still undemocratic totalitarian nation of China with its mix of competitive markets and state-operated businesses, as well as industrialized countries such as France and the United Kingdom. This is, in part, recognition of the power of the price mechanism to automatically coordinate the preferences of consumers with the availability of resources and the capacity of producers. The lack of incentives for efficiency in large government bureaucracies is also a factor. It is safe to say that extreme socialism—with the collective ownership of property, extensive state-operated enterprises, the equalization of income, and all-pervasive economic planning—is, as the Marxists were fond of saying, confined to the dustbin of history. Such terms as market socialism and democratic socialism are used today to represent the path between capitalism and the socialism of command economies.

Research shows that countries with a high degree of economic freedom, including lower levels of government spending as a percent of GDP and lower levels of government transfer payments and subsidies, experience higher rates of economic growth (GDP per capita) than countries with less economic freedom.[4] When it comes to economic growth, competitive markets have the clear advantage. Nevertheless, cultures, traditions and common values still vary among nations. As a result, nations choose to allocate their scarce resources in various ways. Nations with a strong democratic tradition may choose to trade off economic growth for free universal child care or mandatory parental leave benefits. So long as the choice process is democratic, as opposed to coercive or bureaucratic, and the trade-offs explicit (e.g., higher labor costs with resultant product prices that are less competitive), one cannot say the outcome is less preferred.

What guidance does Scripture provide with regard to the alternative roles of government in economy and the choice between socialism and capitalism?

A Christian Perspective
Jesus makes it clear that his kingdom is not of this world (Jn 18:36). Throughout his ministry on this earth, when Jesus preached the gospel of the kingdom, he used the Greek word *(basileia)* that refers to the right or the authority to rule over a kingdom. As Charles Colson notes, "The Kingdom of God is a rule, not a realm. It is the declaration of God's absolute sovereignty, of His total order of life in this world and the next."[5] The initiation of the kingdom was the major focus of Jesus' preaching and ministry. Through the kingdom we find salvation, a restored and meaningful relationship with God, and the expressed moral authority of God. Until Jesus comes again, the state is ordained by God to restrain sin and promote justice. "While it cannot redeem the world or be used as a tool to establish the Kingdom of God, civil government does set the boundaries for human behavior."[6]

Christians have the same civic responsibilities as all citizens, but as citizens of the kingdom of God we are also to bring God's transcendent standards of righteousness and justice into the public square. Christians are to pay their taxes (Rom 13:6; Mt 22:15-21). Civil authorities are to be obeyed unless they set themselves in opposition to divine law (Rom 13:1-5; Jn 19:11). From a kingdom perspective the individual comes first—before the state or the social order. Ultimately, Christians are "aliens and strangers on earth" (Heb 11:13). Christians are to resist the temptation to use the coercive power of the state to bend society into conformity with our view of the kingdom. We must take care not to fall prey to the secular myth that the state can transform people. The state can constrain or not constrain people. It can influence individual behavior by threatening individuals' property, livelihood, families and lives. But, as shown by the rapid disappearance of communist philosophy's influence on Eastern Europeans in the early 1990s, that does not constitute personal transformation. King Josiah had the Book of the Covenant read to all the people of Judah. He removed the idols from the temple, did away with pagan priests, outlawed mediums and spiritualists, and destroyed the high place where children had been sacrificed to the sun god. Yet these sweeping outward reforms did not last long beyond Josiah's reign because the hearts of the Jewish people were not transformed (2 Kings 22—23).

Christians and the church must also be keenly aware that by standing for kingdom values, they will often be challenging the state's claim to ultimate authority in society. This is the legitimate, yet often lonely and dangerous, role of being the salt and light for God in this fallen world, speaking the truth in love. Beginning in the Garden, God gave men and women the freedom to choose to do what is right. This is the heart of democracy. Given fallen human nature, political systems tend to seek after power. In a centralized socialist system this may involve a small elite group seeking to impose its views on the majority, whether from altruism or from material greed. In a democracy this may require elected officials to pander to the sinful desires of various segments of society in order to get the funds and votes to win a campaign. Whenever the state sets itself in opposition to divine truth, Christians are called to prayerful civil action and even civil disobedience, to enter the public square in a stand for divine truth. Martin Luther King Jr.'s nonviolent resistance to the state is one of the twentieth century's supreme examples of faith in action in the public square.

With respect to government involvement in economic affairs, Scripture seems to generally support the views of Adam Smith. As discussed in chapter one, because humans are steeped in sin, we need the state to administer justice, to protect against aggression and to provide for public works (1 Kings 10:9). For the same reason, concentration of civil (and economic) power should be kept limited, with appropriate checks and balances, and complete freedom in economic affairs is rejected. As one observer commented, "We are sinners, and our economic life always shows it." The judiciously constrained coercive powers of government are to be used to encourage economic competition and minimize exploitation in product and resource markets (e.g., antitrust legislation, limiting barriers to entry, guaranteeing the right to collective bargaining).

God wants commutative justice in economic affairs (e.g., prices are not just when there is fraud or coercion in the market). Weights and scales are to be honest, a full measure (shaken down) is to be given (Lev 19:35-36; Deut 25:15; Prov 20:23; Lk 6:38), and currency is not to be debased by inflationary monetary policy or other means (e.g., mixing lead with silver). Lies and deceit are not to enter into economic transactions. Procedural justice requires that contracts and commitments be honored (Lev 19:13). Neither consumers, nor borrowers, nor lenders, nor suppliers are to be exploited. Absence of commutative and procedural justice in an economy raises the costs and reduces the frequency of transactions, reducing overall economic well-being.

God also desires justice when people are wronged economically, so that they get back what is lost. In cases of accidental loss the costs of restoration are to be borne partially or fully by the negligent party (Ex 21:33-36; 22:5-8, 10-15). In cases of crimes against property or persons the perpetrator's punishment may include public confession, multiple financial restitution and even death. With false accusations, the accuser is generally given the penalty associated with the alleged crime (Deut 19:16-19).

The Bible supports decentralized private ownership of most resources (chapter four) and God clearly warns about the dangers of centralized material, political and economic power (1 Sam 8: 6-18). There is consensus among both conservative theologians such as Michael Novak and liberal theologians such as Ronald Sider that, when it comes to economic growth, competitive markets are the clear winner over planned economies. Observes Pope John Paul II, "On the level of individual nations and of international relations the free market is the most efficient instrument for utilizing resources and effectively responding to needs." He adds, however, "But there are many human needs that find no place on the market."[7] The benefits of the free market economy come at a price. That price includes an unequal distribution of wealth and sinful individuals doing bad things to themselves, their families and their communities.

But is the government responsible for distributive justice? Economists disagree. So do Christians. As shown in chapter nine, neglect of the poor is not an option for Christians. All persons are made in the image of God. Each life is sacred and precious in his sight. Every person should have access to the basic provisions necessary for life (e.g., food, clothing, shelter, health care) and the opportunity to participate as an accepted member of the community. God is on the side of the poor, the weak and the oppressed, and so he clearly wants his people to fight economic injustice. People are to be treated equitably, without partiality. Every person who is able to work should have access to the productive resources necessary for dignified participation in the economy. We see a bias against a growing inequality in the distribution of wealth in the Old Testament traditions of the sabbatical and Jubilee years—times when debts were forgiven, property was restored to its original owners, and persons who had sold themselves into servitude to satisfy debts were set free.

In a democracy citizens have the right to voluntarily redistribute wealth and provide charity through private means. We can also elect officials who will take public actions to help the needy. But as detailed in chapter nine, there indeed exists great variation among democratic industrialized nations with respect to the extent of their social welfare spending. The caveats are twofold. First, as Michael Novak observes, "All sectors of society desire more, so politicians promise more. They spend money not their own, money the system does not have. The structural flaw in all welfare democracies is the desire of every population to live beyond its means."[8] Collecting that money through high or extremely progressive taxes helps to destroy the incentives that generate economic growth and may lead to a diminished economic base for all citizens. Second, rhetoric about compassion is often a vehicle used by politicians to obtain power. And political allocation of resources, regardless of its stated purpose, tends to be biased in favor of certain elite interests. According to economists James Gwartney and Richard Stroup, "Politicians are led as if by an invisible hand to reflect the views of special interest groups, even though this leads to wasteful policies."[9]

In our competitive market economy, as the traditional Christian values of self-discipline have given way to self-indulgence and hedonism, most firms and investors simply see new opportunities for making money. The boom in pornography (chapter thirteen) and gambling (chapter twelve), for example, is simply a matter of suppliers meeting consumers' demand for entertainment. The destructive spiritual impact on individuals, families and communities; the accompanying nihilism; and the degradation in the eternal value of each soul are ignored. Christians and the church are obligated to bring God's transcendent standards into the public debate on the regulation of these activities, into the management decision-making structure of corporations (chapter eleven), and into the lending decisions of financial institutions.

The rapid growth in productivity and prosperity in market-based economies has also led to rampant consumerism. Rampant consumerism, a sin of both the rich and the poor, is idolatry, a state of discontent built on covetousness and the substitution of "having" for "being." While God does not want Christians to live in abject, oppressive poverty, we are called to be content in all things and to put the Kingdom first. Prosperous Christians are warned by Jesus to give serious consideration to focusing less on consumption and saving (building bigger barns, Lk 12:18-21) and more on charity.

Government certainly should not allow interest paid on unsecured consumer debt to be deductible from taxable income, and high taxes could be placed on such things as luxury goods and vacation homes. Despite rhetoric from some social activists, research generally indicates that advertising doesn't create demand, rather it shifts demand among alternative substitutes. People actually do enjoy and value their VCRs and their cell phones. And advertising does inform consumers regarding the range of prices and characteristics of products and services. Nevertheless, government certainly can and should play a role in limiting false advertising and advertising of harmful products (such as tobacco).

Aside from taxing and spending, government has enormous impacts on economic activity through the regulatory process. Scripture clearly prohibits discrimination by economic class (Jas 2:1-4) or gender, race, ethnicity or age (Acts 2:17-18; Gal 3:26-29). Government should be aggressive in legislating against discrimination and prosecuting those who commit acts of discrimination. Government regulations should also protect workers from employers who would expose them to unsafe conditions or would steal from their pension funds, just as it protects them from unions that would deny them the right to work. Over-regulation, however, represents a serious danger for a number of reasons. First, it allows regulated industries to take advantage of government-erected entry barriers to raise prices and lower the quantities of products and services. Second, it attracts special interest groups of all stripes to seek special advantages from legislators and bureaucrats, a process that may involve corruption and bribery. Finally, particularly extensive and onerous governmental regulations will encourage disobedience and reduce citizens' respect for the authority of government (contrary to what Scripture desires).

Conclusion

So, which is the appropriate choice of economic systems for Christians: capitalism or socialism? Recent history shows that nations are increasingly voting in favor of democratic capitalism, and less government. Good stewardship of resources provides a scriptural affirmation of that movement. At the same time,

God's concern for the poor is in strong evidence from the beginning to the end of his Word. Certainly the competitive market system has demonstrated its superior ability to generate a rising tide that tends to lift all ships. Yet, disagreement remains among both Christians and nations as to what constitutes an acceptable minimal standard of living and how that minimal standard should be provided. The choice appears to lie on a continuum between mixed capitalism (such as in the United States) and the market socialism found in many Western European democracies.

Whatever the choice, it does not constitute the major threat to the survival of these societies. Differences in GDP per capita income are important but not essential. Democracy is essential. The real threat is the movement of nations into the post-Judeo-Christian era of relativism. Can these affluent societies, can any society, thrive and survive in defiance of the absolute transcendent authority of God? Without a moral foundation can democratic institutions function? Without democratic institutions there is not freedom of religion. And without religion there is no institution to challenge the power of government. Observes Christoph Schonborn, "His kingdom is not of this world, but it comes into this world."[10] Every time Christians apply their faith to economic issues, whether in the public square or the corporate boardroom or the nonprofit management structure, they have a chance to bring decision making back into accord with the values of the kingdom, protecting us from the natural destructive consequences of our sinful natures.

Discussion Questions

1. From a Christian perspective why did Marxist communism fail?

2. Which is a more Christian form of government: democratic capitalism or democratic socialism?

3. What functions does government have to undertake because of fallen human nature?

4. Should Christians concern themselves with the regulatory activities of government? If so, what areas of regulation are most significant?

7

OVEREMPLOYMENT
The Growth of Work
& the Loss of Leisure

We worship our work, work at our play, and play at our worship.

LELAND RYKEN

Whatever you do, work at it with all your heart, as working for the Lord, not for
men, since you know that you will receive an inheritance from the Lord as a reward.
It is the Lord Christ you are serving.

COLOSSIANS 3:23-24

SYNOPSIS

*As employees become increasingly expendable, American workers seek a deeper sense of
meaning and fulfillment on the job. For Christians there is sanctity in all labor, and without God's involvement human labor is futile. In whatever they do, Christians are to do it
heartily as unto the Lord, for we do not labor for the food that perishes, but for the food
which endures to everlasting life. This work may be in the labor force or in the home. Lack
of growth in real wages has helped bring married women into the labor force in unprecedented numbers, leading to less time with their children. Society places little value on
work in the home. Christians have to battle against the desire for material well-being at
the expense of invaluable leisure time spent with spouses and children.*

The situation has been ugly. Encouraged by Wall Street investors, many
companies over the past decade have slashed their full-time work forces,
reduced benefits and demanded more output from the remaining workers. The result, naturally, is an alienation between the company and the
employee. Many workers sense that they are merely expendable components of
an impersonal production process involving the manipulation of employees for
the sole objectives of the maximization of profit and shareholder value. They feel
like spare parts. No one seems to care that their own needs are growing. To a

large degree, employees are prisoners of increasing consumer debt, and many homes have extraordinary child care and evolving elder care pressures.

Not surprisingly, recent surveys find that American workers want a deeper sense of meaning and fulfillment on the job—even more than they want money and time off. Religious discrimination filings by workers grew 40 percent between 1992 and 2000. As religion plays an increasing role in the life of Americans, workers resent employers who try to strip them of their civil and constitutional rights, rights reaffirmed by the Civil Rights Act of 1964.[1] That might explain why spirituality in the workplace is suddenly a hot corporate topic. Driving this movement is mounting evidence that spirituality brings increased productivity. Those who work for organizations they consider to be spiritual are less fearful, less likely to compromise their values and more likely to throw themselves into their jobs.[2]

Whether this is just another passing corporate management fad or not, Christians see all life as spiritual. We're not driven by the bottom line, but by a higher calling. We seek to make decisions about all aspects of life within a spiritual context. So assuming that "work" includes both paid time and unpaid domestic labor, how should Christians balance work and leisure? In this chapter we first examine the trends in work and leisure in the United States. We then review and expand upon our Christian ethical framework, and finally consider what the Christian response to the recent trends should be.

Recent Labor Market Trends

During the past 25 years the structural changes in the U.S. labor market have been extraordinary. The most significant element is the inflation-adjusted average hourly earnings for wage and salary workers. It peaked in 1973 at $14.78 (expressed in 1999 dollars), declined precipitously through the 1981-1982 recession, recovered slightly only to decline again in the 1991-1992 recession. The annual average for 1999 was only $13.24, more than 10 percent below the 1973 peak. This decline in the inflation-adjusted wage has been most severe for workers with less education and for young males, especially young black males.

The decline in the inflation-adjusted wage is attributable to numerous factors. Among these are the entry of the "baby-boom" generation into the labor market; the growth of legal immigration over the past two decades, reaching its highest levels since the 1900-1920 period (see chapter fifteen); a decline in the size and strength of unions; the lack of sufficient increase in the minimum wage; slow growth in productivity; a shift in occupational demand from low-skill to high-skill occupations with a doubling of the earnings premium for college education;

and increased global competition.

There are six major trends tied, at least in part, to this decline in the purchasing power of the average wage. First, inflation-adjusted median household and family income peaked in 1973 and did not surpass its 1973 high until 1995. Expressed in 1997 dollars, median household income was $35,745 in 1973 and $35,887 in 1995. Similarly, median family income was $40,979 in 1973 and $42,769 in 1995. The increase in inflation-adjusted median family income was concentrated among married-coupled families who had two or more wage earners active in the labor market.

Second, married women entered the labor force in unprecedented proportions (being in the labor force means they are either working outside the home or actively looking for such work). Obviously, the drop in hourly earnings meant families needed more hours of work, and many wives began working in order to maintain the family standard of living. Social changes also led to rising levels of formal education and broader occupational choices for women. According to the U.S. Bureau of Labor Statistics, the proportion of females in the labor force rose from 44 percent in 1970 to 70 percent today. Nearly half of this increase was due to the entry of married women into the labor force as their participation rate rose from 41 percent in 1970 to over 61 percent in 1999. The rise was particularly high for married women with children, going from 49 percent in 1970 to 77 percent in 1999 for married women with children ages 6 to 17 and from 30 percent to 64 percent for married women with children under the age of 6. Over half the married mothers with children under a year old are now in the labor force, and two-thirds of these mothers work full-time. Nearly one out of five of their under-1-year-old children are cared for in organized child care facilities. Among all preschoolers whose mothers are employed, 29 percent are cared for in organized child care facilities, 15 percent in family day care homes and 45 percent in their own homes (frequently by a relative).[3]

Third, although the evidence is mixed, over the past two decades the average workweek among Americans working at least 20 hours or more has increased by anywhere from 1 to 4 hours, with the average increase for females ranging as high as 6 hours—the equivalent of an extra month a year.[4] Again, this appears to be an effort to maintain a rising standard of living. Even if the workweek has not risen, Americans are increasingly feeling crunched for time as they hustle to balance career, home and leisure. The percent of Americans under age 65 who said that they "always felt rushed" rose from 24 percent in 1965 to 38 percent by 1992. The share of people claiming they almost never had excess time on their hands rose from 48 percent in 1965 to 61 percent in 1995. The National Center for Health Statistics collected data on people's perceived stress levels over almost a decade, finding increased stress levels for virtually all demographic groups. On the latest survey, 56 percent of adults reported "a lot" or "moderate" stress in the past two weeks. Not surprisingly, as with the detailed data on adults who feel "rushed," women feel more stress, on average, than men, as do people with children. Stress peaks among persons aged 35 to 44 and drops sharply after age 54. Persons who work outside the home, compared to housewives, students and retirees, experience far more stress. Those with more education also feel more stress, possibly because their jobs involve greater managerial and financial responsibility.[5]

Fourth, between 1970 and 1998 the number of multiple jobholders has nearly doubled, from 4 million to 8 million. Almost 42 percent of these are working multiple jobs in order to meet regular household expenses and pay off debts. Nearly two million of them are married women whose spouses are present.[6] The population of nonfarm self-employed workers has risen from 5.2 million in 1970 to almost 9.0 million in 1998, and over 4 million of these are home-based businesses, many of which are part-time, supplementing earnings from a primary job.[7] Both multiple jobs and part-time self-employment contribute to family income.

We must also consider unpaid domestic work. As more American women have entered the paid work force, they have reduced their housework time, but not enough to compensate for their increased time on the job. As a result, their total hours of paid and unpaid work have increased dramatically. Men, on the other hand, are doing less paid work and more housework, but their increased housework time doesn't match the decrease in women's housework time. In short, everyone is working more, especially women, and there is still more work to do.

On average, women who are employed spend 3.3 hours each day directly in child care compared to 7.0 hours for women who are not working. While contact is maintained with children during other household work such as shopping and cooking, and the trend is to fewer children per family, certainly the increased labor participation of women has reduced the direct hours of care received by children.[8]

Fifth, during this period when the inflation-adjusted average wage was falling and median household income was flat, income inequality in the United States increased. Income inequality has traditionally been measured using the shares approach. Households are ranked by income from lowest to highest and then divided into quintiles (fifths) and the share of overall aggregate income of each quintile is calculated. Between 1975 and 1997 shares of aggregate income for all but the top quintile in the U.S. distribution declined (see table 7.1). While the top quintile's share rose from 43.2 percent to 49.4 percent, the shares of all the other quintiles dropped. The average household at the 95th percentile in 1997 had $126,550 in income, 8.2 times that of the household at the 20th percentile ($15,400). In 1967 the household at the 95th percentile had just 6.5 times the income of the household at the 20th percentile. When various adjustments are made for work benefits, taxes, the earned income tax credit and government transfers (both means-tested and non-means-tested), lessening the income inequality, they don't have much impact.

Table 7.1. Household Income Dispersion, 1975-1997

Income Quintiles	Shares 1975	Shares 1997
Lowest quintile	4.4%	3.6%
Second quintile	10.4%	8.9%
Third quintile	17.1%	15.0%
Fourth quintile	24.8%	23.2%
Highest quintile	43.2%	49.4%

Source: U.S. Department of Commerce, Bureau of Census, in "Money Income in the United States, 1997," *Current Population Reports, P60-200,* p. xi.

Sixth, the decline in the inflation-adjusted average wage is not the only factor behind the growth in income inequality in the United States. About one-third of the increase in inequality is due to the changing demographic composition of households,[9] most particularly the rapid increase in female-headed families due to divorce, separation and out-of-wedlock births. Divorces per thousand marriages have risen from 320 in 1970 to 490 in 1997. The median duration of marriage is now 7.2 years. More than a million children are involved in a divorce each year. Simultaneously, the percent of births to unmarried mothers jumped from 10.7 percent in 1970 to 32.4 percent in 1997. The out-of-wedlock birth rate is an astounding 70 percent for blacks, having almost doubled over the past two decades. The rate for whites is now 26 percent, increasing almost fivefold over the past two decades![10]

What is the major demographic factor accounting for the growing inequality in the income distribution? Research from a variety of sources points to *differences in the number of workers per family.* The lowest quintile of all U.S. households has only 19 full-time workers per hundred households while the highest quintile has 134 full-time workers per hundred households.[11] You can imagine how the rise of single parenting has affected those figures.

The causes of divorce and out-of-wedlock birth are undoubtedly not just economic but social and cultural as well, and often interrelated. David Blankenhorn notes that fatherhood as a social role has been radically diminished in three ways, significantly contributing to these trends. First, there are fewer things distinctively defined as father's work. Second, within the wider society many influential people argue that fathers are simply not very important. Finally, "and most important, fatherhood has been diminished as paternity has become decultured— denuded of any authoritative social content or definition. . . . It is biology without society."[12] At the same time, family finances have been for decades a major strain on marriages and a precipitating factor for divorce, and the falling real wages of men has not eased this strain.[13] No evidence currently exists on how married women's entry into the labor force has affected the divorce rate. Certainly, having an established source of income gives women more of an opportunity to leave what they see as a bad marriage. Alternatively, if wives find their work emotionally and psychologically rewarding, it may enhance the marital relationship.

The factors behind the rise in out-of-wedlock births are a matter of some contention in the research literature. Nevertheless, four things are clear.

First, contrary to what logic dictates, there is almost no statistically reliable relationship between welfare payments and the out-of-wedlock birth rate.

Second, there is a strong positive statistical relationship between young women's perceptions of their economic prospects and having a child out-of-wedlock, especially in the African-American community.[14] Unmarried young women who believe they face a bleak work future are far more likely to have children.

Third, the decline in the pool of "marriageable" black males age 25 to 44 due to the precipitous decline in the real wages of young black males, their high unemployment rates, incarceration rates and death rates, has been an important factor in the rise of the black female out-of-wedlock birth rate.[15] Ironically, married white females have been a major competitor for young black males in the labor market—so one trend affects another.

Finally, delayed marriage and what Blankenhorn has labeled "decultured paternity" have contributed to a decline in marriage following the birth of a child among couples who have cohabited.

In 1970, 85 percent of children under 18 lived with two parents. By 1998 that figure had dropped to 68 percent. The percent of children living with their biological father and mother dropped from 75 percent in 1970 to 58 percent in 1990.[16] Meanwhile, the proportion of children living with only their mother more than doubled, from 11 to 23 percent in 1998. Of these, the proportion living with a mother who never married soared from less than 1 percent to more than 9 percent. Of the approximately 25 million children today who do not live with their fathers, 40 percent have not seen their fathers for at least a year, and 50 percent have never once stepped inside their father's house.[17] Not surprisingly, studies are showing that single mothers have more difficulty than working married mothers in finding time to spend with their children, as they try to squeeze into a day the multiple tasks that can overwhelm even two parents. Moreover, the poverty rates of female-headed families are over three and a half times the poverty rate for all persons. Even though almost 79 percent of female heads of families[18] are working, their annual median income is 36 percent of the annual median income of married-couple families with children under 18.

Besides the stress on single mothers, consider the negative impacts of divorce, separation and out-of-wedlock birth on children. Research shows that, compared to children from two-parent families, these children are "more likely to have emotional and behavioral problems, [have] academic trouble, drop out of high school, become pregnant as teenagers, abuse drugs, commit crimes, become mentally ill, or get in trouble with the law. Children of never-married mothers are 75 percent more likely to fail a grade in school and more than twice as likely to be expelled or suspended. Eighty percent of all adolescents in psychiatric hospitals come from broken homes and seventy percent of the juveniles in state reform institutions grew up in fatherless homes. Single parenthood is a better predictor of criminal activity than low income."[19] The costs of fatherless families to children and society are simply staggering.

In summary, the trend in the United States has been falling real wages, accompanied by falling real average household and family income. In response people are working longer hours or more jobs, and women have entered the labor force in unprecedented proportions. The result is more total hours devoted, especially by women, to paid and unpaid (domestic) work and a rise in the proportion of persons under age 55 who feel more stress. Simultaneously, the time given to child care by working women has decreased. As the falling real wage contributed to growing inequality in the income distribution, it also contributed to the rising rates of divorce and separation and out-of-wedlock births. The resulting explosion in female-headed families has raised the poverty rate, placed enormous stress on single mothers and imposed a staggering emotional and behavioral toll on a generation of children.

We should note that since the early 1990s some of the factors behind the declining inflation-adjusted average wage are starting to shift. The "baby bust" is now entering the labor market and entry-level wages are rising. New laws restricting social services to legal immigrants are raising their contribution to domestic income and consumption. Unions are helping to stabilize wages in some service sectors and, for better or worse, are growing rapidly in the public sector. Productivity has risen, driven in part by computer technology and increased capital per worker. Growth is occurring in service sectors that have higher wages and are higher value-added (e.g., engineering services, information systems technology), although formal education is still a critical determinant of wages. And the devaluation of the dollar, together with significantly reduced trade barriers and high-interest, low-risk investment opportunities have begun to shift the balance of trade, including international capital accounts, in the favor of the United States. So we can expect to see the inflation-adjusted average wage to continue to rise of the long term.

Social trends don't change as quickly as the economy. We still see alarming inequality in income and the continued weakening of families. Even with an upturn in real wages, there's still a generation of children growing up without enough parental care. The church and Christian ministries are facing a generation of potential walking wounded—adults who appear whole on the surface appear but whose emotional and spiritual lives are in turmoil.

Ethics Revisited

In our ethical framework we learned, through the creation and Fall, that men and women have a right and an obligation to work. God's call to work preceded the Fall, so work itself can be considered good. But the Fall made work more difficult, and the consequences of not "subduing" the world became more dire. "I went past the field of the sluggard . . . thorns had come up everywhere, the ground was covered with weeds, and the stone wall was in ruins. . . . A little sleep, a little slumber, a little folding of the hands to rest, and poverty will come on you like a bandit and scarcity like an armed man" (Prov 24:30-34). If people are able to work, they are to do so. If they choose not to work, they are to be held accountable. Says the apostle Paul, "If a man will not work, he shall not eat" (2 Thess 3:10).

Work not only satisfies basic needs, it can be a privilege from God. "A man can do nothing better than to eat and drink, and find satisfaction in his work. This . . . is from the hand of God" (Eccles 2:24). Why should work bring enjoyment? The creation narrative shows God to be a worker, a diligent laborer. God neither slumbers nor sleeps as he watches over the lives of his people day and night (Ps 121). Likewise Jesus was a worker, "My Father is always at his work to this very day, and I, too, am working" (Jn 5:17), whose food was "to do the will of him who sent me and to finish his work" (Jn 4:34).

Made in God's image, men and women find that it is natural and rewarding, in many cases dignifying, to be engaged in productive work. According to Pope John Paul II, as God creates, so too do individuals create with God through work. This spirituality further dictates that work is not only needed for our human material condition (food, family, leisure, savings) but is also part of our subjectivity, creativity and artistic personality. Labor gives food for our bodies and meaning to our lives.[20] As a consequence, to deny or deprive others of work is an offense against the image of God in them. Everyone should have the opportunity to participate as an accepted member of the community. All should have access to the productive resources for dignified participation in the economy.

God has endowed individuals with differing talents and skills (1 Cor 12; Rom 12). We see this as early as Genesis 4 and 5 where one man is called to be a herder, another a tiller, another a metal crafter and another a musician. In the early missionary church Paul was called to preach to the Gentiles and Peter to the Jews (Gal 2:7-9). Based on these Scriptures, we can conclude that markets and economic institutions should facilitate the exercise and development of individuals' talents and reward them appropriately ("the worker deserves his wages" [Lk 10:7; Col 4:1]). The individual then has the responsibility to develop his or her talents (Lk 19:11-26; 2 Tim 1:6), and to use the talents and the subsequent fruits for the glory of God (1 Cor 10:31).

The Reformation established the notion that work was a calling, a yielding to God, and that people could serve God in any honest occupation. Martin Luther remarks that household work "has no appearance of sanctity; and yet these very works in connection with the household are more desirable than all the works of all the monks and nuns. . . . Seemingly secular works are a worship of God and an obedience well pleasing to God."[21] The theme of work as a calling was expounded by John Calvin, and later labeled as the "Protestant work ethic" by agnostic sociologist Max Weber. Philosopher John Locke believed that to be good Christians, to build God's kingdom on earth and to evince the highest of civic virtues, Christians should labor for human progress in obedience to God's specific call to them. "The Lord," says the apostle Paul, "has assigned to each his task" (1 Cor 3:5). For the Christian, work is a calling from God. It has spiritual significance, whether it produces the necessary, the useful or the beautiful. All work is thus entitled to respect and all workers are equal in dignity.

While the world may place occupations into a hierarchy, for Christians there is sanctity in all labor. This is especially true because our ultimate focus is on the kingdom and the impact our work has on the world for Christ, whether directly through ministry or indirectly through our witness in the workplace and the world. Our attitude toward whatever work is assigned to us, our work ethic, our servant spirit in carrying out the least task may be used by God to speak to others. As the apostle Paul notes, "Not many of you were wise by human standards; not many were influential; not many were of noble birth. But God chose the foolish things of the world to shame the wise; God chose the weak things of the world to shame the strong. He chose the lowly things of this world and the despised things—the things that are not—to nullify the things that are, so that no one may boast before him. It is because of him that you are in Christ Jesus, who has become for us wisdom from God—that is our righteousness, holiness, and redemption. Therefore, as it is written, 'Let him who boasts, boast in the Lord' " (1 Cor 1:26-31).

Without God's involvement, human labor is futile. "Unless the LORD build the house, those who build it labor in vain" (Ps 127:1). Martin Luther believed that work done through faith in God and in obedience to his commands saves us from the paralyzing fear of human ineffectiveness and from the arrogance of human achievement. God's blessings come to us through our labors, and at times without our labors, but never because of our labors.[22]

Because of variations in supply and demand, different occupations command different levels of remuneration. Consequently, within societies we find an unequal distribution of earnings, even for equal hours worked. As noted by Arthur O'Sullivan and Steven Sheffrin, "There is substantial variation in wages across occupations. Most professional athletes earn more than medical doctors, who earn more than college professors, who earn more than janitors. The wage for a particular occupation will be high if the supply of workers in that occupation is small."[23] Wide earnings disparities may exist between management and production (salaried) employees. Laborers should be free to organize in order to counterbalance the concentrated power of management, but they should not be jealous of the variations in talents and skills endowed by God. Christians called into management have an obligation to ensure that wages are just (Lev 19:13). "Woe to him who builds his palace by unrighteousness, his upper rooms by injustice, making his countrymen work for nothing, not paying them for their labor" (Jer 22:13).

While sloth is a sin and Christians in whatever they do are to do it heartily, "as working for the Lord, not for men" (Col 3:23), this is not exhortation to workaholism. For we serve the Lord Christ (Col 3:24) and we are not to turn our work into idolatry. "Do not work for the food that spoils, but for the food that endures to eternal life, which the Son of Man will give you" (Jn 6:27). For what does it profit someone to gain the whole world only to lose their soul? Larry Burkett classifies as workaholism "anything that interferes with your relationship to God or your family and is out of balance according to God's Word."[24]

Similarly, in the drive for success in the world of work, Christians are not to allow other laborers to be exploited (e.g., dangerous working conditions, the withholding of wages)[25] or tempt laborers to place work before God and his priorities. As established by the law of the sabbath (Ex 20:8-11), the annual feasts of the Old Testament and the behavior of Christ (Mk 6:45-47; Lk 6:12), for example, persons have both a right and an obligation to rest. This affords time to enjoy creation, serve others (starting with our families) and spend time in communion with and in corporate worship of God. "Is it our desire to be self-sufficient, to be independent, to provide for our own needs?" asks Calvin Beisner. "By commanding us to rest one day in seven, God vividly reminds us that it is not by our own efforts or our own goodness that we flourish, but by His gracious blessing. The Sabbath commandment attacks the selfishness that can motivate economic activity, and suggests another motive altogether: faithful service to God as stewards of His household. By resting, Christians commemorate the completeness of God's creative and redemptive work (Ex 20:11; Deut 5:15; cf. 6:10-14), acknowledging that all of our work is not for ourselves but for the Lord and His Kingdom (Col 3:23-24; cf. Eph 6:5-8; 1 Cor 7:22)."[26]

Given the unequal distribution of talents among persons and the differential endowment of wealth that results, it would be foolhardy to imagine that Scripture condemns wealth as such. Through investments, wealth allows for the improvement in the material well-being of all persons by facilitating economic growth. Through charity, wealth allows for the relief of poverty. Wealth, at the same time, is fraught with spiritual dangers. Work, and the money that comes with it, can easily lead us into self-reliance and a focus on self-fulfillment. This is exactly the opposite of the Christian ideal of total reliance on God, seeking to do His will and focusing on self-sacrifice.

For modern organizations seeking technical efficiency, specialization makes most productive work a cooperative venture, where individuals join together in a common task. Observes Pope John Paul II, "It is characteristic of work that it first and foremost unites people. In this consists its social power: to build a community."[27] The primary rules for Christians in community are clear. We are to give up our lives for others, we are to love our neighbors and even our enemies. By doing this, we reflect the love that Christ has for those people. Fellow employees are not to be seen simply as instruments in the production process or as objects for exploitation, but as neighbors in a community of work. Jesus did not work alone. The disciples were sent out two by two. At various times Paul had Silas, Barnabas, Luke and others as coworkers. It is in community (e.g., family, church) where one learns to exercise and accept Christian love, and this includes the wide variety of work communities. Furthermore, James Halteman asserts, "The fact that wisdom is imparted through the group, not through individuals alone, is a prominent theme in the New Testament. . . . The effectiveness of the group in decision-making and ministry derives from the way in which God has endowed the community of faith with an assortment of gifts."[28]

The Christian Response

What can we do? In light of these recent trends, our ethical framework calls for action on the individual, corporate, civic and public levels.

Individually, a flippant response might be to get a good education; find a full-time job, stick with it and do it well; get married and stay married; and save money. On average, the earnings of college graduates are more than three times the earnings of high school dropouts, and the average earnings of persons with professional degrees more than five and a half times higher. We must remember, however, that God has endowed individuals with differing talents and skills, and not everyone is suited or called to higher education. The individual's responsibility is to develop his or her talents and to use these talents to the glory of God. If God has called you to get a college degree, then do it diligently, recognizing the privilege you have been afforded. But at the same time, you should recognize and honor the sanctity of the work to which your friends and others have been called, whether mechanic, janitor, truck driver or full-time parent.

People who enter the work force and stay there, see their earnings grow as they grow older, at rates well above inflation. This reflects, in part, a reward for work experience and knowledge. Because work is a calling for Christians, this commitment to whatever career path or career paths God presents to you over time is natural. You will do the work well because that is part and parcel of your workplace witness, as you work "for the Lord, not for men."

While it is not God's will for all persons to enter into the sacred relationship of marriage, if you do and are blessed with children, you will place your family responsibilities before your material lifestyle and increased consumption. You will maintain a balance between paid work, family time and spiritual time. You will honor and commit part of your scarce time to your spouse. God saw that it was not good for man to be alone. So, "He made us a two gendered people, with the capacity to feel exquisite physical pleasure, to long for emotional intimacy, and to give ourselves in stable, enduring relationships."[29] Moreover, "Sons are a heritage from the LORD, children a reward from him. Like arrows in the hands of a warrior are sons born in one's youth. Blessed is the man whose quiver is full of them" (Ps 127:3-5). You are to train up your children in the ways of the Lord (Prov 1—9) so that, when they are adults, they will not depart from his ways. "And all your children shall be taught of the LORD; and great shall be the peace of your children" (Is 54:13). The peace of the Lord, a heritage beyond value, will be passed on to your children as a result of your faithfulness, discipline and commitment to the balance between paid work and family commitments.

If, within that balanced life, God blesses you with unusual wealth, you will not let it interfere with your total reliance on him. You will see yourself as a steward of that wealth for the cause of his kingdom. You will give freely, for freely you have received, and you will never allow wealth to be your idol. As a Christian you are fully aware of how easily the desire for material goods can turn your heart away from God, and the insidious trap of the work-and-spend cycle.

Moreover, the issue is not just individual. Because God calls you to be concerned with justice and to build community, as a Christian you have corporate, civic and public responsibilities as well. As much as possible, you should seek justice in society. That means all people having the opportunity to participate in dignified work. That means workers receiving fair compensation and benefits and being provided with a safe working environment. That means giving workers a chance to strike a balance between work, family and leisure. That means making sure that single parents and their children have sufficient resources to participate as functional members of the community, and that individuals have access to education and training. It also means that all members of the community—employers, employees, parents and children—are held accountable for their choices and behavior.

With that goal in mind, Christians should be actively concerned with the impacts of the current economic stresses on the working poor and single mothers. We should get involved with debates over raising the minimum wage, increases in the Earned Income Tax Credit, refundable Dependent Care Child Tax Credits, public service employment programs for the long-term unemployed, universal health care coverage, portable health care benefits, the availability of quality education for all children, preschool educational programs for disadvantaged children, the rights to collective bargaining, flextime and job sharing, parental leave and occupational licensing.[30] You, particularly, can bring your conceptual training in economics to bear on the analysis of the proposed alternatives to these issues, supporting those alternatives that efficiently achieve the proposed end and integrate with your Christian ethical framework.

Finally, there is the major issue of the battle between the spirits of this world,

the strong currents of the mainstream culture, and the will of God. We can provide people with opportunities to restore more of the balance between paid work
and other activities (including family activities), but that doesn't mean people
will avail themselves of the opportunities. In her exhaustive study of the progressive Amerco company, sociologist Arlie Hochschild found that, even though the
corporation provided a broad range of family-friendly options through a Work-
Life Balance program, working parents did not use the options. Surveys indicated
that working parents were indeed worn down, feeling stressed, experiencing a
"time famine" and feeling guilty about the lack of time and energy devoted to
their spouses and children; this program should have been just what they needed.
Why didn't they use it?

Although a somewhat hostile attitude among management played a role, the
major reason working parents did not participate was the "devaluing of what was
once the essence of family life. The more women and men do what they do in
exchange for money, and the more their work in the public realm is valued or
honored, the more, almost by definition, private life is devalued and its boundaries shrink. For women as well as men, work in the marketplace is less often a
simple economic fact than a complex cultural value." Workers appreciated themselves more at work than at home. Although Amerco parents loved their children,
they often found life at home less interesting than life at work. Hochschild sees
"Day care for children, retirement homes for the elderly, wilderness camps for
delinquent children, even psychotherapy, in a way, as commercial substitutes for
jobs a mother once did at home. The main 'skill' still required of family members
is the hardest one of all—the ability to forge, deepen, and repair family relationships."[31]

Conclusion

In our ethical framework we noted that, made in God's image, men and women
find that it is natural and rewarding, in many cases dignifying, to be engaged in
productive work. Critics of the market economy have claimed that specialization
and profit-seeking would lead workers to lose interest in their work, would stifle
the individual creative spirit and would cause work to lack significance; however,
survey data contradict this. As reported by John Richard Bowen, "Few workers
indicated that their jobs are monotonous or lack interest; most had a strong sense
of the importance of what they do. Sometimes this importance was expressed in
terms of the significance of their work to society, and sometimes in terms of the
significance of their tasks to the team of workers (or the firm) of which they are a
part. Few indicated that their jobs did not make full use of their talents and capac-

ities. It was found that one of the most important values people find in their work is the human associations it offers. These associations are with fellow workers, customers, sellers, and so on. What people miss most keenly when they do not work is these associations; and what determines whether they like or dislike their jobs is the quality of the human relations involved."[32]

The challenge to Christians and to the church, it would appear, is not to denigrate paid work, but rather to express the importance of unpaid work devoted to family. Ever-higher standards of living cannot overcome the emotional damage wrought by the lack of meaningful family relationships. The opportunity costs of society's current direction are obvious and tragic.

On an even more global plane, we should stress the importance of what Leland Ryken terms the "calm acceptance of time as God's gift"—acknowledging that "this is the day the LORD has made; let us rejoice and be glad in it" (Ps 118:24). We can yield ourselves each day to God's will and purpose, knowing that daily time is kingdom time.[33] And therefore, "Go, eat your food with gladness, and drink your wine with a joyful heart. . . . Always be clothed in white, and always anoint your head with oil. Enjoy life with your wife, whom you love. . . . Whatever your hand finds to do, do it with all your might" (Eccles 9:7-10).

Discussion Questions

1. In many families with young children both the father and mother are working outside the home to maintain a middle-class lifestyle. What are the impacts of this on the family? Is there an alternative?

2. Given the recent trends in the U.S. labor market, what can government do to encourage healthy families?

3. What factors make labor force participation more attractive than raising children and maintaining a household?

4. Over their lifetimes college graduates earn twice as much as high school graduates. Is this fair?

8

CATCHING YOUR INTEREST
Lending & Borrowing
in Scripture & History

Lending money at interest is akin to murder and pimping.

MARCUS PORTICUS CATO (234-149 B.C.)

**Man never fastened one end of a chain around the neck of his brother,
that God did not fasten the other end around the oppressor.**

LAMARTINE

**"Investment" means putting capital to work. It aims at increased productivity,
and thereby benefits all, not just the investor.**

DAVID CHILTON

SYNOPSIS

*Interest, the price paid for the use of money, was a controversial issue in the early church.
The Old Testament forbids usury, a word in Hebrew that means "to bite, to strike with a
sting." In the New Testament, however, Jesus encourages the earning of interest, or tokos,
a word in Greek that means "to bear, bring forth." There are sensible reasons for charging
interest, but in doing so Christians are not to oppress or hurt the poor. Christians should
limit their borrowing to what can be secured with collateral. Both in low-income inner-city
neighborhoods and in developing countries Christians should fight against usurious interest rates by offering funds at more reasonable rates.*

Have you rented any money lately? You probably have. If you currently
have a student loan, those rent charges are amassing even now, adding to
the amount you borrowed. If you have a credit card, you're probably
being charged a high rent every time you flash it. You would expect to pay rent
for the temporary use of an apartment or a car or a big-screen TV to watch the
Super Bowl. But you also pay rent for the money you borrow. We call it *interest*.

Interest is *the price paid for the use of money for a specific period of time*. This
little economic detail has been the subject of major controversy over the centu-

ries. Even now, people rail at the high interest rates enslaving consumers to credit card companies, and national economies rise and fall on the prime interest rates set by major banks.

Market economics presents four logical reasons for the charging of interest. First, during the period of the loan the lender is deprived of alternative uses of his or her money, including the return on alternative investments. Second, there is the time preference for money; most individuals prefer the ability to use their money today as opposed to the possibility of being able to use that money at some future date. Third, there is always the risk, even with collateral, that all or part of a loan may not be repaid. Finally, the persistence of inflation in most societies requires a portion of interest to be levied simply to maintain the purchasing power of the original loan principle.

These all seem like sensible reasons for lenders to expect the payment of interest. And potential borrowers are free to bid for available loanable funds. What is that money worth to you? You could borrow money to buy a house, and thirty years from now, your house should be worth more than all you paid for it, including interest. You could borrow money to pay for your education, which should net both monetary and quality-of-life rewards in the long term. Or you could borrow to buy a brand new Corvette, if you think that the satisfaction you get is worth the payments you make. If interest rates are too high, you might decide not to buy that house, that education or that car—or you might seek a more reasonable lender.

Thus the range of prevailing market interest rates is a function of the supply and demand for funds. Low-risk investments, such as U.S. Treasury bonds, sell at low interest rates because willing suppliers are plentiful, and unsecured (uncollateralized) loans, such as credit card debt, sell at high interest rates because suppliers run a higher risk of default. Similarly, demand for Treasury bonds is steady because risk is low and demand for revolving credit card loans is high because the vast majority of borrowers believe they will pay the loans before any interest is accrued.

What should the position of Christians be with regard to interest on loans? Should Christians borrow money at all? If so, should Christians ever have uncollateralized debt? Should Christians charge interest to other Christians? To the poor? What constitutes a "fair" rate of interest? Should Christians actively work to outlaw loan sharks and support usury laws? What about the infamous moneylenders preying upon the poor in the rural and urban areas of the Third World?

We may find answers by looking at the history of loan interest. This fascinating journey involves detailed theological arguments over Scripture, interpretation of specific Hebrew and Greek terms, the self-interest of the church at various points in time and the changing perspective that accompanied the shift from a primitive agrarian economy to an international marketplace where billions of dollars are electronically transferred in seconds. This study can also teach us about Bible interpretation, especially the needs to consider the specific context of individual verses and to look for the broad sweep of biblical truth.

Usury

The term *interest* is not found in the King James Version of the Bible. It uses the word *usury* fifteen times in the Old Testament and twice in Jesus' teachings. While Jesus used the term positively, the Old Testament is generally negative, referring to excessive interest that oppresses the borrower. This reflects differences in the two different original words from Hebrew and Greek. The Hebrew word used in the Old Testament, *nashak*, comes from a root word meaning "to bite, to strike with a sting (as a serpent)." You can understand how a borrower might feel "bitten" by a loan shark. By contrast, the Greek word Jesus used in the New Testament, *tokos*, comes from the root word *tikto*, "to bear, bring forth," as the earth would bring forth its fruit. *Tokos* could even refer to the acting of birthing offspring. Modern translations use the word *interest* in both the Old and New Testaments, but we must keep the distinction in mind as we take a more detailed look at the verses. While the Old Testament ruled against the exacting of "biting" interest rates (which I prefer to call *usury*), Jesus seemed to approve the "fruit-bearing" quality of sensible investments.

In the Old Testament law laid out in Exodus, Leviticus and Deuteronomy, the people of Israel were explicitly prohibited from charging usury (interest) to their fellow Israelites, particularly the poor, but they could charge interest to the unbeliever (the stranger, the foreigner). Typical is Deuteronomy 23:19 20 (NKJV): "You shall not charge interest to your brother—interest on money or food or anything that is lent out at interest. To a foreigner you may charge interest, but to your brother you shall not charge interest, that the LORD your God may bless you in all to which you set your hand in the land." If a lender took a poor man's cloak for collateral, it was to be given back to the borrower each night so he might keep warm. In fact, this use of collateral may have had less to do with securing the loan than preventing the poor man from using the same collateral for more than one loan.[1]

Moreover, every seventh year (the "sabbatical year") all debts to brethren fellow citizens were to be forgiven (or at the least payments on the debt were suspended for a year).[2] Every 50 years (the "Jubilee year") all property was to be returned to its original owners. This typically involved the redistribution of land, although houses are mentioned and even individuals who sold themselves into slavery. If a family had been forced to sell or mortgage their property, or if they lost it as collateral on loans (e.g., Neh 5), every fiftieth year they would get it back.

Note that these guidelines applied only to interactions with other Israelites. There was no limit on the interest rate that could be charged to foreigners; neither did the sabbatical or Jubilee years apply to them.

The law against usury is supported throughout the remainder of the Old Testament. Psalm 15:5 reads: "[He] who lends his money without usury, and does not accept a bribe against the innocent. He who does these things will never be shaken." The prophets (e.g., Isaiah, Jeremiah, Ezekiel) roundly condemned Israelites who applied usury to their brethren and particularly the poor. Says Ezekiel (18:13), "He lends at usury and takes excessive interest. Will such a man live? He will not!" Rebuking Jerusalem for her many sins, the Lord says through Ezekiel, "You take usury and excessive interest and make unjust gain from your neighbors by extortion. And you have forgotten me. . . . I will disperse you among the nations and . . . put an end to your uncleanness" (Ezek 22:12, 15). Disobedience with respect to the sabbatical year was also a reason given for the Babylonian exile and dispersion of the people of Israel.

Ron Sider asserts that, like the Old Testament principles on usury, the sabbatical and Jubilee years are significant not as specific provisions but rather because they represent the seriousness of the commitment God wants his people to have toward the poor.[3] This compassion and responsibility for the poor is reiterated constantly by Jesus throughout his ministry. Christians are not to engage in economic practices that oppress or hurt the poor.

But at the same time, in his parable of the talents (Mt 25; Lk 19), Jesus has the master chiding the servant who simply buries the talent in the ground, saying, "You should have put my money on deposit with the bankers, so that when I returned I would have received it back with interest" (Mt 25:27). Certainly the major principle of the parable is that disciples of Jesus need to be productive for the kingdom of God. But what does this imply about the charging of interest? Apparently it is acceptable. Note that this sum of money, a talent, is considerable—equivalent to approximately 15 years of wages for a day laborer (in Luke the parable uses a *mina*, a lesser sum, although still equal to 3 months' wages). Jesus' choice of the Greek word *tokos* clearly indicates that the faithful servant was to bring forth fruit from this principal.

In the parable of the rich fool (Lk 12:13-21), Jesus clearly differentiates between investment (putting money to work, especially for the kingdom) and hoarding, condemning the latter. Jesus gives another clear warning in the parable of the rich man and the beggar Lazarus (Lk 16:19-31). From his accumulated wealth the rich man would not even give the scraps of food from his table to the beggar who lay at his gate. Ultimately, from his torment in hell the rich man begs Father Abraham to allow Lazarus to dip the tip of his finger in water and cool his tongue, "because I am in agony in this fire."

This turnabout is reiterated graphically in the Epistle of James (5:1-6):

> Now listen, you rich people, weep and wail because of the misery that is coming upon you. Your wealth has rotted, and moths have eaten your clothes. Your gold and silver are corroded. Their corrosion will testify against you and eat your flesh like fire. You have hoarded wealth in the last days. Look! The wages you failed to pay the workmen who mowed your fields are crying out against you. The cries of the harvesters have reached the ears of the Lord Almighty. You have lived on earth in luxury and self-indulgence. You have fattened yourselves in the day of slaughter. You have condemned and murdered innocent men, who were not opposing you.

In 1 Timothy (6:17-19), Paul offers further cautions to the rich: "Command those who are rich in this present world not to be arrogant nor to put their hope in wealth, which is so uncertain, but to put their hope in God, who richly provides us with everything for our enjoyment. Command them to do good, to be rich in good deeds, and to be generous and willing to share. In this way they will lay up for themselves as a firm foundation for the coming age, so that they may take hold of the life that is truly life."

There is a principle underlying all these Bible passages: All wealth ultimately belongs to God. It is God who "gives us all things richly to enjoy." Israel's land could be re-deeded and debts canceled every so often because God owned all of it. No Israelite had the right to gain unfair profit (usury) from the money he or she owned, because it was ultimately owned by God. Both the rich fool and the rich man who neglected Lazarus had to give account to God for what they did (and didn't do) with their wealth, but so did the timid servant who buried his talent in the ground. Wealth should be used not to "bite" others, to gain an unfair advantage over them, but to "bear fruit." In essence, we are workers in God's garden. We must not claim the garden as our own, but at the same time we must not neglect it.

The Changing Economy

In part, Jesus' position on interest and investment reflects the evolution of the economy in the region. In the largely agrarian village economy of Old Testament times there were basically three uses for income: present consumption; tithes and offerings; and saving for future consumption. The idea that savings would go to investment in production that would eventually lead to future growth and greater prosperity was uncommon. The pool of resources and output was fixed, and economics was a zero-sum game. The economic pie couldn't get bigger; it could only be divided differently. "This no-growth subsistence orientation to economic life [led] naturally to strong admonitions against accumulated wealth and to concentrated focus on income distribution questions rather than production questions. If accumulated wealth was primarily a storing process for future consumption while others were starving, it is not surprising that so many biblical writers . . . spoke [against it]."[4] If a loan were necessary to keep a brother and his family from starving, certainly it seems appropriate that it be given either as charity or at least interest-free. "Commercial loans to establish or extend a business were not common. Most loans were needed by a poor person or by someone in an emergency. . . . The legislation on interest [was] part of an extensive set of laws designed to protect the poor and to prevent the creation of a class of desperately poor folk with no productive resources."[5] The fact that the borrower and the lender were typically from the same tribe and even village made the charging of interest even less likely.

Over time, as trade among villages and regions grew, there arose a demand for loans for the fitting out of ships and caravans. Enlarged markets allowed for specialization of labor, and the resulting artisan class required loans for equipment and materials. Increased trade also facilitated growth in financial institutions due to the need for letters of credit and currency exchange (e.g., the moneychangers in the temple). People began to realize that if they saved money by limiting their consumption, it became a valuable resource that could be used to increase trade, productivity, employment and general economic well-being.

Also, except in times of famine or siege, inflation was generally unknown or minimal in Old Testament times. As central governments came into being, rulers realized that through the printing of money or other means of expanding the money supply (e.g., debasing the currency), they could indulge in expenditures on impressive buildings or military ventures without increasing the tax burden. This is obviously in violation of biblical ethics, since it amounts to stealing from those who have currency by decreasing its value. The increase in the prevalence of inflation provided another logical justification for the charging of interest.

The Evolution of Church Doctrine

As the economy changed over time, so did church doctrine. The Council of Nicea (A.D. 325) banned clergy from lending money at interest,[6] but shortly St. Jerome (340-420) issued a dictum saying that Deuteronomy and other Scriptures prohibited *anyone* from taking usury. The Council of Chalcedon formalized this ban. It was generally accepted that usury ran contrary to the Christian obligations of love and mercy. The writings of St. Ambrose (340-397) supported this view, but with a notable exception. The Old Testament allowed usury in dealings with "strangers" (i.e., foreigners), and Ambrose interpreted these as the foes of God's people who illegally withheld the lands the Lord had promised to the chosen people.[7] With the onset of the crusades, the church's acceptance of Ambrose's position became a thorn in the flesh. Nobles sought loans to underwrite expensive military expeditions, using their estates as collateral, but Christians were forbidden from lending money at interest. So Jews and other non-Christian moneylenders who had official permission to exact usury from Christian borrowers rushed into the gap. In seeking to close the "Brother vs. Other" (stranger) usury door, the Second Lateran Council (1139) "declared the unrepentant usurer condemned by the Old and New Testaments alike and, therefore, unworthy of ecclesiastical consolations and Christian burial."[8] This, of course, was no threat to Jewish lenders, and they continued apace, leading Thomas Aquinas (1225-1274) to go so far as to claim that the special permission granted to Jews in Deuteronomy had "long elapsed." His claim had no effect.

The next crisis arose from the convergence of the Reformation with the emerging mercantilist economy in Europe toward the end of the Middle Ages. Martin Luther in his early sermons stood against usury and even said that Christians should be prepared to forfeit their principle: "Lend to them without expecting to get anything back" (Lk 6:35). Luther's support of the early church's position won him favor with the debt-burdened farmers, peasants and lower classes. Following the peasant revolts of 1524-1525, under pressure from princes and "annuity-owning creditors," Luther shifted his position and declared that "he stood four-square against the radical claims that both individuals and governments were eternally obligated to observe the Mosaic and Gospel prohibitions of usury."[9]

The demand for capital from rapidly expanding crafts, industry and commercial trades continued to put pressure on the church's official ban on usury. The tide began to turn with a controversial tract by French jurist Carolus Molinaeus (1500-1566), who argued that "usury is not forbidden and unlawful according to divine law, except insofar as it is contrary to charity." He reasoned in favor of interest because

> money . . . even when it has to be returned after a time, yields meanwhile a considerable product through the industry of man. Indeed, without gain-seeking activity, the mere delay itself yields a not inconsiderable profit, since the debtor can meanwhile procure enough from the product of his estates or otherwise to pay back the principle

without any grievous and irreparable breaking-up of his patrimony. And sometimes it deprives the creditor of as much as it brings to the debtor . . . so it is not inappropriate that some part of the profit be given to the creditor: since in giving an appreciable use of money, he does give something, though he does not bear the risk.[10]

Reformer John Calvin delivered the knockout blow to the old doctrine prohibiting usury. Calvin reinforced Luther's position, stating that "the Mosaic and Gospel rules were to be translated in light of individual conscience, the equity of the Golden Rule, and the requirements of public utility. . . . Scripture forbids only biting usury, usury taken from the defenseless poor." The precept to lend without usury was a part of Jewish polity and not a universal "spiritual law," since foreign nations were under no prohibition against the charging of usury. "Usury is not now unlawful, except in so far as it contravenes equity and brotherly union. Let each one, then, place himself before God's judgment seat, and not do to his neighbor what he would not have done to himself, from whence a sure and infallible decision may be come to."[11] It should come as no surprise that Geneva, Switzerland, where Calvin spent most of his ministerial life, is still a world banking center.

The Catholic church followed suit in the late 1600s by generally permitting interest on the basis of (a) *damnum energens*, the risk endured by the lender, particularly if the loan was not repaid on time; (b) *lucrum cessans*, the gains relinquished by the lender because he or she was prevented from investing his money in an alternative productive enterprise; and (c) *societas*, the partnership between the lender and the borrower where the lender retains some control over his funds.[12] Other than a few references to "rapacious usury" and "low interest rates" for farmers, the papal writings of the twentieth century have ignored the issue of interest, focusing instead upon private property rights, the ownership of the means of production, the just wage, workers' right to organize and the appropriate role of the state in economic matters (particularly important during communism's heyday).[13]

Conclusion

Some things change. Some things stay the same. Certain central truths persist throughout Scripture and over time—like the importance of compassion for the poor and oppressed. But other ethical issues, such as the payment of interest on loans, may evolve with changes in culture, economic structure and what is in the best interest of individuals and society. But let's return to the questions asked at the chapter's beginning.

What should the position of Christians be with regard to interest on loans?

Based on our scriptural study and our brief tour of historical views, we can arrive at some conclusions. Interest payments are warranted for loans made to persons or organizations for the purposes of investment in productive activity. Loans to the poor are to be interest-free or at low interest (e.g., in order to maintain a viable microenterprise-loan fund against erosion by inflation). Christians are never to participate in a system where charging interest benefits the rich at the expense of the poor. In fact, when led by the Spirit, Christ would have us lend, even to our enemies, hoping for nothing in return (Lk 6:33-36)! Larry Burkett notes that "if you live by God's principles, your ability to collect a delinquent debt will be greatly curtailed because many common means of collection are unscriptural. . . . In seeking the correct balance, remember always that God is more concerned with the salvation of people than with the collection of debts."[14]

Should Christians borrow money at all? If so, should Christians ever have uncollateralized debt? Scripture does not prohibit borrowing. Many Christian financial experts would advise, however, that: (a) borrowing should only be occasional (live within your means); (b) long-term debt should be limited (remember the seven-year limit on the debt of the people of Israel); and c) the amount of debt should be limited to what can be secured by collateral (Lev 25:13-17, 23-55). This means that except for durable goods (e.g., a television set), credit cards should be for convenience use only, fully paid off every month. Certainly Christians shouldn't be borrowing just to participate in the rat race of conspicuous consumption, chasing after the latest and greatest goods. "Keep your lives free from the love of money and be content with what you have, because God has said, 'Never will I leave you; never will I forsake you' " (Heb 13:5). Finally, although it goes without saying, Christians must repay what they owe. "Let no debt remain outstanding, except the continuing debt to love one another," says the apostle Paul (Rom 13:8). What kind of witness are we for Christ when we do not honor our debts?

What constitutes a "fair" rate of interest? Should Christians actively work to outlaw loan sharks and support usury laws? What about the infamous moneylenders preying upon the poor in the rural and urban areas of the Third World? As with other economic markets, a fair rate of interest is that price for money that would prevail under conditions of perfect competition. To the extent that competition in the market for loanable funds is inhibited by unfair trade practices, collusion and fraud, Christians should use both the means of the state and their own leverage to remedy the situation. Usury laws are generally not an effective solution. Usury laws are simply price ceilings, and like other price ceilings (e.g., rent control) they create shortages in the locations where they are applied and surpluses in areas where they are not applied. In the late 1970s, for example, high mortgage rates led the State of New Jersey to enact a usury ceiling on mortgages from New Jersey banks. These banks then simply took their depositors' money and issued mortgages at market rates in the Sunbelt which, at the time, was competing directly with New Jersey for population.

So, in the case of loan sharks or moneylenders preying on the poor, most economists favor the use of competition to drive them to their knees. Christians should support government regulations that force banks to make loans and provide financial services in all segments of the communities from which they receive deposits (in the United States this regulation is known as the Community Reinvestment Act). In the Third World this can be supplemented by Christian organizations directly providing low-interest or no-interest loans or even small grants to the poor. Business loans particularly should be encouraged because they provide a means for the poor to break out of the poverty trap permanently through earned income. And evidence from microenterprise-loan programs shows that, in terms of on-time payments and default rates, loans to the poor are less risky than loans to the average business or Third World government.[15]

Discussion Questions

1. Should it be against the law for banks and other financial institutions to market credit cards to young teenagers?

2. What is the economic and scriptural justification for the charging of interest?

3. Should Christians charge poor people interest on loans?

9

A CLARION CALL

Poverty &
Distributive Justice

There will always be poor people in the land.

DEUTERONOMY 15:11

The poor you will always have with you.

JESUS CHRIST (MATTHEW 26:11)

SYNOPSIS

Benign neglect of the poor is not an option for Christians. Every person who is able to work should have access to the resources necessary for dignified participation in the economy. Not surprisingly, education and a decent job typically keep one out of the ranks of the poor. Labor market discrimination contributes to higher poverty among women and nonwhites. Out-of-wedlock births also fuel the ranks of the poor. Government spending on social welfare is enormous; however, much of the spending involves pay-as-you-go insurance programs such as Social Security and unemployment insurance. Direct spending on the poor is limited. Christians should be supportive of programs that make work pay; of church efforts to provide child care, quality health care, food and educational services; and of efforts to combat discrimination by sex, race or age.

It is simply something we will have to live with. No matter how much we legislate, levy taxes or give to charity, it does not go away. Poverty is a part of our world until Christ returns.

Other than warnings against idolatry, no other theme receives as much clear attention in Scripture as the obligation of believers to address the issues of poverty and distributive justice. Again and again God declares his desire for justice toward the poor and we are admonished to act on it. "I command you to be openhanded toward your brothers and toward the poor and needy in your land"

(Deut 15:11). If we neglect the poor, we cannot claim that the love of God is active in us (1 Jn 3:17). Benign neglect of poverty is not acceptable for Christians.

All persons are made in the image of God. Each life is sacred and precious in his sight. Every person should have access to the basic provisions necessary for life (e.g., food, clothing, shelter, health care) and the opportunity to participate as an accepted member of the community. As God is on the side of the poor, the weak and the oppressed, clearly he wants his people to fight economic injustice. God desires that we recognize and protect the sanctity and rights of the individual. People are to be treated equitably, without partiality. James admonishes us, "As believers in our glorious Lord Jesus Christ, don't show favoritism. Suppose a man comes into your meeting wearing a gold ring and fine clothes, and a poor man in shabby clothes also comes in. If you show special attention to the man wearing fine clothes and say, 'Here is a good seat for you,' but say to the poor man, 'You stand there,' or 'Sit on the floor by my feet,' have you not discriminated among yourselves and become judges with evil thoughts?" (Jas 2:1-4).

Because basic needs are to be met primarily by productive work, by the "sweat of the brow," every person who is able to work should have access to the productive resources necessary for dignified participation in the economy. Charity is to be extended to those who are in need, particularly because of circumstances beyond their control. Of particular concern is poverty that results from oppression and calamity, as opposed to poverty emanating from sinful personal choices (e.g., sloth, alcoholism, drug abuse). Oppression of the poor through discrimination, abuse of power, dishonest scales and slavery must cease, and we must find ways to restore poor people to equal participation in the community of opportunity. As shown throughout Scripture, individuals and nations that persist in the oppression of the poor (Babylon, ancient Israel at times) will be punished and even destroyed by God.

But Scripture does not condemn wealth. Abraham, David and Solomon were very wealthy men. Job had his wealth restored as a reward for his faithfulness. Apparently a person can be wealthy without oppressing the poor. Given the unequal distribution of talents and the changing market value of those talents, productive work will always result in a differential endowment of wealth. Through investments, wealth can improve everyone's material well-being by facilitating economic growth. Through charity, wealth allows for the relief of poverty.

At the same time, wealth is fraught with spiritual dangers. It can easily lead to idolatry and can lead men and women into "many foolish and harmful desires that plunge [them] into ruin and destruction" (1 Tim 6:9). As noted above, not the least of these desires are covetousness (greed), conspicuous consumption, and self-indulgent, pleasure-oriented hedonism. Most dangerous of all, throughout Scripture the blessing of wealth has led people, including God's people, to credit their prosperity to themselves and turn from their worship of God. Pursuit of riches seduce men and women into forsaking their children, denying time to those who are hurting, cutting ethical corners and denying the very God who is their ultimate purpose of living and salvation. "Command those who are rich in this present world not to be arrogant nor to put their hope in wealth, which is so uncertain, but to put their hope in God, who richly provides us with everything for our enjoyment. Command them to do good, to be rich in good deeds, and to be generous and willing to share. In this way they will lay up treasure for themselves as a firm foundation for the coming age, so that they may take hold of the life that is truly life" (1 Tim 6:17-19).

Differences among nations in wealth and the average economic condition of households are enormous and are considered in chapter fourteen. Certainly, there is no doubt that in terms of income per person, nations with democratic competitive markets significantly outperform nations under communism or with strongly centralized government. Yet democratic competitive markets do not guarantee equality in the distribution of income. Our focus in this chapter is on poverty in the United States. We will examine the issue of how to identify the poor, explore the major causes of poverty, review current government programs and policies aimed at reducing poverty and conclude with a discussion of the role Christians and the church might take in poverty remediation.

Identifying the Poor

The total number of poor in the United States in any given year is determined by household data collected by the Bureau of the Census in its March Current Population Survey. More than 60,000 households are surveyed and arrayed according to their reported income before taxes in the previous year and by household size. Households with income at or below a designated level by household size are considered to have been in poverty for that year. For example, in 1999 a family of four with an income of $17,029 or less before taxes would be counted as poor, and the members of that family would be included in the determination of the overall poverty rate and the poverty rates for various demographic groups.

Based on this methodology, in 1999, 32.3 million Americans (12.7 percent of the noninstitutionalized population) were poor. This was down from 34.5 million in 1998 and a peak of 39.3 million persons in 1993. A rising tide does lift all ships, even if it does not lift all ships equally. The sustained expansion of the U.S. economy since 1992 has seen a steady decline in the poverty rates and poverty populations of children, the elderly, and all racial and ethnic groups. As of 1999, most of the poor (21.9 million) continue to be white, and yet the poverty rates for both blacks and Hispanics are still three times the poverty rate for whites. The poverty rate inside central cities (16.4 percent) is almost double the rate in the suburbs (8.3 percent), though it is dropping toward the poverty rate found in America's rural areas (14.3 percent). Family structure continues to have an enormous impact upon poverty: the poverty rate for all married-couple families is 4.8 percent compared to 27.8 percent for female-headed families with no husband present. Almost 17 percent of all children are poor, as are 9.7 percent of all persons age 65 years and over.[1]

There is controversy over the methods used to measure poverty. Some aspects of the methodology cause the extent of poverty to be understated and some overstated. While the poverty thresholds have been updated for inflation each year since their institution in 1963, they have not been adjusted for changes in living standards. During the ensuing 36 years when real (inflation-adjusted) average household income has doubled, the real value of the poverty line has remained unchanged. Consequently, the poverty line for a family of four has dropped from 48 percent to nearly 30 percent of the median income for a family of four. A readjustment for rising living standards would raise the poverty rates.

Similarly, exclusion of the homeless and persons in institutions, including nursing homes and prisons, causes the poverty rate to be understated. Current poverty thresholds also do not recognize the reality of costs in the exploding population of single-parent families where there is a need for paid child care, transportation to and from work, and other expenses necessary to hold a job. Fringe benefits, especially medical coverage, are not taken into account. Lack of adjustment for geographic variation in living costs results in poverty rates being understated in older central cities, the Northeast, and the West, and overstated in rural areas, the South, and the Midwest.

On the other side of the ledger, several factors cause the poverty rate to be overstated. These include lack of adjustment for in-kind government benefits. Among female-headed families, for example, 7 out of 10 receive food stamps, 5 out of 10 Medicaid, and 3 out 10 housing assistance. Considering all in-kind transfers together reduces the incidence of poverty substantially. Research also shows that survey respondents, particularly poor people, tend to underreport their income. This helps to explain the widening gap between what poor families spend and their reported income.[2] The use of income after taxes (rather than before) adds to the overstatement of poverty, since the income-reducing impact of social security (FICA) taxes is more than offset by the Federal Earned Income Tax Credit. Poverty reports also exclude wealth, focusing on income. Since wealth is more unequally distributed than income in the United States, it is unlikely that a large proportion of the poor have substantial wealth holdings. However there are some, particularly among the elderly, who have a high level of assets (e.g., a mortgage-free single-family home) and low current income. Finally, the poverty population is not stagnant; there is significant mobility. Some who are poor in 1999, such as graduate students, may very likely not be poor in the year 2000 or 2001. Research shows that only 1 out of 10 families stays in poverty for five years or more.[3]

The Bureau of the Census currently publishes both the official rates and various experimental poverty measurements that take into account the factors just mentioned. Initial results show little impact on the overall poverty rate, but the experimental poverty measures do result in lower rates for children, blacks, female-headed families, persons with disabilities and people in the South. Those experiencing higher poverty rates under the experimental methods include married couples and people residing in the Northeast and West and in suburban areas across the nation.[4]

Whatever adjustments are made to the current methodology, the population of poor persons in the United States is substantial. In allocating their scarce resources—including their time—individual Christians, the church, and parachurch organizations would do well to remember the insights gained from a clearer understanding of who exactly constitutes the "poor."

Causes of Poverty

The major causes of poverty center around employment, education, discrimination and family structure. Work is the primary path out of poverty among the non-elderly. Among the elderly, those who are not poor tend to be those who worked all their adult lives. Earnings from employment constitute 92 percent of the annual income of non-poor families, 64 percent of the income of all poor families and just 29 percent of the income of poor female-headed families. While 76 percent of the nonpoor heads of households with children (including 85 percent of the married fathers) worked full time year-round, the figures are much lower in poor households—22 percent for household heads and 40 percent for married fathers. In 1999 the poverty rate for families with no workers was 29.1 percent compared to 8.3 percent for families with one or more workers. The poverty rate for female-headed families with no workers was 67.9 percent in contrast to 24.4

percent for female-headed families with one or more workers.[5] As economist Bradley Schiller notes, "Millions of American families and unrelated individuals are in poverty because they don't work, or they don't work enough."[6]

Given the extraordinary economic growth and tight labor market over the past decade in the United States, it is not surprising that most of the nonworking poor do not blame their unemployment on a lack of opportunities. The most frequently cited reason is homemaking responsibility, followed by school attendance and then illness or disability. The mobility of the poverty population is reflected among working-age adults. When tracked over a decade, one-fifth of all working-age adults end up out of the labor market due to permanent disabilities, one-tenth are still poor and the remainder have worked their way out of poverty. It is rare for a person to get into the labor market, stick with it and remain poor.[7]

The shift of the U.S. economy out of goods production into higher value-added services has made formal education and training the primary determinants of the level of earnings. The gap in earnings by education has been increasing since the early 1980s, and the size of the gap is accelerating. The median earnings of a worker with a college degree was 68 percent more than the median earnings of a worker with a high school degree in 1999, up from 29 percent in 1979.[8] As of 1997 the median income of families whose head had less than a ninth-grade education was $21,208, compared to $40,040 for families whose head was a high school graduate and $73,578 when the head had a bachelor's degree or more.[9] The mean family net worth in 1995 by education of the householder was $83,000 for heads who had not completed high school, $129,000 for heads with a high school diploma and $379,000 for heads with a college degree or more.[10] Not surprisingly, as formal education rises, individuals' labor force participation increases, as do their hours worked and their occupational status. Of course their likelihood of experiencing a spell of unemployment or poverty falls significantly.

The path out of poverty seems clear: get your education and a decent job with good pay, and the opportunity for upward mobility will follow. This is generally true, but not always—partly due to the effects of racial and gender discrimination. Within the labor market both employment discrimination (the systematic hiring of one group over another) and wage discrimination (paying different wages to equally productive workers in the same occupation) still persist. Although the wage gap between whites and blacks has been closing, it is still large (30 percent for males and 11 percent for females in 1997). Similarly, the gender wage gap has been diminishing, but remains large (42 percent in 1997). Research indicates that controlling for differences in hours worked per year, education, employment history and geographic location, approximately one-fourth of the difference in average earnings results from racial and gender discrimination in the labor market.[11]

The sources of the labor market discrimination are varied. Women are frequently subjected to occupational crowding, steered into jobs as cashiers and nurses and away from occupations such as telephone line repair and engineering. Discrimination in housing markets may produce a spatial mismatch with lower-income blacks trapped residentially in the inner city, far away from the suburban centers of service job growth. Minorities, even holding different jobs within given occupations, are likely to be more concentrated in lower paying industries and may be paid less for the same work.[12] Reliance on word-of-mouth recruitment for new positions, a common practice for most companies, often excludes minorities because the current work force within the companies is mostly white. Unions are notorious for "inside hiring," as reflected in the small proportion of minorities in most of the major craft unions. Recruitment bias also frequently results when companies turn to traditional mainstream white sources such as major newspapers, employment agencies and, increasingly, the Internet.[13]

Increasingly, as the U.S. service economy grows and companies use formal education as a quick screening device for job applicants, a major source of disadvantage in the labor market is discrimination by race in the educational system. African Americans continue to lag behind whites and Hispanics continue to lag behind African Americans in educational attainment in the United States. In part this is because minorities are concentrated in urban schools with deficient facilities, shortages of textbooks and less-than-optimal learning environments. Two-thirds of all the schools in the nation are at least 50 percent minority and one-third are at least 90 percent minority, and individual classrooms are more segregated than schools.[14] The spending per pupil in many of these high-minority schools is half the expenditure per pupil in the wealthy suburban school districts. Compared to whites, Hispanic high school seniors report gangs in their schools almost three times more often, and black students are twice as likely as whites to feel unsafe in their schools.[15] It is not surprising that seventeen-year-old black and Hispanic students read at the same level as thirteen-year-old whites. Less than half as many blacks and Hispanics complete four years of college as whites.[16]

Bradley Schiller argues that this discrimination by race is reinforced by discrimination by socioeconomic class. He writes, "Poor children drop out of high school at over twice the rate of nonpoor children. A substantial number of poor children leave the educational system even before they enter high school."[17] Data from the U.S. Department of Education show that despite a variety of scholarship, grant and loan programs, only 21 percent of the families earning less than

$10,000 have children in college full-time, compared to over 56 percent of the families earning $50,000 or more.[18] A young person with a high IQ from a high income family is almost two and a half times more likely to graduate from college as a high IQ youngster from a low income family.[19]

These obstacles to educational and labor market success are compounded by the rapidly changing family structure in the United States. As already noted, the poverty rate for female-headed families is almost six times the poverty rate for married-couple families. The rapid increase in female-headed families due to divorce, separation and out-of-wedlock births has resulted in what has been labeled the "feminization" of poverty. Divorces per thousand marriages have risen from 320 in 1970 to 490 in 1997. The median duration of marriage is now 7.2 years. More than one million children are involved in a divorce each year. Simultaneously, the percentage of births to unmarried mothers jumped from 10.7 percent in 1970 to 32.4 percent in 1997. The out-of-wedlock birth rate is an astounding 70 percent for blacks, having almost doubled over the past two decades. The rate for whites is now 26 percent, increasing almost five-fold over the past two decades.[20]

One result is that children have the highest poverty rate of all age groups, a rate nearly double that of even the elderly. In 1970, 85 percent of children under 18 lived with two parents. By 1998 that figure had dropped to 68 percent. The percent of children living with their biological father and mother dropped from 75 percent in 1970 to 58 percent in 1990.[21] Meanwhile, the proportion of children living with only their mother more than doubled, from 11 to 23 percent in 1998. Of these, the proportion living with a mother who never married soared from less than 1 percent to more than 9 percent. The weakening of the family, God's designated primary institution for the nurturing of children and the building of community, is having devastating economic consequences.

Government Programs and Policies

As Karl Case and Ray Fair comment, "Debates about the role of government in correcting for inequity in the distribution of income revolve around philosophical and practical issues. Philosophical issues deal with . . . what is 'fair'? What is 'just'? Practical issues deal with what is, and what is not possible. Suppose we want zero poverty. How much would it cost, and what would we sacrifice? When we take wealth or income away from higher income people do we destroy incentives? [Is] the market when left to operate on its own fair? [Does] a society as wealthy as the United States have a moral obligation to provide all its members with the necessities of life?"[22]

Government spending on social welfare in the United States has become huge.

Social welfare expenditures in the United States, excluding education, have risen from 6.1 percent of GNP in 1950 to 15.8 percent in 1995, topping $1.1 trillion. For the past 15 years social welfare expenditures have been increasing at double the rate of inflation. Without question, the most rapid increases are in Medicare and Medicaid, health expenditures for the elderly and the nonelderly poor. Between 1990 and 1995 Medicare outlays rose 50 percent and Medicaid spending soared up by 98 percent.[23] Welfare expenditures (Aid to Families with Dependent Children), meanwhile, have been falling.

Of the outlays on social welfare expenditures, 3 out of every 4 dollars comes from the federal government, with the remainder from state and local governments. Social welfare expenditures now account for over 60 percent of total federal spending and 45 percent of the spending by state and local governments. Table 9.1 shows the percentage distribution of total government welfare expenditures for 1995. Social insurance, primarily social security payments of all types, accounts for almost half of the total social welfare spending. Medicare and Medicaid, together with other spending on health and medical programs, comprise more than a third of the total spending. Public aid is third in line with a 9 percent share of the total, and this includes the much-debated AFDC (welfare) program, which comprises only slightly more than 2 percent of total social welfare spending. Public spending on housing, which also gets much publicity and stirs controversy, limps in with 2 percent of total spending as well.

Table 9.1. Percent Distribution of Social Welfare Expenditures by Public Program, 1995

Social Insurance	47%
Medicare & Medicaid	28%
Health & Medical Programs	8%
Public Aid	9%
Veterans	3%
Housing	2%
Other Social Welfare	3%

Source: U.S. Bureau of the Census, *Statistical Abstract of the United States: 1999*, U.S. GPO, Washington D.C., 2000, p. 387.

To the extent that social insurance benefits, including Medicare and Medicaid, are largely paid for by the eventual beneficiaries, 75 percent of the nation's social welfare spending represents neutral transfer payments. Citizens put money into the system and eventually draw that money back out. This is not completely the case, however. Because the Social Security system has been tapped by Congress as a source of benefits for disabled workers, struck by rapidly rising life expectancies and indexed to inflation, it has ceased being a trust fund. Current outlays are basically covered by current revenues. The obvious redistributive role of Social Security is evidenced by the fact that without their monthly Social Security checks the proportion of elderly in poverty would rise from less than 10 percent to over 50 percent.[24] In an attempt to ensure the future solvency of the system, Congress has instituted a phased increase in the age at which full benefits can be received and is slowly increasing the total annual wages subject to the FICA tax. Meanwhile, the payroll tax added to finance Medicare pays for only about two-thirds of annual expenditures, with the remainder covered by the Federal government's general revenues. So Medicare is far from self-financing, yet without it, approximately one million older persons would slide into the ranks of the poor.[25] Medicaid costs are covered from the general revenues of both the Federal and state governments, and thus represent a true redistributive transfer payment in support of the poor.

Public aid spending, including public assistance payments, food stamps, nutrition programs (e.g., free breakfast and lunch meals through schools) and housing assistance, is always a source of controversy. There's a built-in conflict: you want to ease poverty by helping jobless people, but you don't want to reward them for staying unemployed. You want to support single-parent families, but you don't want to give married couples financial reasons to break up. Research shows that the work disincentives of welfare are not substantial, but also that welfare encourages young women to have children out of wedlock and leave home. This conflict led Congress in 1996 to replace the traditional AFDC program with the Temporary Assistance for Needy Families (TANF) program. TANF places a lifetime cap of five years on the receipt of welfare assistance from federal funds and requires the welfare recipient to engage in some work-related activity (i.e., work, school or training) within two years of welfare receipt. Teenage recipients are required to live with their parents, to attend school and to assist in identifying the fathers of their children. Federal funds for child care were increased substantially and Medicaid eligibility was not altered.

The immediate impact of these reforms, as might be expected, has been a drop in the welfare caseload. The ultimate impact remains to be seen. The reforms are in the right direction: making work pay. On the positive side, research shows that single women with children are willing to leave the government welfare roles if child care and health insurance are available, together with job search assistance, access to training, and lower tax rates through the Federal Earned Income Tax Credit and state tax earnings disregards.

On the negative side, the accumulated human capital of most welfare recipients is less than needed for economic self-sufficiency. It takes a full-time job at 50 to 100 percent above the minimum wage with good medical benefits and low child care costs to allow a single mother to be better off working than receiving public assistance (including welfare, food stamps, Medicaid). Of women on welfare, 11 percent have an eighth-grade education or less and an additional 35 percent have not completed high school. On average, welfare recipients have reading and math skills about the level of the typical eighth grader, and as many as 25 to 40 percent may have learning disabilities. Moreover, the women who tend to have long welfare spells (roughly half of the recipients at any point in time) tend to be high school dropouts with no work experience and have learning disabilities and even substance abuse issues.[26] In the service economy, where education is the key to earnings, these chronic welfare recipients require significant intervention in order to achieve self-sufficiency. TANF allows 20 percent of a state's welfare caseload to be exempt from the five-year cap.

Unlike Social Security, Medicaid, and Food Stamps, which are all indexed to inflation and not under executive control, government spending on education and training programs targeted to the poor has risen and fallen with the political tides. Going from essentially nonexistent in the Kennedy administration, these programs (e.g., Head Start and targeted training for poor adults) expanded rapidly during President Johnson's War on Poverty, grew steadily through Nixon, Ford and Carter, and then were cut back during the Reagan administration. Today they account for barely 2 percent of all social welfare spending. Research generally has found Head Start to have a positive impact on the educational performance of poor youngsters, at least during their primary school years. Adult training has been found to be cost effective, raising the income of participants by one dollar for every dollar spent on training. But even the most successful programs fail to raise the absolute earnings enough to make a large difference in the poverty status of the participants.[27]

To put this all in perspective, despite the rapid increase in social welfare expenditure over the past four decades, our nation spends a smaller share of its income on redistribution than do most other advanced industrialized nations. Our share is approximately one-half the share spent in France, Sweden, Germany and Italy, and one to two percent of GDP below the share spent in the United Kingdom and Canada. Subsequently, our poverty rate for the elderly is nearly four times higher on average than in these other countries, and the poverty rate for children is two times higher. Since there is no evidence that the more substantial degree of redistribution in other nations has led to slower economic growth, through either impacts on the supply of labor or savings, our choice appears to be driven by political rather than economic considerations.[28]

Numerous surveys show that U.S. social welfare spending reflects the majority opinion of American adults. In contrast to citizens of other industrialized nations, Americans place a premium on the values of individualism, self-reliance and social mobility. While Americans express a desire to help the poor, at the same time an overwhelming proportion of Americans believe lack of effort is an important cause of poverty. Consequently, high levels of support exist for government spending on Social Security, medical care and education, and low levels of support exist for spending on welfare, food stamps and other means-tested transfers.[29] According to survey data, those Americans more likely to attribute poverty to flawed character are college graduates, Protestants, professionals, the elderly, Republicans and the more affluent. Those who believe poverty stems from systemic bias and restricted opportunity tend to be nonwhites, females, Catholics, Democrats, independents and the poor.[30]

These views carry over into government actions to combat discrimination and its effects. The vast majority of Americans support equal opportunity and open competition, but are strongly opposed to special preferences such as affirmative action and quotas. Americans believe that individual effort and ability will garner the appropriate awards in the long run. Federal government efforts to combat discrimination in employment through the Equal Employment Opportunity Commission (EEOC) and the Office of Federal Contract Compliance Programs (OFCCP) have been modest, partly due to insufficient legal powers and partly due to political considerations. The same is true for federal, state and local government actions toward discrimination in education and housing. Since past and current discrimination plays a major role in limiting economic mobility, the lack of clear and strong government action means that certain groups, such as African Americans, will continue to be at an unfair disadvantage in the labor market.

The Role for Christians

As made clear in the beginning of this chapter, Christians are obligated to address the issues of poverty and distributive justice. We must, therefore, take the time to understand the causes of poverty and discriminate among the potential remedies based upon both sound economic analysis and biblical principles. And as we commit our time, prayers and resources to the poor, God can minister to the poverty in our spiritual lives and in our souls.

With respect to government social welfare programs, Christians must show discernment. There are certainly directives in the Old Testament to kings and nations to care for the afflicted and the needy (Ps 9:18-19; 72:1-4; Jer 22:15-16).

Yet most assistance to the poor, even the gleaning and the third year tithe, was voluntary. Joseph's well-intentioned exchange of land for food ultimately resulted in the enslavement of the people of Israel to the state (Gen 47:13-26). Scripture makes it clear that if they are able, it is better for men and women to work than to depend upon the state or charity.

While our discussion has only scratched the surface, we have identified four major causes of poverty: employment, education, discrimination and family structure.

With respect to employment, Christians should be supportive of all government and civil programs that "make work pay." This would include subsidized child care, medical insurance and transportation based upon ability to pay. We should support efforts to continue and increase the Earned Income Tax Credit to lift working families out of poverty, to get all states with income taxes to enact their own EITC, and to continue the Food Stamp program and eliminate the asset cap on that and other welfare programs with respect to the ownership of motor vehicles, homes and savings designated for education or training.

Churches can get directly involved in the provision of child care and quality health care (through the operation of medical clinics or vans in low-income neighborhoods) and the donation and maintenance of used cars to poor families. Church-operated food banks and dining halls can help free up earned income for clothing and school supplies for children. Many urban churches operate job referral services and mentoring support for working adults who are coming off the welfare roles or out of prison. Some churches and many Christian nonprofit organizations such as the Salvation Army provide much-needed shelter for the homeless. Financial services—such as tax preparation, assistance in obtaining loans and opening a bank account, education regarding the establishment of a credit history and the availability of various government and civil programs—are desperately needed in poor communities.

With respect to education, Christians should support efforts to equalize the spending per pupil across the nation's school systems. This may entail anything from state or metropolitan area tax-base sharing to a regressive voucher system (i.e., lower-income families receive a larger voucher per child than higher-income families). Vouchers are particularly attractive because they both stimulate competition among schools and allow parents to choose schools that reinforce the religious and moral values they deem essential. Vouchers also promote diversity because students are not limited by the spatial boundaries of their neighborhood school district. Not surprisingly, research shows that black parents and poorer, inner-city parents favor vouchers. Research also shows that private schools, particularly Catholic schools, are more successful with disadvantaged children, and that everyone—teachers, parents and students—is more satisfied with private schools.[31] Beyond postsecondary school, Christians should support the expansion of subsidized student loans and grants for individuals from low-income families wishing to attend community college or four-year degree programs.

Christians, churches and Christian organizations such as Youth for Christ can and do get involved in the support of public schools in low income communities through such activities as volunteer work in the schools and after school tutoring programs. Christians have also been involved in the startup of magnet schools within the public school system. Christians, typically through a church, provide alternative Christ-centered private schools, generally at affordable tuition rates. The Catholic church, in particular, has over time maintained a substantial commitment to the education of poor children by subsidizing parochial schools in low-income urban and rural communities. Many wealthy Christians provide scholarship support for low-income students and general fund support for Christian schools at all levels of education. Many churches, particularly in low-income urban communities, provide tutoring, job skill training (e.g., training in the use of microcomputer word processing) and scholarship assistance to the poor. Some wealthier suburban churches have assisted in these efforts through partnerships with churches in low-income communities.

With respect to discrimination, individual Christians and the church need to fight the complacency of recent years and restore the excitement and commitment that was evident during the 1960s and early 1970s. Christians and the church should be in the forefront of the challenges to major companies, school systems, groups of realtors, developers, unions, and politicians with respect to discrimination. The Jubilee 2000 movement (chapter fourteen) and the Sullivan principles applied to South Africa show the significant impact Christians can have through prayer, peaceful demonstrations and economic boycotts. As important, Christians must face honestly and prayerfully the existence of discrimination within their own churches. It has been said that on a given Sunday, no other institution in America is more segregated, both racially and economically, than our churches. Christians and churches need to increase their efforts to stimulate the dialogue between races and to commit to work toward restoration wherever past discrimination has wounded groups of people.

With respect to family structure, individual Christians, churches and Christian organizations need to face honestly the wave of both sexual promiscuity and divorce that is engulfing not just our nation, but the Christian community. Sex education should not be left solely to the public schools and Hollywood.

Churches and Christian youth organizations should provide young people with a Scripture-based view of sex, marriage and the family. Some are already doing this. Some are also helping to provide counseling for the emotional trauma that accompanies separation and divorce. Some churches are recognizing the special needs of overwhelmed single parents, particularly women trying to escape the welfare system. In some counties individual churches have adopted every woman in the local welfare caseload, with significant results. In addition, laws that make divorce painless need to be challenged. Premarital and marital counseling and retreats should be commonplace in our churches. Pastors should not marry young people until they show a clear understanding of the marriage vow taken in the sight of God. The church and Christians should back government efforts to secure child support payments from absent parents.

Conclusion

There are, of course, many more areas of service that could be discussed—such as care for the disabled elderly and support for the caregivers of the disabled elderly. And we cannot conclude without recognizing the pervasiveness of poverty as seen by Jesus. The Greek word used by Jesus when speaking of the poor, *ptochos*, means lacking in anything, destitute of wealth *and* destitute of spiritual virtue. As theologian Robert Linthicum observes, "Who, truly, are the poor? According to Jesus, all of us are! For the hungry are not only those people who lack bread, but those who lack love. The thirsty are not simply those who need water; you and I may thirst for righteousness. The naked are not simply those who seek to be clothed; you and I may long to be clothed in dignity, with a sense of being worthwhile or really wanted by someone."[32]

The harvest is plentiful and laborers are welcomed. Go as the Holy Spirit leads, but do go.

Discussion Questions

1. Is it fair for government to levy higher tax rates on the incomes of richer households? Why or why not?

2. What role does discrimination play in determining who is poor and the extent of poverty?

3. What do you anticipate as the long-term impacts of welfare reform?

4. What are the three most effective things a local church can do to help reduce poverty?

10

TENDING THE GARDEN
Environmental Stewardship

Pollution: the act of defiling; the contrary of consecration.

DR. SAMUEL JOHNSON, 1783

Many people mistakenly view humans as principally
consumers and polluters rather than producers and stewards.

THE CORNWALL DECLARATION ON
ENVIRONMENTAL STEWARDSHIP

SYNOPSIS

From the beginning of creation in Genesis, God calls men and women to stewardship of the environment. We are not to damage the substance of his creation. Sound research shows that we face severe and growing environmental challenges today, from the forests to the sources of fresh water to the ozone layer and global warming. A variety of policy options place the costs of pollution on the generators of that pollution. A holistic approach to development, where the real costs of consumption are taken into account, is in accord with the Christian call to creation stewardship.

The story explodes in Genesis 1. God brings light to scatter the darkness and creates sky and land to intersperse the expanse of the waters. The land is filled with seed-bearing plants of all kinds, the water is teeming with living creatures and the sky with winged birds, livestock and wild animals move throughout the earth, and finally man and woman are created. Significantly, "God saw all that he had made, and it was very good" (Gen 1:31). This earth, this creation, is a good thing in God's eyes.

Adam and Eve were put in the Garden of Eden to "work it and take care of it" and were "free to eat from any tree" except the tree of knowledge of good and evil (Gen 2:15-17). As the only element in the whole earth made in the image of God (Gen 1:27), Adam and Eve were explicitly given the special responsibility of stewardship for creation. They strolled in the Garden and named the animals. And we all know what happened next.

Their sin resulted in judgment. After the Fall, their physical survival now involved a previously nonexistent element of toil, sweat and struggle (Gen 3:17-19), but even then the stewardship obligation was not withdrawn. Human beings have an asymmetrical relationship to nature: we are to respect nature even if nature does not respect us. We have been granted by God the right of enjoying the earth and deriving from it all the profit or benefit it may produce (Gen 9:1-3), as long as we don't alter or damage the substance of his creation. As emphasized in our ethical framework (chapter one), men and women have a God-designated responsibility to care for the earth even as we use its resources to meet our needs.

This is the environmental ethic to which this book subscribes. But there are several other "theologies of the environment" that people hold. Some have looked at God's directive in Genesis 1 for man and woman to "be fruitful and increase in number; fill the earth and subdue it," and developed a theology of economic growth. According to this view, popular during the Enlightenment, material progress will lead to an increased focus on the spiritual aspects of life. This sounds promising, but many modern environmentalists see this theology leading instead to a melding of greed and need, where rampant consumerism is required to keep the economic engine running at full tilt. Some critics, such as Lynn White Jr., even go so far as to claim that the environmental crisis of the twentieth-century is a result of the apparent green light that God gave us in Genesis, with Christians sallying forth under a divine mandate to profane the earth.[1]

Perhaps in response to the excesses, others have gone too far in the other direction. They hold that the special stewardship responsibilities we read in Genesis amount to an anthropocentric view, putting humanity at the center of the universe. They react to that perspective by claiming that men and women should not be considered as any better than other species.

Over the past three decades, this root principle has spawned the rapid growth of environmentalism as a secular religion. From a sociohistorical standpoint, we can see that the circumstances in the United States in the 1970s were ripe for this worldview. The war in Vietnam had ended and many persons of social consciousness were looking for a worthy cause. A variety of environmental crises (such as Cleveland's Cuyahoga River bursting into flames in 1969 because of its load of volatile chemicals) had put to rest the age-old premise that the oceans, rivers and air were self-cleansing and the residue could be simply buried under the dirt. The recalcitrance of industry to take responsibility for clear instances of serious environmental degradation became increasingly apparent. It was easy to see humankind as the enemy, victimizing the defenseless co-inhabitants on our earth. Judeo-Christian tradition, with its emphasis on the specialness of humanity, was viewed as the sponsor of environmental abuse. Thus, certain environmentalists rejected the Judeo-Christian God and placed all nature on an equal footing, with every living element being equally sacred. This became, in essence, a secular religion, which has many adherents even today. At its extreme, ecotheology regards human beings as "the cancer of the earth" and sees salvation for the environment in minimizing the human presence in the universe.[2]

Research shows that people who doubt the existence of God and consider the Bible a book of fables are more likely to be concerned about the environment. These persons tend to be younger, better educated, have a more liberal political agenda and, if religious, have a more benevolent view of God. Among Christians there seems to be a clear division regarding environmental views. Biblical literalists (who believe that the Bible is the actual word of God and is to be taken literally, word for word) do *not* tend to show environmental concern, while Christians who consider the Bible the inspired word of God but not literal tend to be concerned with environmental issues. Does this mean we have a serious ethical disagreement among Christians with regard to Scripture's mandate to environmental stewardship?

No. The differences between the "literalists" and "inspired Word" Christians disappear when political views and moral rigidity (i.e., the need for certainties) are taken into account. In other words, biblical literalists who are politically liberal are as likely to be concerned with the environment as are their nonliteralist counterparts. Comments researcher Andrew Greeley, "Those who believe in God and the Bible, and Christians who reject the various levels of rigidity, are as likely as anyone else to support environmental spending."[3] The gap between conservatives and liberals, even among Christians, is apparently due to concerns about the impact of environmental regulations on economic growth and on individual liberties. As Bradley Schiller notes, "To reduce pollution, we have to change our patterns of production and consumption. This entails economic costs, in terms of both restricted opportunities and more expensive ways of producing or consuming goods."[4]

Accepting that we have a mandate as Christians to environmental stewardship, the remainder of this chapter will consider three issues. First, how serious are our current environmental conditions? Second, what policies are currently being applied to address environmental concerns? And third, are these policies compatible with economic growth and Christian ethics?

Is There an Environmental Crisis?

Through the centuries there have been many examples of environmental damage resulting knowingly and unknowingly from the activities of human civilization. For instance, in southern Mesopotamia from 3500 to 1800 B.C., the Sumerian practice of irrigating flat land without proper drainage caused such infiltration of salt into the water table that the resulting evaporation left the soil surface salt-encrusted and unable to produce crops. Today these areas in Iraq and Iran are still unable to support agriculture.[5] Pre-twentieth century cities throughout the world were awash with human excrement, animal wastes and carcasses, smoke from burning wood and coal, poor drainage and ventilation, contaminated water supplies and the prevalence of diseases such as typhus, cholera and consumption. Industrialization accelerated and intensified this environmental degradation.

Technology, planning and regulation, sewer and septic systems, water treatment and increased safeguards for workers in industries utilizing toxic substances (e.g., hat and mirror making, where mercury poisoning was widespread) helped ease many of these conditions, but they spawned new issues as well. The automobile, for example, reduced population densities in central cities from levels that contributed to the rapid spread of diseases, but the nitrogen oxides and hydrocarbons in automotive exhaust fumes have become a major source of air pollution. Pressures on the ecological system have also been intensified by increased rates of population growth, rising levels of per capita consumption and the "natural" inclination of polluters, both in the private and public sectors, to avoid bearing any direct costs for the environmental damages they may generate.

As we enter the new millennium, we are encountering serious environmental concerns. Although there may be shades of disagreement among participating parties (e.g., corporations vs. government regulatory agencies vs. nonprofit advocacy organizations) regarding their severity, most environmental problems today are substantiated by empirical data, frequently from very rigorous, causal scientific research. Within the biosphere, the thin membrane around the earth, biologists have identified between 1.5 million and 1.8 million species, and estimates of the total number of living species range up to 3.6 million. These species inhabit five major types of ecosystems—forests, freshwater systems, coastal/marine habitats, grasslands and agricultural lands—all of which are showing signs of deterioration.

Forests, home to two-thirds of all species, reduce flooding and topsoil erosion; enhance the health of streams, rivers and lakes; slow the buildup of carbon dioxide in the atmosphere; and serve as a source of new medicines. Except for Russia and Canada, industrial nations have cleared almost all of their original forests. The original forest area from Maine through North Carolina extending west to the Mississippi, for example, has been reduced by 98 percent.[6] For decades, perhaps even centuries, the new second-growth forests are not able to provide the same substantive support for habitat as original old-growth forests. Besides the tree loss, the initial destruction of the forest results in a drastic reduction in biodiversity that involves many more species. This is critical because biodiversity is necessary for a healthy ecosystem to function.

The size and shape of a forest also matters. While total forested acreage actually increased in the mid- to late 1900s, in many urban and rural areas of the United States it consists of fragmented parcels. Unfortunately, these fragmented parcels are too small to provide food and living space for many species. Neither can they act as a significant deterrent to regional flooding. Two years ago deforestation contributed to floods in China that killed 3,600 people and left 14 million homeless. Meanwhile, in less-developed countries, forests are being cleared at an alarming rate to provide land for crops and cattle ranching, fuel and other life basics for the desperately poor, as well as timber for export markets. The search for firewood alone has caused deforestation estimated at 10,000 square kilometers per year. Cattle ranching in Brazil and Central America causes another 15,000 square kilometers of deforestation per year.[7] The rain forests, covering a space as large as the contiguous United States, are currently losing forest area about half the size of Florida each year.[8]

According to the Psalms, "He makes springs pour water into the ravines; it flows between the mountains. They give water to all the beasts of the field; the wild donkeys quench their thirst. The birds of the air nest by the waters; they sing among the branches. He waters the mountains from his upper chambers; the earth is satisfied by the fruit of his work" (Ps 104:10-14). However, human water consumption rose at twice the rate of population growth in the past century. People currently use 54 percent of available freshwater. A joint report by several UN agencies states that 2.3 billion persons currently face water shortages, and the outlook for freshwater is rated unequivocally "grim."[9] So much freshwater has been drawn from major rivers in mega-urban areas that we're seeing saltwater moving from the ocean up such rivers as the Nile, the Yellow, the Rio Grande and the Hudson. Extensive paving and storm-sewer systems in urban areas have retarded the percolation of precipitation into aquifers, rushing storm waters into swollen rivers and on toward the ocean. In some coastal areas aquifer levels are so low that saltwater is intruding. In addition, more than 40,000 large dams around the world help to stabilize the supply of water for human uses, but these have had disastrous impacts on thousands of species that resided in the former streams, rivers and forests. After damming, channeling and diversion in the Florida Everglades, 68 of the region's resident species have become endangered, which also jeopardizes a $14 billion ecotourist industry. The forthcoming UN report estimates that 20 percent of freshwater species have vanished or been driven toward extinction in recent decades. Meanwhile, we continue to see cities developed in areas so arid that warm-blooded mammals are nonindigenous.

Coastal areas are home to 2 billion people. Two-thirds of all harvested fish depend at some point in their lives on coastal wetlands, sea grasses or coral reefs.[10] Estimates are that two-thirds of all coral reefs are now impaired by human activity, and at least half the world's wetlands have been lost over the past century. Explains Carl Safina, "Gravity is the sea's enemy. Silt running off roads and clear-cut forests . . . pesticides and other toxics sprayed in the air and washed into rivers find the ocean. The biggest sources of coastal pollution are waste from farm animals, fertilizers and human sewage. They can spawn red tides and other harmful algal blooms that rob oxygen from the water, killing sea life." At the turn of the twenty-first century, the mid-Atlantic states of the United States have seen numerous fish kills and even a few human illnesses attributed to these algal blooms or toxic microbes. Moreover, despite numerous international agreements, the lack of clear ocean property rights continues to lead to abuse by certain nations and individuals. It is estimated that Europe's North Sea, New England's Georges Bank and Australia's Queensland coast are all scoured by trawlers four to eight times per year. A foreboding event was the recent collapse of the North Atlantic cod industry that put 30,000 Canadians from 700 communities out of work. While some countries, such as New Zealand and the Philippines, have established marine reserves and are adopting harvesting techniques that protect endangered species, other nations, such as Japan, treat the ocean as an inexhaustible resource and a garbage dump as well.[11]

According to the United Nations, an estimated 80 percent of grasslands worldwide are suffering from soil degradation and 20 percent of drylands are in danger of becoming deserts. Including savannas, shrublands and tundra, grasslands support large mammals, migrating birds and livestock. Grasslands are being lost to development and global climate changes. According to the National Wildlife Federation, 70 percent of the short-grass and mixed-grass prairies that once covered the United States are gone, while tall-grass prairies comprise 1 percent of what they once were.[12] Some mammals and birds are being hunted to extinction. The extensive losses of grasslands that have already occurred have limited the habitat available to a broad variety of mammals and birds, and the habitat that remains is increasingly less productive and more fragmented.

One-third of the world's land is used for agricultural production. Although agricultural production continues to outpace population growth, three-quarters of the land devoted to agriculture has poor soil, and half of that (particularly in less-developed countries) is threatened by significant erosion, nutrient depletion and water stress (70 percent of the earth's rainfall is already being used in agriculture). The "green revolution" and other new production-enhancing technologies have increased food production in less-developed countries, but negative side effects can occur. Pessimists argue that use of heavy machinery, irrigation and large doses of fertilizers and pesticides produce quick jumps in productivity, but reduce fertility in the long run. In addition, fertilizers and pesticides may damage biodiversity directly and through storm water runoff. When Indonesia spent $150 million annually to subsidize pesticide use, it killed the pests but also wiped out birds and other creatures that ate the pests. It also caused human illness. And if, as predicted, the fertile, arable land per person in the world drops from 0.28 hectares in 1989 to 0.19 by 2030,[13] the laws of diminishing marginal productivity can take effect as increasingly marginal lands are brought into production. Solutions may lie in the reduction or elimination of all world trade barriers on agricultural production together with a more appropriate use of natural technologies.

In addition to these potential problems, the agricultural crop species may also be at risk. Although all grains and cultivated plant species originated in grasslands—over 7,000 species in all—today only 20 species provide 90 percent of the world's food, and three—maize, wheat and rice—supply more than half.[14] Rather than maintaining a variety of plants and spreading the risk, we are narrowing our precarious foodstock future and concentrating the risk. Currently unknown or unforeseen blights or diseases could be disastrous to these crops, particularly in less-developed countries.

Affecting all the major ecosystems are the major environmental issues of global warming and the depletion of the ozone layer. After years of research, according to the 1995 report of the Intergovernmental Panel on Climate Change sponsored by the UN Environmental Program and the World Meteorological Organization, the verdict is in. Global warming has begun and the results could be serious. Besides the impact on agriculture, melting polar ice sheets will raise global ocean levels, putting the huge populations in coastal areas at risk and altering the role of the coastal areas in the marine food chain. Storms, and drought periods, may be more severe and tropical diseases may spread more rapidly.[15] To stop this trend, we must slow the release of carbon dioxide through curtailed burning of coal, oil and gasoline for heat, electricity and transportation. This will require everything from more efficient use of these resources, to the adoption of wind and solar technologies for energy production, to the use of hydrogen fuel cells for fossil-fuel-powered automobiles and trucks (with the residual carbon dioxide stored in underground aquifers).

In 2001, nearly 180 nations, exclusive of the United States representation, agreed to implement the 1997 Kyoto Protocol's legally binding limits on emissions of carbon dioxide and other greenhouse gases. As the world's leading contributor to emissions that increase global warming, the United States' absence from the implementation agreement places the fate and effectiveness of the treaty in doubt. Through the Kyoto Protocol the United States and thirty-seven other developed nations had agreed to cut their carbon dioxide emissions beyond what is necessary to stop further increases in global warming. This reduction would give less-developed countries, which are less able to afford rapid changes, time to adopt new technologies. With their crowded megacities, overwhelmed water supply and sewage systems, vast coal reserves, surging combustion engine markets and extreme poverty, such countries may not give high priority to environmental concerns. Similarly, spurred on by the Vienna Convention on Protection of the Ozone Layer in 1985, at the 1992 Montreal Protocol on Substances that Deplete the Ozone Layer, the United States and other developed nations agreed to radically limit the emission of ozone-depleting chemicals, with the United States completely halting the production of chlorofluorocarbons as of 1996 and taxing their emission.[16] Comments Paul Portney, "The principle environmental challenge for the developed world today is helping the developing countries to increase their standards of living in ways that help them skirt, to as great as an extent as possible, the pollution-intensive period the developing countries underwent."[17]

Site-specific toxic pollutants from industrial plants, landfills or agriculture also cause serious concern. It is true that current environmental laws and regulations in the developed countries are much more rigorous than in the early part of the twentieth century. Also, industry waste disposal facilities and agricultural practices in developed countries are often going beyond requirements to reduce their pollutant emissions. But still problems exist. And due to the persistent nature of many toxic substances, the impact of industrial waste disposal, as well as agricultural practices, from the early and mid-1900s, is still being felt. Highly toxic substances such as polychlorinated byphenyls (PCBs), mercury, cadmium, lead, arsenic and assorted pesticides can be found in the soils around old factories, landfills, or farmland, and in any crops grown on that land. The substances are often discovered in the groundwater beneath such sites or in the waterways nearby.

Animals and people alike are victims of toxic pollution, with young children (especially infants and developing babies in the womb) often being much more sensitive. These harmful compounds may also become more concentrated in the tissue of organisms as they pass up the aquatic food chain: minute levels of toxins in water become more concentrated in the microscopic plants, which are eaten by microscopic animals, which are eaten by the small invertebrates, which are eaten by the small fish, and so forth. At each level of the food chain the toxin is concentrated so that the concentration level of a toxin in a predator bird may be as much as ten million times the level present in the water. The decline in the 1970s and 1980s in large predator bird populations like eagles and pelicans is one of the most best-known examples of the dangers of toxic bioaccumulation. Fish consumption advisories for humans are common today in much of the United States for the same reason.

Although the introduction of toxic wastes to the environment has slowed in developed countries, the expense of safe practices and the lack of regulation in developing countries exposes those populations to many of these problems. Moreover, as has been painfully realized in the developed world, the impacts of these toxins are long term.

Policy Options

As quickly as environmental damage issues are being identified, so are policy alternatives for addressing the issues. To be sure, economists have neither the expertise nor the social mandate to set the acceptable environmental standards for any society. But once standards have been set, economists can recommend the most efficient means for achieving those standards. The common means used in industrialized countries today include individual bargaining, the tort system (law suits), direct governmental controls, taxes, fines, markets for externality rights, opportunity cost pricing, public works and information programs.[18]

Direct bargaining between those causing environmental harm (the damage to natural resources) and those affected by them works best if property rights are clearly defined, the number of persons involved is limited and bargaining costs are negligible. Suppose that I enjoy hosting guests at a backyard barbecue every Saturday afternoon, and you are my next-door neighbor. While the guests are not noisy, you value the privacy of your own backyard and Saturday afternoon is the one day you get to spend time gardening and relaxing. Consequently, you offer to plant shrubbery as a screen between your backyard and mine. My right to host a quiet barbecue on my private property is not violated, and the benefits of privacy to you obviously exceed the costs of the screening—otherwise you would not have proceeded.

If, however, you believe that my Saturday barbecues were unduly noisy and a violation of your rights to peace and quiet, you may proceed to bring legal charges against me. The court might put an end to my barbecues or compensate you for your damages, or both. If I suspect that my barbecues are unduly noisy, I might try to settle out of court, stopping the gatherings on my own. The same is true with environmental costs. Often the mere threat of a lawsuit will prevent a problem—especially if clear regulations are in place. For example, I cannot use my residential property as a dump for used automobile tires. I might be tempted to flout these zoning restrictions, if I saw profit in it, but your threat of legal action would probably prevent me.

As mentioned above, in order to maximize profits or minimize costs, the inclination of polluters, both in the private and public sectors, is to avoid bearing any direct or indirect costs for the environmental damages they cause. In the past this was possible because most people were unaware of the danger of industrial or agricultural spillover, such as the release of toxic materials into rivers or the air. But increased facts on environmental consequences have changed the balance sheet. Private firms downstream from polluting parties now realize that they have to pay the costs of cleaning the water before it can be used in their production processes. Measures of ambient air quality have clearly shown the health hazards from pollutants released into the air. Through websites it is now even possible to learn the estimated air-quality impacts of a specific plant or business on your neighborhood.

In order to force businesses to absorb the costs of the environmental damages generated as part of their operations, the government uses direct controls, taxes, fines and markets for externality rights. Under direct controls, maximum levels of pollutants for specific plant and business sites are set and regulated, often by an agency such as the U.S. Environmental Protection Agency (EPA), established in 1970. The list of regulations enacted over the past three decades in the United States includes the Wilderness Act of 1964, the Clean Air Act of 1970, the Endangered Species Act of 1973, the Clean Water Act of 1972, the Superfund Law of 1980 (limiting the storage, disposal and transportation of hazardous and toxic wastes) and the Clean Air Act of 1990.

In the case of direct controls, manufacturing plants and businesses are given specific dates by which minimal emissions targets must be achieved. For exam-

ple, under the Clean Air Act of 1990, requirements for the year 2000 included a
90-percent reduction in the emissions of 189 toxic chemicals, a 50-percent reduction in the use of chlorofluorocarbons to ease the depletion of the ozone layer,
and a 50-percent reduction in sulfur dioxide emissions of utilities to ease acid-
rain impacts. These direct control targets require companies to purchase, install
and operate equipment that does not typically increase productivity, but raises
costs and prices. The higher costs can reduce profits. The higher prices may also
reduce the quantity demanded. So, since the companies themselves have little
incentive to follow such costly guidelines, government regulators have to spend
substantial time and resources on enforcement. There is certainly no mystery
why business has used the courts to prolong the battle over what constitutes
"appropriate" emissions standards. Investigation and enforcement by government
regulators is also necessary in those cases where fines and taxes are levied as a
means of raising the costs to firms that persist in noncompliance. However, some
politicians are lax in enforcing environmental regulations on local companies that
provide jobs to voters and offer significant campaign contributions.

There's another policy option that might sound strange at first, but it is gaining
momentum—markets for the trading of pollution rights. This has been proposed
by economists for decades but is just currently working its way into government
regulations in the United States and elsewhere. Essentially, the government gives
companies the right to pollute the environment a certain amount, but these rights
can be bought and sold. Rather than investing in pollution-reduction equipment,
one company might buy air pollution rights from another firm whose pollution
output is well below required standards. As long as the total amount of rights
granted falls within healthy standards, this approach has the advantage of achieving macroenvironmental targets with the minimal direct expenditure. These markets also offer conservation groups the opportunity to buy up and withhold
pollution rights in order to reduce the achievable macroenvironmental target.
Moreover, as growth occurs in a particular region and the allowable macroenvironmental targets stay fixed, the price for pollution rights will rise, encouraging
the development of more efficient technologies for pollution reduction.

On an international level, the Clean Development Mechanism demonstrates
this kind of policy. As part of the 1997 Kyoto Protocol, this grants credits to
developed countries that finance reductions of greenhouse gas emissions in less-
developed countries. These credits can be used by the developed country to meet
future greenhouse gas reduction obligations or to sell to others. A key environmental concern is setting the macro targets at levels that adequately protect
human health and biodiversity.

An often overlooked but essential issue in economic environmental stew
ardship is setting prices to represent opportunity costs. A price set at opportunity cost ensures that resources are priced at least at the value of what they
would have produced in their next best alternative use. This ensures that individuals and firms are paying the true cost of resources. Prices set below opportunity costs generally lead to distorted resource markets, higher quantity
demanded than would exist if costs were properly represented, and environmental abuse.

While imperfections in the operation of markets may result in prices set below
opportunity cost, typically the worse offenses occur because of the intervention
of politicians and government. How else can one explain that water prices in San
Diego, where annual precipitation averages less than 10 inches per year, are
lower than water prices in Philadelphia where annual precipitation is over 41
inches per year? In Tunisia water is priced at one-seventh of what it costs to
pump. Metropolitan areas build huge reservoirs and even consider dams to prevent water shortages during summer peak load periods, rather than follow the
lead of electric utilities that have merely raised prices during times of peak
demand. Why are developers allowed to build vacation homes on fragile coastal
dunes and taxpayers forced to underwrite the rebuilding of those homes after hur-
ricanes hit? Shouldn't the prices of tires reflect the high costs to communities of
their ultimate disposal? A microcomputer is basically a box of hazardous materials. Shouldn't computer manufacturers bear some of the responsibility for funding the disposal or recycling of machines where the useful life is rapidly falling to
three years or less? Why is the U.S. Forest Service allowed to sell timber below
competitive market prices? As suburban developments are built further and further from central cities, why are existing homeowners asked to subsidize the
extension of utility infrastructure, roadways and new school buildings? The UN
estimates that throughout the world $700 billion in annual government subsidies
spur the destruction of ecosystems.

Frequently, direct government involvement is necessary for common areas
and natural resources that exhibit the characteristics of public goods (i.e., the
good is indivisible and it is difficult or impossible to exclude persons unwilling
to pay from consumption). For example, no individual or group of individuals
is willing to pay for maintaining Grand Canyon National Park; user fees are
low enough to allow access to a cross-section of the public, but too low to cover
the cost of maintenance. Still, it's a common area worth funding with general
tax revenues. Since the price system has broken down in such cases, the optimal supply of common areas must then be determined through the democratic

process and provided through public works. With respect to common natural resources such as oceans, without active enforcement and penalties by governmental entities, history indicates that the ultimate result will be overuse, degradation and, in some cases, even destruction. A first come, first served mentality prevails.

Finally, as consumers in developed countries have become more environmentally informed, either through government programs, education programs of nonprofit organizations, the news media or other sources, some of these consumers are steering their consumption dollars to companies that exhibit a concern for the environment. Between 1975 and 1985 more than 300 of the Fortune 500 companies were convicted of serious environmental pollution offenses.[19] It is very, very unlikely that these companies are willing to risk the market impact of such a high incidence of offenses today. It took Exxon years to recover market share following the disastrous Exxon *Valdez* oil spill incidence. McDonald's and other fast food restaurants moved quickly to cardboard and other disposable containers when the environmental damage from Styrofoam was exposed. Research has found that firms with the highest return on assets typically have reputations for going above and beyond their competitors in pollution control or waste reduction.[20] Local government has stimulated substantial household recycling simply through making consumers aware of the environmental benefits from recycling, and complemented this in some communities through lower prices on refuse collection when households place refuse in recycling containers. Influencing consumer spending and behavior is a powerful tool whose use by environmental advocacy groups is just in its infancy.

Holistic Development: The Example of Cambodia and Community Forestry
The recent efforts of the Mennonite Central Committee (MCC) in Cambodia provide a wonderful example of holistic stewardship where environmental enhancement is accomplished together with economic development and individual liberty.[21] The Cambodian population is 85 percent rural and relies directly on forest resources to meet daily needs for food (vegetables, fruits, nuts, wildlife and fodder for livestock, as well as fish from forest streams), medicine, construction materials (houses and farm implements), and fuel (wood and charcoal). Deforestation is a major issue, with estimated forest cover falling from 73 percent in the 1960s to 58 percent today. Deforestation not only undermines the ability to meet the daily needs cited, it also causes soil erosion, silting of lakes, decreased stream flow in the dry season, and loss of native plant and animal species.

The Cambodian deforestation is driven primarily by (1) the poverty of the growing local communities who do not have substitutes for the forest products and (2) the sale of logging rights by senior government urban elites for self-enrichment. The MCC program targets the lack of clear land-tenure rights for the poor. In cooperation with the Cambodian Department of Forestry, the MCC sponsored a Cambodian staff person to attend a six-month training course at the Regional Community Forestry Training Center in Thailand. A reserve of 1,600 hectares was then assigned to twelve rural villages. Villages were guaranteed access to defined forestlands.

Initially trees were made available by the government for villagers interested in planting them either on public or private land. The trees were almost entirely fast-growing species used to alleviate fuel wood and timber shortages. In the fourth year loans were made available for villages to start their own nurseries. The village nurseries soon produced 10,000 to 20,000 trees per year at half the price that the government charged. Under the land agreement with the government, farmers needed to plant a minimum of 1,500 fast-growing and 150 long-term trees per hectare. For short-term trees the farmer is guaranteed 15 years protection and for long-term trees a 60-year land guarantee is provided. The result, naturally, is that the farmers and villages became stewards of their forest resource. Indiscriminate logging ceased.

In addition, and of great importance, through surveys and meetings with community groups, the MCC determined that in order to minimize the temptation for indiscriminate logging, the villagers needed food security, followed by credit access and drinking water. Consequently, in collaboration with World Food Program a rice bank was established for the villages. In this way everyone would have guaranteed access to rice during transplanting time. Borrowed rice was paid back at 20 percent interest and a rice bank committee of villagers was formed to manage the bank.

A year later, groups of interested families formed credit funds in each village with seed capital from the MCC. Loans were limited to a maximum of $25, interest was 3 percent per month, and a village committee administered the fund. Eventually, 30 percent of the interest became compensation for the fund managers and the remaining 70 percent was added to the available capital. As the project expanded into new villages, the original villages provided $5,000 from their own funds as start-up capital.

Two staff people were then employed to provide training on basic health topics such as clean water, safe food and personal hygiene. Over 400 latrines were constructed and birth spacing methods introduced.

Finally, Village Development Committees and an Inter-Village Community Forestry Development Association were formed to enforce and continue the evolution of the policies initially put into place. The Association is funded by interest earnings from the village credit funds.

The value of the forest products is increasing. Villages have posted rules, including fines, in order to deter thieves. In some cases guards have been hired to keep an eye on the plantations. Forests comprising fast-growing species are increasingly available to meet immediate needs, although those needs are less desperate now that the economy is more fully developed and more balanced (e.g., more stable rice crops); forests of long-growth species will be available for future generations to enjoy and wildlife to inhabit.

Conclusion

Certainly there are individual instances where the environmental policies presented above may be applied inappropriately or unjustly. And there will be disagreements over specific issues that may never be resolved to the satisfaction of all (e.g., a cost-benefit study was done on spotted owl preservation in the Northwest old growth forests, but no value was placed upon the preservation of species diversity and ecosystems; the study found the value of the net benefits at that time to be approximately negative $24 billion).[22] And there are legal and philosophical issues that are still unresolved (e.g., denying an individual the use of part of his or her private property for the public good, such as for the maintenance of species habitats, is a taking and should be compensated). Nevertheless, the policies presented simply force the prices of resources, goods and products to reflect true social costs, and they expand the definition of economic growth from an increase in output per person (chapter five) to an increase in quality of life per person.

The policies also place value on the natural world as God's creation, providing incentives to better stewardship. If individuals want higher levels of material consumption, they should have to pay prices that reflect the opportunity costs of the production of those goods, including all environmental externalities and the impacts on the global environmental quality of life. This is a more holistic view of development where the real costs of consumption decisions must be taken into account, and is in accord with our Christian ethical call to creation stewardship. We recall the vision of the prophet Jeremiah spoken during a time when God's people were living in rebellion to his will, "I looked at the earth, and it was formless and empty; and at the heavens, and their light was gone. . . . I looked, and the fruitful land was a desert; all its towns lay in ruins before the LORD, before his fierce anger" (Jer 4:23-26).

Discussion Questions

1. Is the protection of endangered species a biblically mandated responsibility for Christians?

2. Is the survival of salmon in a particular river as important as providing hydroelectric power to a community?

3. Comment on the following statement: The natural creation is God's handiwork and worship of creation is therefore worship of God.

4. Human actions inevitably improve conditions for some aspects of the environment while adversely affecting others. How should Christians choose among alternative policies that all have environmental consequences?

11

WHO'S RESPONSIBLE?

Business & Social
Responsibility

There is one and only one social responsibility of business—
to use its resources and engage in activities designed to increase profits
so long as it stays within the rules of the game.

MILTON FRIEDMAN

SYNOPSIS

Recognizing that human nature is fallen, Adam Smith anticipated that some businesspersons would use underhanded means to earn a profit. Ample examples of such behavior exist today. Should profit maximization be the sole objective of business, or does business have a responsibility to society that extends beyond the bottom line? Conservative economists would say that a business's one social responsibility is to maximize profits. Other economists would argue that issues like human rights, environmental stewardship and community impacts should all be on a business's radar screen. While being advocates for the free enterprise system, Christians should be prepared to bring Christian ethics into the marketplace.

In his textbook, economist Michael Parkin comments: "If you asked a group of entrepreneurs what their objectives were, you'd get lots of different answers. Some would talk about making a quality product, others about business growth, others about market share, and others about work force job satisfaction. All of these objectives might be pursued, but they are not the fundamental objective. They are means to a deeper objective, which is achieving the largest possible profit."[1]

Maximizing profits. Economic theory assumes that this is the objective of business. And it makes a lot of sense. In the long run if a firm's revenues do not cover its costs, the doors will have to be shut. Controversy rages, however, over three issues. First, are all methods used to achieve profit maximization acceptable? Second, should profit maximization be the sole objective of business, or does business have a responsibility to society that extends beyond the bottom line? Third, if some methods for achieving profit are immoral or if business has a social responsibility beyond the generation of profit, what should be done about it?

Certainly, within the market enterprise system, businesses make a significant contribution to social well-being *by* maximizing profit. Jobs are created. Goods and services are produced at competitive prices, meeting the demand of consumers and the production needs of various industries. Input prices generally reflect their opportunity costs (the value the inputs could command in their next best alternative use). This is all in keeping with our ethical framework (chapter one) where we established (1) that men and women have a right and an obligation to work and the right to have their needs met by that work; and (2) that stewardship of creation, which includes the pricing of resources at their opportunity costs, is a mandate. Thus, profit maximization cannot be rejected. Yet there remain many serious ethical issues that Christians may have to consider when making decisions that affect profits.

Expect Anything!

As discussed in chapter one, all people are sinners (Rom 3:23) and live in a fallen world filled with self-centeredness, greed, lust, fear and injustice. As a result we should look for and expect sin in economic relationships. As noted in chapter two, this truth was the major reason Adam Smith withheld an unqualified blessing of "the unconstrained pursuit of self-interest." What type of behavior did Smith observe in the relentless pursuit of profit? "People of the same trade seldom meet together, even for merriment or diversion," he noted, "but the conversation ends in *a conspiracy against the public or in some contrivance to raise prices*"[2] (emphasis added). With regard to the compensation of workers Smith commented: "Masters are always and every where in sort of tacit, but constant and uniform combination, not to raise wages of labour above their actual rate."[3] Smith also recorded that British manufacturers used high duties or absolute prohibitions (quotas) to restrain the importation of foreign goods and obtain "either altogether, or very nearly a monopoly against their countrymen."[4] When prices for a particular commodity were rising, suppliers were "generally careful to conceal this" lest the great profits attract entry (note: new competitors) and cause prices to be reduced "to the natural price or even below it."[5]

Smith's views were significantly influenced by David Hume, who believed that, while benevolence may be found in almost all persons, the dominant force is self-love. Whether one is referring to businesspersons, policymakers or civil servants, "avarice, or the desire of gain . . . is an universal passion, which operates at all times, in all places, and upon all persons."[6] It would be logical, therefore, to expect almost anything in the relentless pursuit of profit.

Following are a few modern examples of unethical behavior in business.

Dancing with the devil. In his well-documented book, *Trading with the Enemy*, Charles Higham writes:

> What would have happened if millions of Americans and British people, struggling with coupons and lines at the gas stations, had learned that in 1942 Standard Oil of New Jersey managers shipped the enemy's fuel through neutral Switzerland and that the enemy was receiving Allied fuel? Suppose the public had discovered that after Pearl Harbor the Chase Bank in Nazi-occupied Paris was doing millions of dollars' worth of business with the enemy with the full knowledge of the head office in Manhattan? Or that Ford trucks were being built for the German occupation troops in France with authorization from Dearborn, Michigan? Or that Colonel Sosthenes Behn, the head of the international American telephone conglomerate ITT, flew from New York to Madrid to Berne during the war to help improve Hitler's communications systems and improve the robot bombs that devastated London? Or that ITT built the Focke-Wulfs that dropped bombs on British and American troops? Or that crucial ball bearings were shipped to Nazi-associated customers in Latin America with the collusion of the vice-chairman of the U.S. War Production Board in partnership with [Hermann] Göring's cousin in Philadelphia when American forces were desperately short of them? Or that such arrangements were known about in Washington and either sanctioned or deliberately ignored?[7]

The participants justified these relationships under the flag of "business as usual" and profit before patriotism. President Roosevelt chose not to intervene, fearing both the loss of the participation of major corporations in the American war production efforts and the adverse public reaction. Following the war there were few prosecutions, and Nazi friends were placed in prominent positions as businesses in the United States and Germany swung into production to fight the Cold War.

Among the most chilling relationships were those in the financial community. The Bank for International Settlements (BIS) was created in 1930 by the world's central banks for the ostensible purpose of providing reparations from Germany to the Allies for World War I. BIS quickly became a mechanism for supplying American and British funds for the building of the Nazi war machine. Then when the Nazis began to sweep across Europe, the gold looted from countries such as Austria, Czechoslovakia and Belgium flowed into the BIS and was promptly loaned to Hitler. Beginning in 1942 and continuing through the remainder of the war, gold bars created by melting down jewelry, spectacle frames, watches, cigarette cases and gold dentures confiscated by the Nazis in concentration camps and from occupied territories moved through the Reichsbank to the BIS. Following the war, Harvard graduate Thomas Harrington McKittrick, president of BIS, was given the position of vice-president of the Chase National Bank.[8]

In August 1998, after more than five decades of denials and stonewalling, Swiss banks agreed to a $1.25 billion settlement with Holocaust victims—but only when forced by the release of hundreds of historically damaging documents. Swiss banks had not only laundered gold looted by the Nazis, they had denied Holocaust survivors and their heirs access to accounts established to protect family funds from Nazi theft. When claimants came to the Swiss banks after the war, they were asked for account numbers that had perished with victims. If claimants had an account number, they were asked for a death certificate—but of course no Nazi concentration camps issued death certificates. In some cases the banks simply lied, saying the accounts did not exist.[9] Despite the size of the ultimate settlement, the estimated true present value of the funds stolen by the Swiss banks is $7.0 billion.[10]

Price fixing. God desires commutative justice in economic affairs (e.g., Lev 19:11-13, 35-36; 25:14). That is, prices should be fair and markets should function without coercion. Price fixing occurs when a group of firms making a similar product agree to set a price higher than that which would occur under competitive market conditions. Sometimes price fixing involves limiting the supply of a product, as companies agree to produce less than they would under competitive market conditions. There are numerous charges of price fixing brought by the U.S. Department of Justice each year. Recent cases include: a $200 million settlement by the three largest makers of baby formula charged with price fixing for at least a decade, an out-of-court settlement by the major record companies for fixing the minimum price retailers could charge for compact discs, a $165 million fine levied by the European Union Commission against 19 manufacturers of carton board and a $21 million settlement by ConAgra and Hormel for fixing the U.S. price of catfish.

One of the most extensive recent cases involved the Archer Daniels Midland Company (ADM). It started when ADM decided to enter the market for lysine, an essential amino acid used to stimulate animal muscle growth and a common component in feed for hogs, poultry and fish. ADM's aggressive efforts to gain a 30-

percent market share led the price per pound of lysine to drop from about $1.30 to $0.60. The drop in price, combined with above average production costs, had ADM losing money on lysine. Meetings were held with ADM's two major Japanese competitors in the lysine market, and the result was three years of continuous agreements on global production volume and prices. When confronted with FBI evidence, ADM ultimately pleaded guilty to price fixing (not just for lysine, but also for citric acid) in exchange for immunity from prosecution in a price-fixing investigation involving high-fructose corn syrup (HFCS). Allegedly, ADM would buy sugar cane and inflate the price so HFCS would be a lower-cost substitute for beverage companies (a $3 billion market). According to one ADM executive, a common ADM phrase was: "The competitor is our friend, and the customer is our enemy."[11]

Squeezing labor. Our ethical framework recognized that each human life is sacred. Therefore inhumanity to others, oppression or exploitation of labor is unacceptable to God. Compared to other nations throughout the world, labor generally fares well in the United States with respect to its share of total business earnings, regulations protecting health and welfare, unemployment insurance and mobility. Yet our hands are far from clean in the pursuit of profits. It took until 1865 and a Civil War with over half a million casualties to legally eliminate the use of slaves as labor. One study of 71 cotton textile plants in 1820 found that 55 percent of the workers were children under the age of ten.[12]

Among the U.S. sources of energy, coal was king in the latter 1800's, peaking with an 80-percent share of the energy market in 1920. The demand for coal was derived from the Industrial Revolution with the use of steam power in manufacturing, the growth in railroads, the increased use of iron and steel, and the rise in the price of wood. The demand for men to work the mines rose as rapidly as the demand for the black ore. The work was hard and dangerous, and due to immigration and the lack of collective bargaining, miners were, according to Bill Bryson, "infinitely expendable." Observes Bryson: "When the Welsh got belligerent, you brought in Irish. When they failed to satisfy, you brought in Italians or Poles or Hungarians. Workers were paid by the ton, which both encouraged them to hack out coal with reckless haste and meant that any labor they expended making their environment safer or more comfortable went uncompensated. . . . Explosions and flash fires were common. Between 1870 and the outbreak of the First World War, 50,000 people died in American mines."[13] Isolated in deep valleys in the mountains and eventually in the Great West, coal company towns were notorious for high rents and high prices for food and clothing at company stores. In their efforts to save on warehouse space, some companies even forced families to store explosives in their homes and, naturally, there were occasions when whole families were killed by accidental detonations. In Alabama from 1880 through 1922 an estimated 100,000 inmates, mostly African Americans, were leased to private coal mines to pay off fines and court costs for crimes ranging from eavesdropping to vagrancy to murder. Beatings were common. A state inspector reported that 165 inmates at one mine received 137 floggings with a whip during one month of 1899. Death rates were high, with inmates dying from cave-ins, asphyxiation, pneumonia, tuberculosis and attempted escapes. This forced labor system generated between $225 million and $285 million in today's dollars for the state in the first two decades of the twentieth century.[14] Despite court approval of unions as early as 1842,[15] it wasn't until the passage of federal laws and after years of brutal and bloody strikes that the abuses of mine labor eased and tangible gains were realized. Coal mining today still has the highest fatality rate per 100,000 workers among United States industries, but total deaths per year are now only between 30 and 40.[16]

Restricting imports. While almost all nations, including the United States, use tariffs and import quotas to protect particular domestic industries, the Japanese are the masters of nontariff barriers. David Landes observes that imported baseball bats are drilled to make sure they are all wood. Obviously the market for wooden bats with holes drilled in them is not large! High-tech new medical equipment is allowed in, but the procedures using this equipment are excluded from health insurance coverage. "Once, vexed by increasing imports of French skis, the Japanese tried to exclude them on the pretext that Japanese snow was different."[17] The consensus in the research literature is clear. Countries that engage in trade protectionism have lower rates of economic growth, higher price-cost margins and reduced productivity, and may inhibit the diffusion of technology that occurs through imported capital and intermediate goods.[18] Japan's trade policies have generated monopoly/oligopoly profits for a number of domestic industries, but the Japanese consumer has suffered high prices. This protectionism has also resulted in industrial over-capacity relative to market demand, one of the major factors behind the sluggish performance of the Japanese economy in recent years. Trade barriers benefit a minority while punishing the majority, and thereby run contrary to a variety of major Christian ethical economic principles.

Shifting costs. Production or consumption costs that can be evaded and shifted to others are considered external costs. The most common external costs involve environmental pollution. It is tempting for firms, in the interest of enhancing profits, to avoid absorbing the costs of environmental degradation. While there are many examples of polluting by manufacturing firms, petroleum refineries and ocean liners, a classic case is that of the oil tanker Exxon *Valdez*. In 1989 with the captain asleep in his bunk, partially drunk, an unqualified third mate ran the tanker aground on a reef in Prince Williams Sound. Oil spewed from the ruptured hull and within a week an oil slick covered 2,600 square miles of coastline and sea. The environmental disaster was enormous. Besides being a major fishing ground, Prince Williams Sound is home to the world's largest concentration of killer whales, one-fifth of the world's trumpeter swans, one-fourth of the U.S. sea otter population and hundreds of species of birds.

The environmental disaster was a direct result of the Exxon Corporation's attempts to minimize costs. In order to get permission to export oil from that area, Exxon had agreed to double hulls for tankers and a comprehensive contingency plan for handling spills at the *Valdez* terminal. But Exxon managed to convince the Coast Guard that the double hulls were unnecessary, and so the Exxon *Valdez* was constructed with a single hull, saving $22 million. While the contingency plan called for a crew of at least 15 persons on site at all times, by 1989 the total crew working at the terminal had been cut to 11 to save costs. And at the time of the disaster some of the crew were off for the Easter holiday weekend. Between 1985 and 1989 at least nine of Exxon's oil spill experts and its chief environmental officer had left or retired without being replaced. The spill control operation was supposed to have three tugboats and thirteen oil skimmers, but had only two tugs and seven skimmers. It needed 21 thousand feet of boom for containing spills, but had only 14 thousand feet. Ultimately, Exxon agreed to a civil settlement totaling $900 million and a criminal plea agreement of $150 million. Exxon has appealed an accompanying $5 billion punitive damage award.[19]

These examples just skim the surface of questionable behavior engaged in by businesses in the pursuit of profit. We could also cite other actions such as: pursuing government regulations that will limit competition, false advertising, tolerating discrimination if it reduces labor costs, using bribes to obtain contracts, tolerating the existence of unsafe working conditions, selling products that are known to be unsafe or of poor quality, and stealing intellectual property. When a survey published in the *Journal of the American Medical Association* found that 51 percent of children between the ages of three and six recognized Joe Camel as associated with Camel cigarettes, a spokeswoman for the R. J. Reynolds Company responded innocently, "Just because children can identify our logo doesn't mean they will use our product." And yet research showed that since the introduction of Joe Camel, Camel's share of the under-eighteen market had climbed from 5 percent to 33 percent.[20]

One can easily criticize big companies for their unscrupulous profit-mongering, but we see similar behavior in individuals, and sometimes in ourselves. We must not forget that the unscrupulous decisions we have just criticized were all made by people. In each case, someone decided that profits were more important than safety, justice or fair prices. As a company pursues profits, its profit motive filters down to its workers. Employees who keep their companies in business tend to remain employed; conversely, those who allow their companies to go broke will find themselves jobless. Employees who contribute significantly to the company's bottom line are more likely to be financially rewarded.

Where does that leave the individual Christian? It is natural to want a well-paying job with good benefits, perhaps in an established firm. As we have already seen, it is good to work and to get paid for it. And the sense of security that accumulated wealth provides is a continual temptation. However, we all need to be careful about the decisions we make and the corporate decisions to which we contribute. There is considerable pressure on individuals in business to participate in a range of unethical behavior in the pursuit of profit.

Beyond the Bottom Line?

Are all methods used to achieve profit maximization acceptable? That was the first controversy about profit, and we have answered with a resounding *no*. We have seen several examples of unjust, irresponsible methods, and there are many more examples that could have been cited.

The second controversy mentioned at the beginning of the chapter was this: *Should profit maximization be the sole objective of business, or does business have a responsibility to society that extends beyond the bottom line?* In the natural course of pursuing profits, businesses make substantial contributions to societal well-being through the generation of jobs, the supply of goods and services at competitive prices and the creation of resource markets where prices approach opportunity cost. But do businesses have social responsibilities that *exceed* these contributions?

The classic free market position of the social responsibility of business comes from Nobel laureate Milton Friedman. His position is clear and succinct: "There is one and only one social responsibility of business—to use its resources and engage in activities designed to increase its profits, so long as it stays within the rules of the game, which is to say, engages in open and free competition, without deception or fraud."[21] Suppose a company spends some of its resources on socially responsible activities—perhaps contributing to a charity. While that might seem like a noble thing, it could reduce dividends to stockholders, raise prices for customers or lower the wages of employees. In essence, company executives are taking the voluntary right for decisions on social spending away from those individuals. The rights of these individuals are subordinated to the views of some executive as to what is socially responsible. However, Friedman says that company managers have one responsibility—to maximize profits within the bounds of the law.

Friedman's position has merit. What makes company executives particularly qualified to identify social needs? And by paying taxes and conducting their operations within the legal code, businesses are conforming to the established mechanism for the expression of the general social interest, the democratic state. The government makes decisions about redistributing money to enhance the social welfare and about proper business conduct that furthers rather than harms the public interest. In Friedman's view, business should leave that to the government. Quite literally, it should "mind its own business."

This assumes, however, that adherence to the law is a reasonable limit for business and individual ethical obligations. History renders this view absurd. When it comes to social change, the law has almost always lagged behind rather than led. Government is often under the control of special interests, and violent social movements are frequently required for the law to change in a positive direction with respect to individual and social rights. Advocates for business social responsibility point out that businesses are members of their communities, are charted by the state and have, therefore, all the rights and responsibilities that any other member of society has. In the early nineteenth century, in fact, only enterprises that were thought to serve a socially useful purpose could be incorporated.[22]

Advocates of social responsibility present such beyond-profit concerns as

☐ human rights, including the treatment of workers and working conditions in less-developed countries; racism (e.g., apartheid in South Africa); and tribalism (e.g., Rwanda)

☐ equal employment opportunity

☐ environmental stewardship extending beyond current legal requirements

☐ social justice issues (e.g., economic development of extremely low-income urban communities; minority scholarships)

☐ community impacts (e.g., from plant closings or downsizing)

To encourage such activities, social responsibility advocates use strategies such as public protests, shareholder resolutions and boycott movements. Consumer pressure is also an important tool that grabs the attention of management. Following the Exxon *Valdez* disaster, for example, sales of Exxon products plummeted and it took years for Exxon to recover its market share. If profits were always generated in competitive markets by perfectly ethical individuals and corporations were not granted special rights under the law, then Friedman's straightforward position could stand. This is not the case, however, and advocates of social responsibility deserve a hearing.

Coming from a biblical perspective, Hershey H. Friedman points out that in ancient Israel farms were the equivalent of big business and there were numerous laws prescribing what farmers must do to help the poor. The corners of the field were not harvested and stalks that fell from the sickle were left behind (Lev 19:9). "If a bundle of grain was accidentally left in the field during the harvest, the owner was not permitted to return for it. This sheaf had to be left behind for the poor." Similarly, the gleanings to be gathered by the poor were to be left on grape vines and olive trees (Deut 24:20-21). Farmers were expected to make a special tithe for the poor (Deut 14:28-29).[23]

What Should Be Done?

Without a doubt, some individuals and firms in the pursuit of profit have engaged in behavior that is unethical and even abhorrent. At the same time, the majority of businesses and their employees conduct their work within the law and often adhere to ethical standards well above the law. In addition the commitment of business to social responsibility is reflected in the $8 billion of corporate donations to U.S. charities made each year, and a sizable portion of the 20 billion hours of volunteer time donated annually to charities comes from Americans who are encouraged, supported and even loaned by their businesses to engage in such activities.[24] Nevertheless, given fallen human nature, we can expect unethical behavior to continue. And we can't expect all businesses to attend to matters of social welfare. What can we do about this?

First, Christians should be advocates for the market enterprise system, alert to attempts to limit competition. Nothing fights ethical abuse better than knowing there are alternative competing companies with products and jobs to offer. There is strong research evidence that a positive relationship exists between good ethics and profits. When businesses supply products in an environment of mutual respect and perceived fairness, they experience higher customer retention rates. A direct relationship has been found between customer loyalty and the customer's ethical rating of a business. A similar direct relationship exists between employee commitment and employees' ethical rating of a business. Lack of employee commitment leads to lower productivity and higher turnover, both of which raise labor costs and reduce profits.[25] For these reasons, firms that over time build and maintain a reputation for ethical conduct and social commitment increase their likelihood of being profitable. Some firms now even integrate ethics into their strategic planning as one component for enhancing competitive advantage. Also, there is mounting evidence that a significant proportion of stockholders believe ethical and social concerns should constrain wealth maximization. This is seen in the rapid annual growth in the introduction of shareholder social policy resolutions, the active stance of major institutional investors (including four of the world's five largest pension funds) on corporate actions that undermine basic human rights or dignities, and the establishment of mutual funds sensitive to such issues as environmental degradation.[26]

Second, Christians should be willing to move into upper-management positions at firms and even start their own for-profit companies with explicitly Christian objectives. Successful Christian companies include Auntie Anne's Pretzels, Cardone Industries and Chick-fil-A Inc., which closes its 1,000 stores every Sunday. The four core values of the high-profile Fortune 500 company ServiceMaster ("In the Master's Service") are "to honor God in all we do, to help people develop, to pursue excellence, and to grow profitability." According to C. William Pollard, ServiceMaster chair and CEO, "If people do not have a purpose and meaning beyond generating profits, you will come up against the law of diminishing returns. In the long run, you are not going to have consistent production of quality products and services unless people see a mission beyond profit. People work for a cause, not just for a living."

Third, since there is not a perfect correlation between ethics and maximum profits, Christians should encourage government to enforce existing laws and regulations prohibiting unethical business conduct. We should also encourage the enactment of additional laws and regulations if clearly merited. Yet Christians must not be naive about the way regulatory systems function. We should remain vigilant and intelligent, making sure that the laws we propose have their desired effects. Thomas McCraw observes, "Regulation has served as a versatile tool whose handle has been seized at different times by reformers, business managers, bureaucrats, and lawyers—and manipulated as often for the particular interests of one of these special groups as for the general interest of the American public."[27]

While the Consumer Product Safety Commission and the Occupational Safety and Health Commission have brought positive gains in safety for consumers and workers, consumers have also suffered from the protection and cartel-building of industries under the Interstate Commerce Commission and the Federal Communications Commission. Once again, not surprisingly, the inefficiencies arise because fallen human nature infects the public sector, just as it does the private sector. Specifically, in this case, small numbers of people or firms or special interest groups who stand to receive large gains from changes in laws or regulations are far more likely to win in the legislative process than a larger number of individuals who stand to suffer small losses. For example, after decades in which regulation was used to maintain oligopolistic profits and high wages, deregulation in airlines, trucking, railroads, financial markets and telecommunications have led to significant increases in the number of competitors and significant decreases in prices. Meanwhile, the Environmental Protection Agency, despite opposition from sore industries, has advanced the public interest through significant gains in the restoration of the quality of water in many of the nation's major lakes and rivers through the Clean Water Act.

Conclusion

Finally, having been forewarned that we live in a sinful world and are always subject to temptation ourselves, individual Christians should be prepared to be confronted by and to respond to unethical behavior and choices in business affairs. Whether as an employee, a manager, a customer, a politician, a lawyer or a social advocate, each of us should be ethically prepared before the situation occurs—otherwise knee-jerk, and hence ineffective, reactions will predominate, yielding potentially negative effects. We must know where we stand. Unconditional loyalty can never be given to any institution, corporation, organization or individual. We must weigh all our loyalties in accordance with God's law and revealed will.

Knowing what we should do is insufficient unless our inner lives are transformed. We must each day put on the full armor of Christ, our feet shod with the gospel through daily devotions and constant prayer in the Spirit (Eph 6:13-18). Then, perhaps, we can be a positive force, taking the benefits of the profit-driven competitive enterprise system—which is motivated by the continual striving of individuals for security through money, power, and position—and integrating them with the kingdom of God.

Discussion Questions

1. Recognizing the product's addictive nature and health hazards, should a Christian work for a tobacco company?

2. Why does regulation tend to reduce competition in industries?

3. Should companies be required to give six months' notice and outplacement services before they shut down a plant?

4. When a company focuses solely on the bottom line, what type of behavior is encouraged among its employees?

12

FALSE HOPE

The Boom in Legalized Gambling

The only way to really beat a slot machine is with a sledge hammer.

FRANK SCOBLETE

Lotteries are a voluntary tax on the stupid.

SIR WILLIAM PETTY (1623-1687)

Governments may not be able to control vice,
but surely they ought not to encourage it.

BLAKE HURST

SYNOPSIS

Gambling is the world's oldest hobby. Throughout U.S. history, official sanctioning of gambling has waxed and waned. Currently, government at the state and local levels is throwing the doors wide open to gambling of all types, and through lotteries is a direct provider in many states. One of the largest industries in the country, gambling is a regressive tax and, unfortunately, for many people it is addictive. The odds on lotteries, slot machines and other forms of gambling amount to legal extortion. The amounts of money involved have resulted in government corruption as suppliers of gambling relentlessly seek new venues. Gambling undermines the biblical work ethic, disregards the sovereignty of God and violates our love of neighbor.

Gambling may be the world's oldest hobby. Archeological evidence indicates that it has been a common human activity as long as prostitution. Gambling in the United States dates back at least to the seventeenth century. In fact, a lottery in England was used to underwrite the first settlement in Jamestown, Virginia. But the American people have long had a love-hate relationship with games of chance, and historians can trace three cycles of public sentiment over the centuries.

Despite the Jamestown project, other seventeenth-century Americans—especially those in the Plymouth colony and the Puritan settlements—strongly opposed gambling. Games of chance were thought to encourage habits of idleness and improvidence, and considered disrespectful to God.[1] The famous Puritan preacher Cotton Mather condemned gambling as theft and as productive of nothing. In 1699 the clergy of Boston labeled lottery agents "pillagers of the people."[2]

Sentiment started to swing, however, in the face of the rising need for capital. With only three banks, lotteries were a major source of public and private funding for everything from the building of roads, water supply systems, canals and bridges to the construction of colleges (e.g., Yale, Harvard, Princeton, Pennsylvania) and even churches. Between 1744 and 1774 the colonies sanctioned approximately 158 lotteries whose proceeds paid for the building of canals and roads, 27 churches and 12 financial institutions, and the start-up costs of five new industries.[3] The Continental Congress used lotteries to supply the Revolutionary War troops. Following independence, since taxes were so unpopular (apparently even taxation *with* representation was a problem), lotteries paid for a variety of public works.

The government legitimization of lotteries naturally led to the initiation and growth of state and private lotteries. Between 1790 and 1850, lotteries were used by 24 of 33 states, more than 50 colleges, 300 lower schools, and 200 churches.[4] In 1832 an estimated 420 lotteries held in eight states raised gross revenues of $66 million, a sum more than five times the federal government expenditures for that year.[5] The growth of lotteries was accompanied by an increase in horse racing and gaming of all types. In 1812 the first steamboat offered gambling on the Mississippi River, and in 1827 the first casino opened in New Orleans. As has been the pattern, however, the rapid expansion of gambling eventually led to corruption[6] and that resulted in a public backlash. For example, governments were in the habit of contracting out lotteries, and in 1823 the agents conducting a lottery to beautify Washington, D.C., disappeared with the funds.[7] Riots at casinos in the west culminated in the lynching of professional gamblers. Finally, in reaction to the growing scandals, lotteries were outlawed in most states by 1840.

The second wave of gambling started during the Civil War as troops used gambling of all types to while away the hours. After the war, financially strapped states, particularly in the South, used lotteries to rebuild the social infrastructure. Riverboat casinos soon began to cruise the Mississippi once again. Card playing was considered the equivalent of speculating on the stock market. And in 1895, the slot machine was invented, spawning new gambling halls in such major cities as New York, Chicago and Baltimore.

Again, as gambling grew at an exponential pace, corruption and scandal soon followed. For example, the Louisiana state lottery, aptly named "The Serpent," had gross revenues as high as $5 million per annum in the late 1880s, with purchases coming from all over the country. Half of all the mail coming into New Orleans was for the lottery. Yet payouts were virtually nonexistent, as were contributions to state projects. Consequently, in 1890 Congress prohibited the use of the federal mails for lottery sales and, in 1895, invoked the Commerce Clause to forbid shipments of lottery tickets or advertisements across state lines. The Serpent, together with almost all other lotteries, was snuffed out.[8] Growing public outcry, particularly from religious groups and the Progressive movement, against the social costs of gambling and alcohol led to state bans on lotteries, horse racing and casinos. By 1910 Nevada became the last state to close its "gaming" houses.

The third wave began shortly after the onset of the Great Depression as Nevada legalized casinos in an effort to build its tourism industry. In 1933 Massachusetts legalized bingo, and New Hampshire, Michigan and Ohio legalized betting pools for horse and dog races. By 1950 pari-mutuel betting (on horse and dog racing) and low-stakes charity gambling was once again legal in the majority of states. Then in 1964 New Hampshire voters approved the establishment of a state lottery. Since 80 percent of the tickets were sold to out-of-state residents, surrounding states began to press for the approval of lotteries. Gambling was approved in Atlantic City, New Jersey, in 1976 with the first casino opening its doors two years later. During the 1980s 25 states ratified lotteries as well as off-track betting, video poker and keno. In 1987 the U.S. Supreme Court affirmed the right of Native Americans to establish casinos on reservations and in 1988 Congress passed the Indian Gaming Regulatory Act, opening the floodgates to gambling on reservations. In 1989 Iowa became the first state to permit riverboat gambling (casinos on water), followed quickly by Louisiana, Illinois, Indiana, Mississippi and Missouri.

As the dust settles, today only two states, Utah and Hawaii, have no form of legalized gambling. In the section that follows we will briefly examine the total scope of legalized gambling in the United Sates today. We will then weigh the social benefits and costs, review proposed public policy recommendations and reflect upon legalized gambling from the viewpoint of Christian ethics.

The Ante
Legal gambling in America now totals more than $560 billion a year. That's a

conservative estimate, but it still adds up to more than $2,000 for every man, woman and child. Americans spend more on gambling than the U.S. government does on national defense. Legal gambling now dwarfs all other spending on all other forms of entertainment combined. As stated in the recent report of the National Gambling Impact Study Committee: "Legal wagering has increased every year for over two decades, and often at double-digit rates. And there is no end in sight."[9] Over the past decade betting on legal gambling has grown at almost twice the rate of total personal income.[10]

Casinos. By market share, casinos have sprung quickly to the front of the pack, accounting for 84 percent of the total gross revenues wagered, and one-sixth of that activity occurs at Native American casinos. Pari-mutuels, whose market share has fallen steadily as gambling substitutes have arisen, capture about the same 7 percent market share as state lotteries. The remainder of the legal wagering goes to charities and miscellaneous convenience gambling.

Because the average payout per dollar wagered varies significantly by gambling type, we need to distinguish between net gambling revenue (the "hold") and gross revenues wagered (the "handle"). Casinos have a payout rate of approximately 93 cents out of every dollar, pari-mutuels 81 cents and state lotteries only 51 cents. (The states, of course, often justify their take by proclaiming that it funds worthy public causes, such as education or senior citizens' projects.) The payout rate for charity bingo is typically 74 cents. When we determine market shares of the hold rather than the handle, the casinos' share dips to 54 percent, while the states' share rises to 30 percent. Pari-mutuels run third at 13 percent.

Casinos have only recently come to dominate the legal gambling scene. Prior to 1990 legalized casinos operated in only Nevada (429 casinos) and Atlantic City, New Jersey (14). But casinos are now legal in 32 states, including 30 states with Native American casinos and 12 states where non–Native American casinos are legal. There are nearly 100 riverboat and dockside casinos in six states and approximately 260 casinos on Indian reservations.[11] Between 1990 and 1996 casino visits rose almost four-fold from 46 million to 176 million. An estimated 70 percent of all Americans now live within 300 miles of a casino.[12] The current trend in Las Vegas is to attract families by adding Disneyland-type attractions that appeal to kids—a movement toward theme parks with crap tables. Las Vegas now draws more than twice as many visitors as Orlando.

Casinos are big business. Thirteen of the world's twenty largest hotels are found in Las Vegas, where the occupancy rate averages 90 percent. The Las Vegas MGM Grand cost $1.03 billion, has 5,005 rooms and more ATM machines than any other single building in the world.[13] Casinos are owned by hotel chains and conglomerates, and many are listed on the New York Stock Exchange. Graduates of Harvard, Cornell and Penn's Wharton School today run casino companies. CEO base salaries can be as high as $4 million, with options ranging over $10 million.

Sophisticated methods are sought to increase the handle. The odds for casino games were originally developed in 1980 by Jess Marcum, who also assisted in the development of radar and the neutron bomb. In its never-ceasing efforts to deepen and broaden its market, the casino industry regularly employs Ph.D.s doing state-of-the-art marketing research, mathematicians developing new games, "theming" consultants creating mythical dream worlds and demographers conducting segmentation surveys to target the socioeconomic profiles of potential players.[14] These consultants consider everything—from the impact of the color of slot machines and various air fresheners on the frequency of play to the ability of alternative architectural schemes to keep visitors in the gaming area. Data from video cameras, house credit cards or slot cards, and information from other sources are fed into computers for analysis and customer targeting.

All casino games give the house a mathematical edge. Consequently, the longer a player gambles, the greater the house's chance of winning. (Simply put, .9 x .9 = .81 and .9 x .9 x .9 = .73.) Casinos vary the odds on slot machines to keep players moving between machines and staying in the gaming area longer. Slot cards, used by as many as two-thirds of all players, allow the house to identify high volume bettors and ply them with free alcohol, rooms, food and other compensations to keep them coming back. The result is that slot card users tend to lose more than three times the amount of money per visit than players without cards do. Add whirling lights, fast action games, no clocks, no windows and no direct path to the exit door, and the casino has an almost captive audience.

Lotteries. There is nothing new about governments using lotteries to raise money—Emperor Nero used a lottery to rebuild Rome after it burned. What is new in the United States is the state monopoly, its rapid proliferation and the variety of games. From the modest beginning of the New Hampshire lottery in 1963, a decade later lotteries were operating in 7 states with total sales of $2 billion. By 1997 lotteries operated in 37 states plus the District of Columbia and sales exceeded $34 billion.[15] Unlike the first two waves of legalized gambling, lotteries today in the United States are an exclusive privilege of state governments.

Economist Roger Miller observes that the odds of winning the lottery are "the same as the odds of a poker player drawing four royal flushes in a row, all in spades, and then getting up from the card table and meeting four total strangers who were born on the exact same day."[16]

As with casinos, in order to increase sales, lotteries have become increasingly sophisticated. Executives found that, when the sales of one game plateau, the introduction of new games does not reduce sales of existing games but just increases total wagering. Thus, today state lotteries offer far more than the traditional raffles they began with. There are instant games, daily numbers, lotto, electronic terminals for keno and video lottery terminals programmed with a wide variety of games. Because lottery sales are insensitive to the payout rate and driven by the size of the jackpot, states have also shifted toward games where the jackpot rolls over and where jackpots are combined among a consortium of states.[17]

While casinos have the largest market share, participation in lotteries far exceeds participation in casino gambling. In 1998, 29 percent of Americans visited casinos compared to 52 percent of Americans who played the lottery once or more.[18] Most lottery players adhere to budgets, but the law of the "heavy half" applies: 50 percent of total sales come from 10 percent of the players. (The top 20 percent of players account for 65 percent of lottery sales.)[19]

Convenience gambling through video lottery devices (VLDs) such as video keno and video poker have helped to drive this participation rate upward at an explosive rate. More than 110,000 VLDs are run in eight states, closely regulated by lottery authorities. Delaware has fewer than 3,000 machines, but South Carolina has 34,000, which can be played 24 hours a day in everything from bars and restaurants to convenience stores and gas stations.[20]

Lottery revenues as a percent of state general revenues range from 1.5 to 5.0 percent.[21] Of the 37 state lotteries, 10 place the revenues directly into their general funds, 16 designate the funds for education and the remainder target the funds for a broad range of worthwhile uses such as parks and recreation, economic development projects, police and firefighter pensions, and general tax relief.[22] Certainly, lotteries have rapidly come from nowhere to become a substantial portion of the revenue base in many states.

Pari-mutuel. The pari-mutuel industry, consisting primarily of betting on horse racing and greyhound racing, has been in steady decline as a direct result of the legalization of casinos and the initiation of state lotteries. As a sport, horse racing has a long history, and it has long been associated with wagering. Pari-mutuel betting on horse racing is now legal in 43 states. Most wagering now takes place away from the track at Off-Track Betting (OTB) sites where simulcasts from multiple tracks permits larger betting pools. Despite OTB, participation in wagering on horse racing has fallen from 14 percent of all adults in 1975 to 7 percent in 1998, and that decline has been most rapid in states with casinos.[23] Greyhound racing is legal in 15 states, and its 49 tracks have been harder hit financially than even the horse racing industry by the competition from casinos and state lotteries. The racing industry is fighting back by lobbying states for the right to place slot machines and video lottery terminals in their facilities, thus moving toward becoming casinos with racing on the side. The state of Delaware was the first to approve such an arrangement.

Charity. Charity gambling is quickly becoming a basic component of fund-raising by nonprofit organizations. Big Brothers and Sisters of Spokane County, Washington, for example, covers 95 percent of their annual $400,000 budget from bingo.[24] Total charity gambling is growing more than 12 percent a year, and it is expected to exceed $100 billion. Charities retain approximately 10 percent of the handle,[25] with the majority of money wagered going to private companies that run the various games. Charitable gambling is legal in all but five states; the games include bingo, casino or Mardi Gras nights, pull-tabs and jar tickets. Bingo is still the most popular, with a 45 percent market share. New computerized machines allow gamblers to play as many as 600 cards simultaneously. As with pari-mutuel betting, charity gambling has suffered from the growing competition with casinos, and charities are fighting back by establishing their own national lobbying organization and pushing the envelope to allow new types of gambling and to lift restrictions on the size of prizes and hours of operation.

Sports and Internet. The last two segments of the U.S. gambling industry are sports wagering, illegal in all but two states, and Internet gambling. Sports wagering is estimated to total anywhere from $80 billion to $380 billion per annum, making it the most widespread and popular form of gambling in America.[26] Point spreads are published in major newspapers and widely followed. Internet gambling is an infant wild card that has the U.S. casinos and state governments scared stiff and scrambling for congressional prohibitions. Internet gambling is available through 300 websites (up from 15 sites three years ago) with 22 international offshore casinos operating in such locations as Ireland, Monaco, Antigua and Aruba. Players use digital cash in the form of credit or debit cards with an access code. The integrity of Internet gambling through offshore casinos is ostensibly guaranteed by international accounting firms and financial institutions. Estimates have the total handle exceeding $1 billion and doubling each year since 1997.

Social Benefits and Social Costs
The benefits of legalized gambling, as trumpeted by the industry, are simply

stated: jobs, state and local tax revenue, and entertainment. According to the industry, gambling directly and indirectly (through multiplier effects) creates more than 1 million jobs with a payroll in 1995 of $21 billion. Casinos have brought new economic life to older manufacturing centers undergoing deindustrialization such as Gary, Indiana, and to isolated, played-out mining towns such as Deadwood, South Dakota. A frequently cited example is Tunica, Mississippi, a predominantly African American county in the swampy delta region that was so poor that Jesse Jackson labeled it "the Ethiopia of the U.S." Since the opening of 10 casinos, Tunica county's unemployment rate has been cut in half, as has its welfare caseload. The county now has more jobs (13,000) than residents (8,300).[27] Indian reservations, where unemployment rates have typically exceeded 50 percent, have realized over 280,000 jobs from casinos and related services.

Besides netting over $18 billion in lottery proceeds, states and localities collected over $20 billion in gambling privilege taxes in the year 2000. Gambling accounts for 42 percent of Nevada state revenues, 6 percent of New Jersey state revenues, and 1 to 3 percent of the total revenues in the remaining 46 states with legalized gambling.[28] It is easy to see why states prefer legalizing gambling to raising taxes.

More than 56 percent of all Americans gamble at least once a year.[29] With the explosive expansion of casinos, including their ancillary family attractions, gambling has become America's leading form of entertainment. In 1997 Las Vegas and Clark County, Nevada, received 30.5 million visitors; Atlantic City 34.1 million visitors; and Tunica County 17.4 million visitors.[30] In 1996, the hotel occupancy rate in Atlantic City averaged an extraordinary 89.5 percent. Analysis shows that the majority of gamblers are as aware as nongamblers of their low probability of winning, especially winning anything substantial. And many working-class gamblers stick to a disciplined budget.[31] So, obviously, gambling is mainly valued as just plain entertainment, a fun way to while away leisure hours.

What are some of the problems?

With respect to employment there are three complicating issues: cannibalization, missed opportunity costs, and who gets the jobs. Las Vegas and Atlantic City are the only two gambling centers in the nation that draw substantial numbers of gamblers from beyond 150 miles of their location. Consequently, when regional residents spend their discretionary income at the local casino, fewer dollars are spent in local department stores, restaurants and gift shops. In Deadwood, South Dakota, for example, the local retail base essentially disappeared. Even in Atlantic City, with all the casino day-trippers, the retail base has fallen by one-third since the opening of the casinos, with the number of eating and drinking establishments dropping from 311 to 66.[32] The Maryland Restaurant Association opposes the legalization of casinos. The gambling industry would respond that this is life in a competitive economy; if people prefer gambling to other activities, why shouldn't their preferences be respected? Maybe so, but if you're trumpeting the amount of money casinos pump into an economy, you have to acknowledge that much of this is being pumped out of other businesses.

The missed opportunity costs are the new business ventures that might have been started or nurtured by state and local governments had these governments not been spending so much time and resources on the gambling industry. The majority of jobs in the gambling industry are low-paying service occupations such as housecleaning, dishwashing, valet services and waiting tables. The multiplier or spin-off jobs are in pawnshops, cash-for-gold stores and discount outlets. Casinos produce wealth for the few owners fortunate enough to get the exclusive licenses, and the largest casinos that are unionized may provide some opportunities for employment advancement. But if a community wants a viable economic base in the long run, it should be working to develop industries with high value-added products and well-paying jobs with substantive benefit packages, such as pharmaceuticals, computer services and financial services.

Finally, the jobs created by casinos often do not go to local residents, no matter what casino proponents have promised. In Tunica County, for example, most of the jobs, especially the higher paying positions, are held by noncounty residents and although the county unemployment rate has fallen, it remains one of the highest in the nation. County residents are still segregated spatially and institutionally (e.g., African American children attend the public schools and white children attend the private Tunica Institute of Learning). The situation is similar in Atlantic City, where the unemployment rate is 50 percent above the national rate. In Wisconsin, tribal casinos employ 4,500 persons; 2,000 of them are not Native Americans.

With respect to taxes and entertainment there are three major issues: regressivity, compulsive gambling, and government corruption. First, we need to look beyond the total revenues flowing into government coffers and see where it's coming from. Consider gambling monies as a proportion of household income. Even if wealthy people wagered the same amount as poor people, gambling taxes would be regressive (the lower your income, the greater percentage of your income you pay in taxes). But the reality is even *more* regressive, since poor people tend to gamble more. Higher-income people gamble for entertainment. They enjoy the excitement, the social contacts and the diversion from the daily routine.

Low-income folks, on the other hand, view gambling as an opportunity to escape from poverty, an investment alternative to the stock market. The research evidence on this issue is absolutely clear, especially with respect to the lottery. The poorest neighborhoods are where the most lottery tickets are sold. Dissatisfaction with current income is the major reason for buying a lottery ticket. Formal education and occupational level are inversely related to lottery purchases. High school dropouts spend four times as much as college graduates. Hispanics in the western United States and blacks in the east play the lottery more than non-Hispanic whites.[33] Blacks spend five times as much as whites.[34] Lotteries, and increasingly video lottery terminals, take tax revenue from the poor and give it to the rich. States Dr. Philip Cook, leading researcher for the National Gambling Impact Study Commission, "The tax that is built into the lottery is the most regressive tax we know."[35]

Second, compulsive gambling is a serious problem; it is directly related to the availability of gambling and is extremely costly to society. Harvard's Center for Addiction Studies estimates that 3.5 to 5 percent of the U.S. population exposed to gaming can be expected to develop into compulsive or pathological gamblers[36] and another 7 to 10 percent may become problem gamblers. As many as 7 percent of all teenagers are compulsive gamblers and the proportion is rising. Researchers identify gambling as the fastest growing teenage addiction.[37] In 1980 the American Psychiatric Association added compulsive gambling to its official Diagnostic and Statistical Manual of Mental Disorders as an impulse-control disease. According to the APA, compulsive gambling is a chronic and progressive psychological disorder. Compulsive gamblers typically have a history of substance abuse, sexual abuse, spousal abuse, depression and other emotional illnesses. They are more likely to write bad checks, embezzle money, go bankrupt, be absent from work and land in jail or court. Three-quarters of compulsive gamblers have committed a felony to support their habit. Estimates of the average social cost of a compulsive gambler range from $13,000 to as high as $53,000 per year.[38]

John Kindt of the University of Illinois estimates that when gambling is legalized in a state or region "economies will be plagued with 100 percent to 550 percent increases in the number of addicted gamblers."[39] The compulsive gambling population in Iowa more than tripled after riverboat casinos were legalized. With the proliferation of tribal casinos, gambling addiction rates are now at least twice as high among Native Americans compared to the rest of the population.[40] When video lottery terminals, labeled the "crack cocaine" of gambling, were introduced in South Carolina, the number of chapters of Gamblers Anonymous increased from 4 to 27. After the legalization of video lottery terminals in 1988, gambling addiction grew so rapidly in Holland that in early 1994 the Dutch Parliament and cabinet called for the removal of all of the 64,000 machines from stores and other neighborhood facilities by 1998.[41]

Finally, the position that state and local governments find themselves in, once they have started down the slippery slope of legalized gambling, is expressed well by economist John Goodman: "Once you hold 'em, it's hard to fold 'em." State and local governments have become dependent on the tax revenue from legalized gambling. Yet they are finding it increasingly difficult to turn a blind eye to the corrupting influence of this relationship.

The books don't balance. It is estimated that for every dollar in gambling revenue states receive, they face $3 in gambling-related social costs.[42] Second, through their involvement with lotteries, state governments find themselves facilitating addictive behavior, promoting a regressive tax, preying on the poor and uneducated, and playing bait and switch with lottery revenues. By participating and sanctioning gambling, state governments make gambling a more acceptable activity and stimulate the growth of all of gambling's social costs. Research concludes that, while state lotteries have a strong appeal to established gamblers, they also serve as recruiters for commercial gambling, attracting about one-quarter of the adult population who would not otherwise gamble.[43]

Over time, various forms of gambling (including various lottery games) follow the normal life cycle of any product, moving from expansion stage to maturity, where the net gain flattens. And so governments are continually pressed by casinos for regulatory relief and subsidies. State lotteries keep pushing the envelope as well. The Washington state lottery schedules its advertising campaigns to coincide with the delivery of checks to Social Security and welfare recipients. Until stopped by a public outcry, Maryland brought a "Lottery on Wheels" into nursing homes.[44] Unlike the private sector, state lottery advertising is not subject to truth-in-advertising laws, and so abuses are numerous. The probabilities of winning are misstated, as is the true size of jackpots. Advertising targets the poor, the compulsive gambler and the uneducated. The Illinois lottery placed a billboard in a low-income African American neighborhood that read: "This could be your ticket out."

State lotteries justify their aggressive behavior by hiding behind the good ends to which the revenue is to be put. Not surprisingly, research shows that revenues are fungible, and lottery dollars that go into public education equal the amounts that go from public education into state general funds. In other words, public education isn't receiving any more money than it would otherwise—the bait and switch. You might justify your lottery habit by imagining some student getting a much-needed textbook, a music program or a better teacher. But the truth is that the state's share of your wager just goes into the state coffers. The amount spent on public education (or whatever worthy project your state is pushing) does not rise or fall based on lottery sales. And yet those revenues have become crucial to state governments—so crucial that their lottery agencies have very broad mandates, such as "maximizing revenues in a manner consonant with the dignity of the state" or "consonant with the general welfare of the people." The state of Delaware is more up-front, directing its lottery commissioners to "produce the greatest income for the state."[45]

Big money brings corruption. Government grants exclusive territorial rights to gambling franchises, and the value of those rights is reflected in gambling industry profit rates that are at least double the average profit rates across the U.S. economy. Not surprisingly, there has been one political scandal after another. Six legislators in Arizona and seven in Kentucky pleaded guilty to accepting bribes. The governors of West Virginia and Louisiana were sent to prison, as was a Pennsylvania attorney general. Over the past five years the gambling industry and its suppliers have legally spent over $100 million in political contributions and lobbying fees to influence state governments and, since 1993, another $6.4 million in contributions to federal election campaigns, including $500,000 each to Bill Clinton and Bob Dole in 1996.[46]

Involvement with legalized gambling has helped government lose its moral capital. Commentator George Will has summarized it well: "State sponsorship has changed gambling from a social disease to a social policy."

Current Policy Recommendations

As the social costs from the current wave of legalized gambling become more prominent, it is clear why the first two waves ended with general gambling prohibition. In an effort to head off any prohibition movement, gambling interests are actively working with government on policy recommendations that might curb social costs without killing the goose that lays the golden eggs. Recommendations under consideration include the following:

☐ Restrict or ban political contributions from gambling companies.

☐ Require comprehensive gambling impact studies before a state or community can expand gambling. Apportion social costs in the same way environmental costs are apportioned.

☐ Raise the minimum gambling age to 21.

☐ Conduct programs that expose teenagers to the realities of gambling.

☐ Remove ATM and credit machines from gambling areas.

☐ Ban Internet gambling by enforcing the federal law that prohibits using telephone lines for gambling.

☐ Ban all gambling on collegiate and amateur sporting events.

☐ Apply federal truth-in-advertising laws to state lottery advertising.

☐ Ban all advertising for gambling.

☐ Increase oversight and regulation of Native American gambling.

☐ Reduce opportunities for convenience gambling.

☐ Prohibit nonprofits from using gambling to raise funds.

☐ Encourage health insurers to expand coverage for treating compulsive gamblers.

Gambling interests, including addicted state and local governments, hope enactment of some of these recommendations will halt any movement to freeze the legalized gambling industry and develop strategies for phasing it out.

A Christian Perspective

Lots, a form of dice, were used frequently in Scripture to discern God's will. We find lots being used to select a king (1 Sam 10:20-21) and by the disciples to choose Matthias to replace Judas in the ministry (Acts 1:26). Lots were used regularly by the temple priests for the selection of animals for sacrifice (Lev 16:7-10), the assignment of rotations in office (1 Chron 24:5-31) and the assignment of specific duties in the temple (Lk 1:9). Aaron was ordered by the Lord to wear a form of lots (Urim and Thummim) over his heart when going into the inner sanctuary. Lots were used by Joshua to determine who—in defiance of the Lord—had taken forbidden spoils in battle (Josh 7:10-26), to choose who should return to Jerusalem from the first exile to Babylon (Neh 11:1), to divide land and wealth among competing claimants, and to direct Esther in her actions to save her people (Esther 3:7; 9:24). Before the general anointing of the Holy Spirit at Pentecost, lots were a common way to let God lead. This perspective is summed up by Proverbs 16:33, "The lot is cast into the lap, but its every decision is from the LORD."

But these examples of lot casting were not gambling. No money was wagered. The utensils of chance were used with the full confidence that the Lord was directing the outcome. But in these scriptural cases, people weren't placing bets. Gambling was done in the ancient world, but the attitude of Jewish law toward gambling was consistently negative. Jewish law considered it wrong to take money from another without giving services or something of value in return. Time spent gambling was considered wasteful because it took away from time that should be devoted to study or work. Most significantly, gambling meant one was relying on luck rather than divine will.[47] Similarly, the early and medieval Christian church consistently condemned gambling. Gambling undermined the work ethic and encouraged idleness. As God commands in Genesis 3:19, "By the sweat of your brow you will eat your food." Work is both a command and a gift from God, an essential element of human dignity and stewardship. Moreover, gambling encourages covetousness and stimulates greed, materialism and the love of money. Rather than encouraging people to be content in all things, gambling facilitates the idolatry of money.

Perhaps most grievous of all, gambling violates our love of neighbor. While gambling is robbery by mutual consent (the house always wins, and someone always loses), encouraging individuals to gamble lures them into sin. Rex Rogers provides a succinct summary: "Gambling disregards the sovereignty of God and promotes pagan superstitions. Gambling violates Christian stewardship of time, talent, and treasure, and it violates our stewardship of relationship with others. Gambling undermines a biblical work ethic and human reason and skill. Gambling is associated with a host of social and personal vices, thus violating God's command to avoid every kind of evil."[48]

Conclusion

The facts are clear. The social costs of legalized gambling are enormous. The selling of legalized gambling as innocent entertainment is fraudulent and dangerous. Christians need to begin the work of breaking the third wave of legalized gambling in the United States on the beach of common sense and love of neighbor.

Discussion Questions

1. State lotteries, given the odds, amount to extortion, and, given the customer base, are a regressive tax. What actions might be taken to remedy these effects?

2. Should Christians oppose legislation that legalizes casinos in their communities? Aren't casinos simply part of the leisure/entertainment industry?

3. Should churches use bingo and other forms of gambling to raise money?

13

THE NAKED GORILLA

The Ethical & Economic Challenge of the Pornography Industry

The Internet's anonymity and the wide range of fetish and fantasy sites
also create "hypersexuality"— a compulsive need for cybersex
that can choke the life out of marriages and partnerships.

ERIN MCCLAM

[Economics] is incapable of deciding as between the desirability of different ends.

LIONEL ROBBINS

Violence and pornography,
which is a felony against the human spirit,
are the atrocities of despair.

C. EVERETT KOOP

SYNOPSIS

Are there markets for which it is not morally or ethically acceptable to produce? Although in recent decades pornography has come to be accepted as a harmless diversion, it is, in fact, addictive and desensitizes users to degrading and dehumanizing behavior. With the Internet pornography is widely available to even young people. Christians certainly should have nothing to do with pornography, either as consumers or suppliers. As important, Christians need to become active in lobbying for constructive censorship.

Mainstream economics claims to stay neutral in matters of good and evil. It is an amoral, "scientific" discipline that focuses on mechanisms, not morals. It looks at the means rather than the ends. Economics is analytical, value-free inquiry. Right and wrong isn't at issue. As a result, in an academic world where moral relativism reigns supreme, economics finds a happy niche.

The absurdity of this position is obvious. Shall we simply allow the forces of supply and demand to govern the sexual abuse of children? Should workers be exposed to hazardous wastes so long as they are willing to accept the risk of future illness or birth defects? What of the destitute women in India whose aborted female babies are fueling the growing market for fetal tissue and organs in Europe and the United States? Among the many goods and services the economic system is capable of producing, is there anything that is not morally or ethically acceptable to produce? Are there any available means of production that are not morally or ethically acceptable? Yes and yes, especially to Christians. In other words, while the application of a neutrally scientific (technical) worldview may not be absurd when trying to understand the forces driving an economic activity, a value-free worldview toward the acceptability of the activity itself is absurd. We want the league to call balls and strikes neutrally on the field, but we don't expect the league to condone the drug use or spousal abuse of the baseball player off the field. There are economic activities where normative issues must be addressed.

A case in point is pornography. In the modern world, it has become more than a moral issue: it is an economic juggernaut. Pornography is a worldwide industry, earning billions each year. Must we economists accept this industry as just another mechanism of commerce and comment solely on its technical aspects, or may we legitimately rule it abhorrent and unacceptable?

What Are We Talking About?

The word *pornographer* comes from the ancient Greek, referring to one who wrote about harlots. "Pornography" was a description of prostitutes and their trade. Over time the scope of pornography was expanded to include any portrayal of obscene subjects intended to arouse sexual desire. Obscene materials are currently defined as offensive to modesty or decency; lewd; foul; filthy; repulsive; disgusting.[1]

The definition of pornography has evolved as the technology for transmitting pornography has evolved. With the recent arrival of Gutenberg's printing press, in the middle of the sixteenth century, the Catholic Church felt it necessary to publish a list of forbidden books, including books that "professedly deal with, narrate or teach things lascivious and obscene."[2] Within three years of the invention of photography in Europe in 1839 the U.S. Congress passed a law forbidding the importation of "obscene or immoral pictures." A federal law passed in 1865 and strengthened in 1873 forbids the use of the U.S. Postal Service for the mailing of obscene, lewd, lascivious, indecent, filthy or vile articles, matter, things, devices or substances. It remains in effect to this day.

While technology has continued to evolve over the last three decades (e.g., videocassettes, the Internet), there has also been an expansion of the boundaries of pornographic content. Pornography has become increasingly explicit, graphic, violent and bizarre. In 1957 the Supreme Court ruled in *United States v. Roth* that a work could be ruled obscene only if it was found to be "utterly without redeeming social importance." But in 1973 the court moved to much more specific standards. *Miller v. California* sets the following standards for determining whether sexually explicit material is obscene:

> whether the average person applying contemporary community standards would find that the work, taken as a whole, appeals to prurient (i.e., inclined or disposed to lewdness or lascivious thoughts) interest; b) whether the work depicts or describes, in a patently offensive way, sexual conduct specifically defined by applicable state law; and c) whether the work, taken as a whole, lacks serious literary, artistic, political, or scientific value.

Miller temporarily slowed the growing pace of deviancy in the U.S. pornography industry, but lack of enforcement, particularly under the Clinton administration, has seen the pace accelerate.

Given the expansion of pornographic subject matter, and its impacts as discussed below, the typology for pornography first used by the Meese Commission in the mid-1980s seems most appropriate. This typology establishes three categories of pornography: (1) violent, (2) nonviolent but degrading or dehumanizing, and (3) mutual or erotic. The growth in the first two categories is the most frightening, but, as we shall discuss, all three categories are problematic for Christians.

The Economics of Pornography

Total expenditures on pornography in the United States today are estimated at $15-$20 billion. This exceeds the total combined spending on sporting events and live music performances, and equals the total annual contributions to religious organizations. Individual markets include expenditures of approximately $8 billion on the rental of adult videos (5 percent of which is through pay-per-view on cable TV or in hotels and motels), $3 billion spent for pornography on the Internet, $1.5 billion for telephone sex (an estimated 250,000 customers each evening) and the remaining $2.5 billion or so on printed material, video purchases, pornographic software and files, live adult entertainment and miscellaneous sex products. After drugs and gambling, pornography is reported to be organized crime's most profitable business.[3] These figures exclude the massive soft-porn market composed of X-rated Hollywood movies, magazines such as *Cosmopolitan* and *Vogue*, and TV and radio fare such as the *Howard Stern Show*.

On the supply side, the economics of pornography is dominated by the impacts of technology on the average costs of production and distribution. The earliest known hand-carved figures of naked women date to more than 20,000 years ago. The Greeks and Romans not only had carved stone statuettes, they also covered everything from dinnerware to vases to walls with sexual images of all sorts. The rise of Christianity and the Catholic church as a major funder and censor of the arts significantly reduced the production of erotic carving and painting, and for centuries the church controlled the production of handwritten books as well. Quickly following the introduction of the Gutenberg press in the sixteenth century came the production of pornographic written material, including both novels and verse.

The birth of photography in 1839 significantly reduced the skill and costs of producing visual pornography and, as the taking and development of still pictures became increasingly easier and cheaper, moving pictures were introduced. By the early twentieth century steamships, railroads and motor vehicles lowered the distribution costs of pornographic materials, whether books, magazines, pictures or films, and allowed pornographers to skirt the U.S. Postal Service and its obscenity laws. The lower legal risks associated with the alternative distribution channels translated into lower prices and permitted the supply of more deviant materials.

The next major milestone was the initial publication of *Playboy* magazine in December 1953. Dr. Alfred C. Kinsey had issued his first Kinsey Report in 1948, based on supposedly scientific research, advocating a liberal, anti-marriage, prosexual freedom perspective, including pro-deviant sexual practices (e.g., same-sex partners, sex with animals, sex between adults and children). Later investigation showed Dr. Kinsey's work to be nonscientific and nonacademic, using biased data from a largely criminal, deviant population. However, Hugh Hefner, the publisher of *Playboy*, wrapped himself in the Kinsey Report mantle and mass-produced a "gentlemen's" pornographic magazine. Despite laws that could have stopped the distribution of *Playboy*, Hefner got away with it. With evolving technology in offset color printing and economies of scale (circulation at its peak exceeded 6.6 million copies), he became rich. By the time potential competitors realized what was now possible, he so dominated the mainstream market that entry was possible only in complementary markets by supplying more sexually explicit, graphic and violent sexual material (e.g., *Penthouse, Hustler, Oui, Gallery*). At their peak in the late 1970s the total annual circulation of the top seven subscription U.S. pornography magazines was nearly 25 million copies.[4] Pornography was becoming big, legal business.

In 1975 the Sony corporation introduced videocassette recorders. VCR market penetration went from 1 percent of all U.S. households in 1979 to 87 percent in 1998. Through research and development, prices of video cameras and VCRs plummeted and the quality of the images and sound continually improved. Pornography was in the forefront, first through the transfer of old pornographic films onto video cassettes and then through the professional production of pornographic videos. Today, the market is flooded with amateur pornographic videos of all varieties to satisfy any deviant fantasy imaginable. Pornographic videos constitute 26 percent of the home video rental market, are purchased through direct mail, and are viewed on cable TV in the home (at least two-thirds of U.S. households are cable subscribers) and in hotel and motel rooms.

In the 1990s came an even bigger boon to pornography: the Internet, the gorilla of pornography. As with the video industry, ever-improving technology and mass production has brought microcomputers into almost 50 percent of all U.S. homes and into over 80 percent of all workplaces. The Internet, together with scanners, digital cameras and digital imaging, and now video streaming, has brought pornography into the anonymity of the home. The Internet and its associated technology have lowered the barriers to entry to the pornography industry and made it possible for a plethora of small businesses to compete with major, affluent organizations. Every pornography supplier is limited to the same display space (the microcomputer monitor) and no one can gain a locational advantage. There is easy access to distribution channels, the initial capital investment is minimal, production costs are low (hundreds of pictures can be taken in one day with a digital camera and thousands can be scanned), billing methods are reliable and readily available (credit or debit cards charged immediately online), general advertising is relatively cheap (e.g., through search engines) and there is a very large pool of part-time employees.[5] Certainly larger companies have been able to gain some competitive advantages, such as through investment in computer equipment and programming providing higher speed and reliability and the total mix of products provided at a single website (e.g., digital images, video streaming, pay-for-performance, sex chat rooms, games, product sales). Nevertheless, competition is immense with the supply of adult websites currently estimated to range from thirty to sixty thousand, and growing daily.

With the rise of the Internet the pornography industry is taking on all the characteristics of monopolistic competition. As the supply of adult websites is approaching saturation, subscription prices have fallen from $24.95 per month to $24.95 for six months. Product differentiation is on the increase and includes increasingly bizarre content (including material which is illegal), a wide range of materials at a single site, better organization of site material, increased speed, more frequent updating of material, increased hyperlinks to related sites, the latest technology and opportunities to meet the porn "stars" through cyberspace or in person. Ways are constantly sought to improve marketing efficiency such as increasing linkages to other sites (especially affiliate sites, evolving now into commission-based revenue-sharing among affiliates), obtaining priority spots on search engines and advertising in non-Web media. As the marketplace becomes increasingly crowded, however, customer acquisition costs are climbing, and with falling prices, profits are being squeezed.

As the shake-out transpires in the Internet pornography sector, the impact on substitutes has already been enormous. The top seven porno magazines, already challenged by video and hurt by the "baby bust"-related decline in the population of young males, have suffered further with the onslaught of the Internet, dropping in circulation by over 60 percent over the past two decades, with declines for individual magazines ranging as high as 90 percent. Moaned *Hustler* publisher Larry Flynt, "If you ever cruise the Net and see everything that's available, it's glutted with sleaze. It's a nightmare out there. This has to be affecting the revenues of people like myself."[6]

Labor is not a problem. Wages for models on video conferencing sites range between $25 and $50 per hour, well above the average service-economy wage rate. Nontraditional working hours are available and work can often be done from home. Compared to traditional sex occupations (e.g., strippers, prostitutes), the jobs are considerably safer, with minimal exposure to violence and disease. In addition, in an industry where ownership was dominated by males, lower startup costs have now resulted in many women becoming producers and distributors of pornography.

Given the God-created erotic attraction between men and women, the demand for pornography has never been a problem. Given changes in sexual mores and technology, the demand does appear to be growing and changing. Traditionally, men were the primary consumers of pornography (which is more visual) and women tended to erotica (which is more relational and romantic). High production costs meant relatively high prices, which were a constraint for centuries on pornographic consumption. As prices fell due to changes in technology, there was still the stigma and embarrassment associated with being seen purchasing a pornographic magazine or book, entering or exiting an adult bookstore, movie theater or nightclub. Now, through VCRs and the Internet, consumers can indulge their pornographic fantasies in the isolation and anonymity of their homes. An estimated 40 to 50 percent of adult videos are now rented by women.[7] A survey of 26,000 readers of *Redbook* magazine found that nearly half of the women regularly watch pornographic films.[8] Recent research shows that almost 9 percent of people who use the Internet for sex spend more than 11 hours per week surfing for pornographic material and that these numbers are nearly equal for men and women.[9]

As early as 1979 almost 100 percent of U.S. teenage boys and over 90 percent of teenage girls had looked at a pornographic magazine.[10] Cable TV, VCRs and the Internet certainly make access to pornography easier for children. A 1995 survey of 1,100 Canadian children age 4 to 12 years old found that 39 percent said that they watched pornography at least once a month.[11] According to one U.S. study, 84 percent of all high school students have seen X-rated films.[12] Given young persons' familiarity with computers and extensive time on the Internet, one can reasonably assume that many of them are surfing through some of the tens of thousands pornographic websites readily available there.

The Dark Side

What does the Bible have to say about pornography? Jesus made it clear that he came to fulfill the law and even go beyond it, specifically mentioning adultery and lust. The law established that we should not have sex with anyone but our spouse, but Jesus added that those who even look at another person lustfully have already committed adultery in their hearts. If we can't stop such behavior, we would be best to gouge out our eye and throw it away, or cut off our right hand and throw it away, rather than for our whole body to go into hell (Mt 5:28-30). These are clear words and strong words.

Why is Jesus so concerned about sexual lust? Because as he tells us, everyone who sins is a slave to sin (Jn 8:34). Sin thus ensnares us, controls us, dominates us. What starts out as an innocent indulgence can gradually spiral downward until we find ourselves completely enslaved by sin. This is, of course, the plan all along of the great deceiver, the father of lies, the prince of darkness, Satan.

And as we stray from the healthy expression of sexual desire within marriage, what then does the Bible predict in terms of our behavior? We will be given over to shameful lusts and every kind of depravity and perversion. Women will be inflamed with lust for other women and men with lust for other men. We will invent ways of doing evil (Rom 1:26-28). In Leviticus, the Israelites were warned against being corrupted by the practices of the local Canaanites, including abhorrent sexual practices such as bestiality and incest. If God's people fell into those activities, the land would be defiled, and they would invite God's judgment.

The trend in the pornography industry over the past 30 years has been toward increased depravity and perversion with more violence; sadomasochism; oral, anal and vaginal rape; bestiality; homosexuality; sexual abuse of children; sex mutilation and even sexual murder ("snuff films"). Recently, Dr. Ronald Theimann, dean of the Harvard University Divinity School and founder of Harvard's Center for the

Study of Values in Public Life, suddenly had to go on sabbatical when a routine request to turbocharge a data-clogged computer found an extensive collection of hard-core pornography. Theimann, a Lutheran minister, eminent scholar, energetic leader, dynamic fundraiser, crusader for values, and happily married father of two daughters, had to resign his deanship.[13] Does this not sound like enslavement? Like addiction? The growth of cybersex in recent years has also seen the founding and growth of organizations such as Sexual Addicts Anonymous and the National Council of Sexual Addiction and Compulsivity.

What does the research literature have to say about the impact of pornography? First, scientifically conducted public opinion surveys in the United States over the past decade have consistently found that the majority of adults believe that pornography leads to a breakdown of public morals, harms children, leads some people to lose respect for women and causes some men to rape. These beliefs are far stronger among women, older individuals, religiously affiliated individuals, conservatives, less-educated individuals and individuals with less income. Professionals, particularly academicians, are far more likely to view pornography as harmless (even "healthy") and oppose all censorship.

Second, research conducted in laboratory experiments and with convicted sexual offenders over the past 25 years shows a clear correlation between violent or degrading pornography and (a) increased acceptance by males and females of violence against women; (b) increased levels of male aggression toward women; (c) greater acceptance by both males and females of premarital and extramarital sexual relations, a decline in the endorsement of marriage as an essential institution and a decline in the desire to have children; and (d) desensitization among males and females with regard to violence toward women and deviant sexual practices as a result of prolonged exposure to pornography. Exposure to pornography with violent content results in significant increases in male subjects' self-reported likelihood of raping and endorsement of rape myths (e.g., rape is enjoyed by the victim). A majority of child molesters and rapists report significant exposure to pornography prior to the age of 18 and cite pornography as a factor in inciting and preparing them to commit their sexual offenses. Over the past 30 years reported rape rates have risen steadily in all countries where pornography has been made more accessible and pornography laws liberalized.[14] Finally, in societies where there is a more equal distribution of power between men and women, mutual respect, and appreciation for the contribution that women make to society, rape is infrequent or almost nonexistent.[15]

Given the overwhelming data, how can anyone argue in favor of pornography? And yet some do, citing their concern about free speech and their opposition to censorship in general. Underlying these arguments is usually an assumption that all morals are relative, and that no one has a right to tell others what's good or bad to watch, read or think.[16]

Yet as Christians we know that men, women and children are made in the image of God (Gen 1:27). Our bodies are the temple of the Holy Spirit. No one is to be made into an object, either for sexual exploitation or to indulge the sexual obsessions of another person. Marriage is God's provision for the healthy satisfaction of our sexual desires (1 Cor 7:2-5). Pornography and masturbation disengage sex from its relational aspects, making sex self-seeking rather than an expression of mutual love within marriage.

Conclusion

What are we to do with this economic gorilla in our midst? Ban it? Cage it? Tax it? Clearly, Christians are not to engage in the pornography industry as either buyers or sellers. Nor are we to stand on the sidelines as the industry grows, pretending that it is benign (Ezek 3:16-21). Production of pornography is evil and is used by Satan to spiritually destroy individuals and families. Prohibition, given the current liberal First Amendment inclination toward freedom of the press, is unlikely. Nor can Christians expect to match the resources of the pornography industry with respect to prolonged court battles and the lobbying of legislatures. Small actions, persistently applied, may be the course.

Christians can lobby for obviously constructive censorship, such as not allowing children access to Internet pornography in public libraries. We can engage in direct service, such as providing education and job training to single mothers who are leaving the sex industry or counseling persons who have been sexually abused as children. We can propose and vote for taxes and restrictions on the interstate transmission of pornography via the Internet. Most important, we must recognize our own frail and sinful human nature, fleeing from the temptation of pornography (1 Cor 10:13; 2 Tim 2:22), confessing our temptations so we can be free to live for Christ (1 Jn 1:8-9), and praying for all those who are in any way ensnared by this profligate industry.

Discussion Questions

1. Should public libraries offer unrestricted access to the Internet?

2. How can Christians fight against the growing tide of pornography? What can Christians do in their homes, in their communities and in their states?

3. Why, according to Scripture, is pornography so destructive to both the consumer and the provider?

14

A MATTER OF LIFE & DEBT

Debt Relief for
Less-Developed Countries

The rich rule over the poor, and the borrower is servant to the lender.

PROVERBS 22:7

The Jubilee year does not point us in the direction of the communist model
where the state owns all the land. God wants each family to have the resources
to produce its own livelihood. Why? To strengthen the family.

RONALD J. SIDER

International efforts at poverty alleviation are profoundly
under-funded and consequently half-baked.

JEFFREY D. SACHS

SYNOPSIS

*External debt among less-developed countries (LDCs) has reached unprecedented enor-
mous levels. This assumption of debt was encouraged by Western banks flush with OPEC
petroleum dollars in the mid 1970s. Since then, a rise in interest rates together with falling
prices for commodity exports has resulted in LDCs with external debt payments that
exceed the total of their annual exports and in some cases exceeds their annual Gross
Domestic Product (GDP). The most radical Christian response advocates the cancellation
of the external debt among the lowest-income LDCs in keeping with the spirit of the year
of Jubilee and the Bible's admonishment to not oppress the poor. Less radical options call
for more selective debt forgiveness with the condition that the money saved be spent on the
indigenous poor (e.g., primary education, health care) and with the enactment of other
policies that in the long term will provide relief to the poor.[1]*

Imagine two piles of money. First, take the richest 20 percent of the world's
nations and put all their income in one pile. In the other pile put the income
of the poorest 20 percent of nations. Of course the rich nations' pile is bigger, but by how much? Ten times? A hundred times? According to 1998 Gross
National Product (GNP) figures, it's 335 times the size of the poor nations' pile.

Ethiopia has the lowest 1998 GNP per capita at $100, while Switzerland
tops the scale at $39,980. Regional averages range from $430 per capita in
South Asia and $510 in sub-Saharan Africa to $3,860 in Latin America and the

Caribbean and \$22,350 in Western Europe.[2]

The reasons for these disparities are many. They include corruption, political instability and war; the legacy of colonialism and racism; the lack of secure private property rights and human liberties; over-dependence on a small number of export goods; worsening terms of trade; the quadrupling of fuel prices during the two previous OPEC market manipulations; inefficient state-operated enterprises; price ceilings on agricultural products; discrimination against women; tribalism; lack of access to capital for small farmers and entrepreneurs as financial institutions invest available funds in government bonds; and noncompetitive markets due to state licensure. In this chapter we consider the role that international debt has played in growth of the less-developed countries' economies and poverty. We'll also seek Christian responses to the issues.

The History

The debt story began in 1973 as the OPEC (major oil-producing countries) significantly raised their prices. The resulting flow of revenues was deposited in secure Western banks. As the increase in the supply of loanable funds put downward pressure on interest rates, banks desperately sought investment opportunities and turned, among other places, to the less-developed countries (LDCs). The LDCs, whose economies were growing and who needed cash to meet the rising price of oil, were more than willing to borrow, especially given the current low interest rates.

Although a handful of LDCs used the cheaper borrowed funds to repay previous, more expensive debt, generally the money was wasted on spending that did little to stimulate long-term economic development or relieve poverty conditions (e.g., purchases of military arms; diversion of funds into the private bank accounts of government elites). Then in the late 1970s stagflation (rising inflation and unemployment) hit the United States, and interest rates began to rise worldwide. Simultaneously, partly through encouragement by Western banks, the prices for LDC raw material exports such as tea, coffee, cotton, cocoa and copper fell due to a market glut. Caught between double-digit interest rates and falling export earnings, LDCs ultimately had to turn to the World Bank (WB) and the International Monetary Fund (IMF) for rescheduling of their enormous debts.

As economist Joseph Stiglitz points out, "The banks are also to blame for failing to take into account the risks associated with the loans they were making. They should have realized, for instance, that prices for goods like oil are volatile. The banks also placed too much trust in the assurance of foreign governments that the loans would be invested productively."[3]

In exchange for their assistance, the WB and IMF imposed strict economic policies, known as Structural Adjustment Programs (SAPs), on the LDCs. The SAPs are in keeping with the mainstream macroeconomic policies that have been found to be successful in the Western democracies over the past five decades. The major SAP components include reductions in government spending; a tightening of government monetary policy; currency devaluation (typically against the hard currencies such as the U.S. dollar); reductions in barriers to trade, including import tariffs and quotas and controls on foreign investment; privatization of government-owned enterprises; market deregulation (especially with respect to price ceilings and wage floors); and a focus on the production of exports in which the LDC has a comparative advantage.

These are all policies that have been successful in stimulating economic growth and rising income equality in many industrialized nations and some middle-income nations such as Argentina. For many of the LDCs, however, the timing of the policies could not have been worse. The reductions in government spending, naturally, had a recessionary impact, decreasing demand and increasing unemployment. The tightening of monetary policy raised interest rates and helped to further choke off investment demand and access to capital for poor farmers and low-income entrepreneurs. The currency devaluation did make exports cheaper but, as mentioned previously, at a time when export markets for primary goods were over-supplied and prices were falling. Simultaneously, devaluation increased the costs of the hard dollars required to service the external debt and increased interest rates. Import costs also rose, making it more expensive for domestic producers to obtain new technology and replacement parts.

Specialization in low-income export crops put subsistence farmers particularly at risk. According to research, reducing barriers to trade increased the efficiency of most LDC manufacturers, yet one short-term effect was increased unemployment. Further, while privatization of government enterprises also increased efficiency, that was accompanied by downsizing, which resulted in unemployment for thousands of the middle class. Finally, the reductions in government spending came primarily from social expenditures on food subsidies, education, health care and infrastructure, exacerbating the condition of the desperately poor and increasing income inequality. However, research clearly shows that income redistribution through social spending directed toward education, improved health care, greater credit availability and land ownership all unambiguously increase a nation's rate of economic growth.[4]

Overall, according to an internal review by the IMF, "developing countries worldwide implementing SAP programs have experienced lower economic growth than those who have been outside of these programs." Between 1991 and

1995 the annual average growth rate in inflation-adjusted per capita income was essentially zero for all SAP LDCs, it was negative for sub-Saharan African nations.[5] Under the SAPs sub-Saharan African countries have seen their per capita incomes decline to lower levels than in the early 1980s and, at current World Bank projected growth rates, will not retake those levels until 2006.

As a response to this economic crisis and pressure from various nonprofit groups, including the Christian Jubilee 2000 Coalition, in 1996 the World Bank and IMF, together with the governments of various industrialized countries, initiated the Highly Indebted Poor Country Initiative (HIPC). The 41 nations initially targeted include 33 in Africa, 4 in Latin America, 3 in Asia and 1 in the Middle East. The cutoff point for HIPC designation is a fixed ratio of 150 percent for the present value of total external debt compared to annual exports.

Obviously these nations are seriously overextended economically. According to the figures from 1995-97:

☐ Total debt stocks are 349 percent of annual export earnings and 126 percent of annual GNP.

☐ The present value of total external debt is 272 percent of annual export earnings and 98 percent of annual GNP.

☐ Annual debt service is 15 percent of annual export earnings.

☐ The annual interest on the debt is 6 percent of annual export earnings.

The present value of total external debt as a percent of annual GNP ranges from a high of 375 percent (Sao Tome) to a low of 30 percent (Burkina Faso). Annual debt service as a percent of annual export earnings ranges from a high of 81 percent (Zambia) to a low of 2 percent (the Democratic Republic of the Congo). By way of comparison, following World War II, West Germany's debt service was capped at 3.5 percent of export earnings after a 10 percent proposal was rejected as "unreasonable," and was paid only after human development needs had been met.

An HIPC Trust Fund was established with contributions from all multilateral creditors and bilateral donors, including the World Bank and IMF. External debt servicing will be cut by potentially $50 billion (out of total 1997 debt stocks of $201 billion), and when combined with traditional debt relief, the initiative will cut by more than one-half the outstanding debt of more than 30 countries. As of fall 2000, 20 countries have qualified for or are likely to qualify for debt relief packages amounting to approximately $34 billion, a sum equal to 44 percent of the total debt outstanding of these nations. The central goal of the HIPC is debt sustainability, allowing a country to reduce its debt overhang, attract foreign investment, sustain economic growth and, as a consequence, reduce poverty. Eligibility for HIPC, however, requires three years of successful implementation of SAPs. Critics counter that tying the SAP to the HIPC debt relief may salvage the best from a bad credit situation, but will only worsen the condition of the poor in most LDCs.

Consequently, the World Bank has launched an effort to generate Poverty Reduction Strategies in those countries receiving concessional assistance, especially those receiving debt relief under the HIPC Initiative. The strategies are to be "country-driven, oriented to achieving concrete results in terms of poverty reduction, comprehensive in looking at cross-sectional determinants of poverty outcomes, informed by a long-term perspective, and providing the context for action by various development partners."[6] A series of poverty forums have been initiated throughout the developing world to facilitate the sharing of best practices on poverty reduction, the selection of indicators for assessing progress and the drafting of Poverty Reduction Strategy papers. Participants include the World Bank and IMF, government agencies, regional development banks and other multilaterals, bilateral assistance agencies, nongovernmental organizations (including church leaders), academia, think tanks and private sector organizations.

The Christian Response
The most radical Christian position on the LDC debt crisis comes from the Jubilee 2000 Coalition, advocating the cancellation of the external debts of all HIPC countries. The biblical logic is that the debt crisis falls disproportionately on the poorest of the poor in the LDCs and the basic principles of justice and righteousness preclude us (the more economically fortunate) from being oppressors (Lev 25:14: "Do not take advantage of each other"). Moreover, the principle behind the Year of the Jubilee is the equitable restoration of productive resources regardless of ability to pay. "If one of your countrymen becomes poor and sells some of his property, his nearest relative is to come and redeem what his countryman has sold. If, however, a man has no one to redeem it for him but he himself prospers and acquires sufficient means to redeem it, he is to determine the value for the years since he sold it and refund the balance to the man whom he sold it; he can then go back to his own property. But if he does not acquire the means to repay him, what he sold will remain in the possession of the buyer until the Year of the Jubilee. It will be returned in the Jubilee, and he can then go back to his property" (Lev 25:25-28). As Calvin Beisner observes, "The Law of Jubilee was designed not to promote economic equality, but to prevent one family member's destroying an entire family's means of productivity, not only in his own generation but also in generations to come."[7]

Scripture clearly condemns hoarding (Prov 3:27-28; Jas 5:1-6). Christian financial advisor Larry Burkett would add that Christians should never lend more than they can afford to lose because "you will discover that if you live by God's principles your ability to collect a delinquent debt will be greatly curtailed because many common means of collection are unscriptural."[8] God is more concerned with our witness and the salvation of people than with the collection of debts. Regardless of the motivations behind most debt collection efforts, they are unlikely to further promote the kingdom. God's heart for the indebted poor is most clearly illustrated in the incident where the creditor was coming to take the widow's two sons as slaves when, following the instructions of the prophet Elisha, a few small jars produced enough oil to satisfy the debts and provide additional funds to live on (2 Kings 4:1-7).

Stephen Smith raises three important issues with respect to the Jubilee 2000 proposal. First, as stated in chapter one, Christian ethics require that contracts and commitments are to be honored; lies and deceit are not to enter into economic transactions. Second, given the unequal distribution of talent among persons, a just and righteous society should honor and reward work and encourage stewardship and long-term investment. Third, is LDC debt relief both a necessary and a sufficient condition for improving the lives of the desperately poor?[9]

Both the Old Testament (Deut 23:21-23; Eccles 5:4-5) and the incident of Ananias and Sapphira in Acts (5:1-10) make it clear that the breaking of voluntary contracts undertaken as covenants to the Lord is sin. Certainly, the loans to LDCs cannot be considered under the terms of covenants. The word "credit" in the Latin refers to faith, fidelity and trust, and thereby implies that the lender trusts the borrower and believes in their ability to repay. There is no evidence that in the torrent of lending during the 1970s the LDCs deliberately misrepresented their ability to repay their loans or with foreknowledge intended to violate the terms of the contracts. Such actions would be stealing and be forbidden by the Eighth Commandment. There is some evidence that lending nations used loans as political "gifts" to prop up regimes for utilitarian purposes. In the final analysis, as in any financial transaction, the lenders bear the risk that the collateral is not sufficient and the loan will not be repaid. There are numerous instances of millions of dollars of European loans lost in bankruptcies to what appeared to be very sensible and sound investments in U.S. canals and railroads during the nineteenth century.

From a Christian perspective, one could even go a step further with regard to the ultimate sanctity of the LDC loan contracts. Scripture calls for mercy with respect to the repayment of debts owed by the poor. "He who is kind to the poor lends to the LORD, and he will reward him for what he has done" (Prov 19:17). "If there is a poor man among your brothers in any of the towns of the land that the LORD your God is giving you, do not be hardhearted or tightfisted toward your poor brother. Rather be openhanded and freely lend him whatever he needs" (Deut 15:7-8). And

Jesus taught, "If you do good to those who are good to you, what credit is that to you? For even 'sinners' do that. And if you lend to those from whom you expect repayment, what credit is that to you? For even 'sinners' lend to 'sinners,' expecting to be repaid in full. But love your enemies, do good to them, and lend to them without expecting to get anything back. Then your reward will be great, and you will be sons of the Most High, because he is kind to the ungrateful and wicked. Be merciful, just as your Father is merciful" (Lk 6:33-36). Since the total GNP of the HIPC countries equal six-tenths of one percent of the GNP of the major multilateral lending nations, the words of Christ would seem applicable. The call by Jubilee 2000 and the Congressional Meltzer Commission for immediate canceling of the debts of all HIPC countries is not so far-fetched.

With respect to Stephen Smith's second and third issues, many economists and others believe that debt relief to the HIPC and other qualified LDCs must be conditional. These conditions typically include the following:

1. A preferential option for the poor with respect to the spending of the funds saved. This includes increased spending on education, health care systems and degraded or nonexistent infrastructure (e.g., roads, water, sewer); increased access to capital for low-income farmers and micro-entrepreneurs; cooperative extension services to farmers; pre- and postnatal nutritional assistance; and programs for the prevention and treatment of AIDS. While small budget deficits preserve macroeconomic stability, HIPC debt servicing in recent years has exceeded the combined spending of their health and education departments. (In 1997, for example, total debt service was 14 percent of HIPC GNP, while total public expenditures on education were barely 7 percent.)

2. The institution of social security systems. No debt relief should be given to any nation at war with its neighbors (peace-keeping duties excepted) or citizens, and military spending should be capped. Similarly, no debt relief should be given to nations actively engaged in persecution of religious groups (e.g., Christians in Laos) or minorities.

3. Active democracy and participation of civil society in governance; transparency in government affairs, particularly with respect to the budgetary process; and rigorous prosecution of governmental corruption.

4. An independent judicial system operating in accord with generally accepted principles of justice, law and fairness.

5. Export diversification with less emphasis on primary products and industrial strategies to produce exports for which United States and Europe will guarantee open markets (e.g., textiles and garments). Simultaneously, the steady reduction of protectionist barriers to domestic industries. Such barriers are advocated by the left wing to prevent the imperialism of multinational corporations and advocated by the right wing to protect monopoly profits. In fact, research shows that protectionism fosters inefficiency, retards the adoption of new technology, raises consumer prices and reduces the range of consumer choice.

6. *Eliminate domestic price ceilings, especially on agricultural products, that retard the growth in supply.*

7. *Investment by developed countries in technology necessary to foster LDC development*—particularly in such areas as health (e.g., AIDS, malaria, tuberculosis, diarrheal disease), alternative energy sources and more drought-resistant crops.

8. *The institution and enforcement of environmental policies and regulations.*

9. *Programs tailored country by country, rather than applied in cookie-cutter fashion, and with significant participation of domestic economists, public officials, and representatives of other constituencies (such as poor farmers), to include specific limits on long-term debt relative to ability to pay.* This would be facilitated by having voting power with the International Financial Institutions, the World Bank, and the IMF changed from an investment share basis to one member/one vote. This coincides with a sentiment among some experts that the World Bank should return to its original focus, economic development, not banking.

Conclusion

Given the condition of the poor and the governance systems in the HIPC LDCs, unconditional debt forgiveness could be simply pouring water on sand. As Roland Hoksbergen argues, "We must structure our interventions so that all of God's people are respected and honored as image bearers, and are thus progressively encouraged to take responsibility for managing their affairs with justice and righteousness. Forgiving debts without regard to consequences is irresponsible, though forgiving debts with discernment and purpose can be a powerful force for good."[10] It is heartening to observe that debt forgiveness for the poorest of the poor nations is moving forward; it is focused on programs that will provide long-term relief for the poor within those nations; and Christians from around the world played a major role in bringing this issue to the forefront.

Discussion Questions

1. What is the biblical basis for the Jubilee 2000's call for the immediate canceling of the debts of all HIPCs?

2. What conditions do you believe should accompany debt relief to LDCs?

3. Why has the application of the World Bank's standard Structural Adjustment Policies been counterproductive in many LDCs?

15

GIVE ME YOUR TIRED, YOUR POOR . . .

The Economics of Immigration

**No one can surely be enough of an optimist to contemplate without dread
the fast rising flood of immigration now setting in upon our shores.**

FRANCIS WALKER, FIRST PRESIDENT OF THE
AMERICAN ECONOMIC ASSOCIATION, 1891

I was a stranger and you invited me in.

MATTHEW 25:35

SYNOPSIS

*Over the past two decades immigration into the United States has reached levels experi-
enced only in the Great Wave of immigration of the late nineteenth and early twentieth
centuries. There are difficult short-term consequences as wages fall in certain occupations
and as government services, including public schools, are heavily burdened. In the long
run, however, extensive and intensive economic growth may be expected. Beginning with
the Old Testament laws regarding strangers through Jesus' admonition to invite the
stranger in, the biblical position seems to largely favor unconditional immigration.[1]*

Almost everyone reading this book is a descendant of immigrants, people who uprooted, left their home and moved to a new land. Immigration has some interesting economic effects, and there are notable moral issues as well.

Currently about 140 million persons, or approximately 2 percent of the world's population, are immigrants living in countries where they were not born.[2] Immigration takes many forms. We usually think of persons voluntarily moving from one country to another, seeking a new home or greater economic opportunity, but over the centuries there have been many forced relocations. As conquer-ing armies move through a land, refugees flee before them, and vanquished people often migrate to escape the devastation, carnage and tyranny that conquer-ors leave in their wake. Forced bondage, or slavery, has moved many between countries and even continents. Certain nations have also been moved *en masse* by forced resettlements or expulsions such as the flight of the Jews from Spain dur-ing the Inquisition and the removal of Indians and Pakistanis from East Africa in the 1970s—or the Babylonian captivity of biblical times. Finally, much migration is simply temporary or seasonal. During the nineteenth century, for example, migrants from northern Italy left in the spring to work in Switzerland, Austria and France through the fall harvests.

Although there are vast immigration issues throughout the world, in this chap-ter we will focus on voluntary immigration to the United States. Today nearly 10 percent of the U.S. population is foreign-born, but the flow of immigrants has varied significantly over our short history, as has its effect on the overall popula-tion. During the eighteenth century, American economic growth was facilitated by a combination of the labor of free immigrants, indentured servants and slaves from Europe, Africa and the Caribbean. Nevertheless, natural population growth overwhelmed the contribution of immigration to the net change in population. Travel conditions were harsh, with immigrants crowded into small ships plagued with smallpox, yellow fever, typhus, dysentery and lice. According to Thomas Sowell, "In 1749, an estimated two thousand German emigrants died at sea. On one ship in 1745 only 50 out of 400 passengers arrived alive and in 1752 only 19 out of 200."[3] Fierce storms also sank perhaps a dozen emigrant ships a year.

But, as figure 15.1 clearly shows, immigration steadily rose as an important contribution to population growth. As a percent of the net change in United States population by decade, immigration went from 4 percent during the 1820s to a high of 34 percent during the 1850s. Steamships made international travel safer, shorter, more reliable and less expensive. The Civil War dampened the flow a bit, but the period from 1881 to 1924 is known as the "Great Migration," reaching a high of 55 percent of growth from immigration from the turn of the century to 1910. Overall, nearly 26 million persons entered the United States as immigrants (88 percent from Europe) during these four-plus decades, helping to fuel the Industrial Revolution and the development of the West. The misuse of intelli-gence tests, concerns by current citizens about their jobs, and other prejudices caused Congress to enact a national-origins quota system in the 1920s. The quo-tas, together with the collapse in the demand for labor during the Great Depres-sion, saw immigration into the United States to fall from 4.1 million during the

1920s to barely over 0.5 million during the 1930s, contributing only 6 percent to the decade's net change in population.

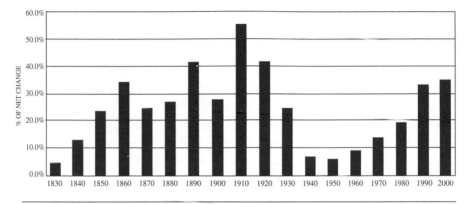

Figure 15.1. Immigration as a percent of net change in U.S. population

The number of legal immigrants entering the United States climbed steadily from one million in the 1940s, increasing approximately one million each decade through 1980. Net immigration was 4.5 million during the 1970s and accounted for 19 percent of population growth. Suddenly, during the last two decades of the twentieth century there has been a revival of large-scale immigration to the United States. During the 1980s one-third of our population growth was due to immigration, as 7.3 million legal immigrants arrived, the majority (almost 80 percent) from Latin America and Asia. The latest estimates for the last decade of the millennium show legal immigration reaching almost 10 million persons, contributing 36 percent of the change in population for the decade. Compared to the 14.5 million immigrants who arrived between 1900 and 1920 during the peak of the Great Migration, over the past two decades more than 17 million immigrants have reached the shores of the United States. This does not, of course, include the approximately 300,000 illegal aliens currently arriving in the United States each year. As some have begun to conclude, the United States is in the "Second Great Migration."

This chapter examines three questions regarding this fascinating issue. First, is immigration good or bad for the economy of the country of destination? Second, what are the U.S. immigration policies (and what could they be)? And, finally, what is the Christian perspective on immigration and immigration policy?

The Economic Consequences of Immigration
The majority of Americans are not favorably disposed toward immigration.

Writes George Church, "In a country almost entirely composed of immigrants and their descendants, heavy majorities—around 70 percent in two polls—favor reducing the flow of people through the Golden Door."[4] There are a number of logical economic reasons why native-born Americans are less than enthusiastic about immigration. These reasons, listed below, surfaced during the Great Migration through newspaper articles, speeches by politicians, and eventually the enactment of legislation, and they are beginning to surface again during the Second Great Migration. They include the following.

Immigrants flood the labor market and drive down wages. This is especially the case for low-skilled native-born workers who face competition from low-skilled immigrants willing to work long hours in poor conditions for below-market wages. One study of recent immigration data showed that U.S. workers with less than a high school degree earn wages that are about 5 percent less than they would without competition from low-skill immigrants.[5] This contributes to the growing inequality in the distribution of American earnings, as wealth is redistributed from less-skilled native workers to those who employ immigrants and use immigrants' services. It is estimated in Texas, for example, that use of low-skilled immigrants has lowered the prices for such services as baby-sitting, housekeeping and gardening 17 to 24 percent below the national average.[6] Over the past two decades, immigrants' level of education relative to natives has declined. Simultaneously a greater inequality of education among the entering immigrants has led to charges that at the secondary and postsecondary levels educated immigrants are "crowding out" native blacks, Hispanics, Asians and whites.[7]

The labor market impact of less-educated immigrants has been particularly hard on African Americans, many of whom compete in the unskilled and semi-skilled segments of the labor market. This is especially true in the six states where immigrants are concentrated: California, Florida, Illinois, New Jersey, New York and Texas.

Immigrants take more in services from government than they contribute in revenues. According to economist George Borjas, an outspoken opponent of indiscriminant immigration, immigrants receive more from the welfare system than they contribute. He also claims that they divert education funds from much-needed programs and technology into bilingual and special education programs, since many immigrant children, even those of high school age, have little or no schooling and are illiterate even in their native language. In the long run, he says, immigrants will have a net negative impact on the Social Security system.[8] The negative fiscal impacts, especially those from welfare and education, hit hardest at the state and local levels where immigrants are clustered. According to one study, in New

Jersey a native-born household pays an average $232 a year to cover the net cost of services used by immigrants. In California the figure is $1,178.[9]

The contribution of immigrants to economic growth is negligible. Says George Borjas, "Subtract the extra costs of immigrants from their contributions to the massive American economy, and the result is a net gain—from $1 billion to $10 billion. That's tiny—a $7 billion gain would equal about 0.1 percent of the national output of goods and services."[10] Rather than generating a positive "multiplier effect" that helps to drive the 3 to 4 percent annual growth in inflation-adjusted Gross Domestic Product, immigrants are, at best, keeping the economy at breakeven.

The contribution of increased immigration to population growth is exacerbating the U.S. environmental problems. Population growth, of which half is coming from immigration, is seen as degrading the nation's natural resources, depleting aquifers, draining wetlands for development and hastening the extinction of species. From this perspective, some say that immigration must be halted in order to save our environmental quality of life.[11] (For a more balanced view see chapter ten.)

All these negative impacts are legitimate concerns. However, upon closer examination they generally turn out to be overstated or just plain false. Most of these arguments involve poor analysis, use of low-quality data or a focus on the short term as opposed to the long term. For example, it is simply poor economics to treat the whole labor market or even the unskilled labor market as if it were selling a product, such as corn. If labor were a single, homogeneous commodity, then basic supply-and-demand analysis might work. But there are thousands of major occupations in the U.S. economy, and the supply-and-demand conditions for any one occupation vary by region, state, metropolitan area, and even local community. Moreover, by taking jobs for which they are better suited, immigrants free up native-born workers to flow into more specialized production.

Roger Miller notes, "According to numerous studies, there is virtually no statistically significant change in unemployment rates when immigration increases. [And] while immigrants definitely increase the supply curve of labor, they mainly affect specific parts of the labor market, and then for only a short time."[12]

The arguments against immigration also use bad data. Jasso, Rosenzweig and Smith found that Borjas's analysis had used an amalgam of legal, illegal and nonimmigrant populations. But when they looked at 1972-1995 Immigration and Naturalization Service (INS) data on legal immigrants, they found that: (1) the labor market quality of legal immigrants has been as high or higher than that of the native-born workers; and (2) while this relative quality fell during the 1970s and early 1980s, there has been a steady rise in quality during the last half of the 1980s and through the 1990s.[13]

The greatest weakness in the current debate is that it concentrates only on the immediate, first-round effects of immigration. Certainly in the near-term there will be some immediate "zero-sum" redistributive effects as millions of persons pour into our country. The question is: What then happens as the normal dynamic effects of an economy come into play? Will the economy be strengthened as new workers become consumers and savers, creating demand for new employment as product and service sales rise, stimulating the demand for productive capital to meet new levels of sales, and making investment cheaper through lower interest rates due to rising savings?

The best way to evaluate the long-term impacts of immigration is by examining the economic consequences of the first Great Migration. In a comprehensive review of the research literature, Susan Carter and Richard Sutch have done just that, and their overall conclusion is that the Great Migration "enhanced the rate of economic growth, improved the welfare of resident workers, moderated the business cycle, and had no impact on the distribution of income."[14] The specific findings are as follows.

In the long run the Great Migration resulted in both extensive economic growth (more people, more output) and intensive economic growth. Labor productivity and inflation-adjusted wages both rose. It also increased the rate of intensive growth. In part this was because immigrants were mostly young adults and, at first, primarily males; also, they had much higher labor force participation rates than the native population.

Despite massive infusions of labor, the capital-labor ratio rose. Savings rates of immigrants were higher than those of natives. This resulted in greater rates of self-employment (after having been in the United States for a decade or more) and higher home-ownership. Moreover, because the supply of savings was elastic, the increase in the demand for capital stimulated by immigration stimulated growth in the capital stock, and interest rates actually fell.

The United States became a magnet for would-be immigrant inventors, scientists and innovators. A brief glimpse at the recent history of science and technology reveals that many of the most renowned American inventors were foreign-born. Attracted by the availability of financing (including venture capital), research institutions, patent rights, laboratory infrastructure and libraries, some of the world's most brilliant people made their way to U.S. shores during the Great Migration. In addition, the fast growth of economic output and capital stock in that period facilitated the adoption and diffusion of the newest technologies.

Overall, immigrants were just as educated and skilled as native-born workers.

In fact, in terms of investment in human capital, the United States gained a great benefit with the more educated immigrants. America didn't have to pay for the development of their abilities but still reaped the returns.

There is no evidence that over time immigrants reduced wages, lowered the living standards of the resident population or raised unemployment rates. Immigration was very sensitive to economic conditions in the United States and actually helped to smooth the business cycle by relieving labor supply bottlenecks during expansions and reducing the labor supply through return migration during recessions (many immigrants are, in fact, "sojourners").

Finally, children of immigrants tend to have noticeably higher education and wages than the children of natives. Other things equal, being a child of immigrants is associated with greater socioeconomic success in the United States.[15] Moreover, when all the concurrent descendants (e.g., U.S.-born children) of immigrants are included in the analysis, the federal, state and local fiscal impact of immigrants is positive.[16]

In summary, immigration is one of the major reasons why the U.S. economy is so robust, diverse, dynamic and resilient. This is not to minimize the negative impacts immigration can have on particular workers, families or communities. But in general, U.S. policy should be supportive of, rather than resistant to, immigration. As described below, U.S. immigration policies have varied over the years.

U.S. Immigration Policy

As a result of political pressures stemming from the Great Migration, in the early 1920s the U.S. Immigration and Nationality Act established immigration quotas by country of origin. The quotas were most definitely biased in favor of Canada and Europe, and against Asia and Africa. The abolition of the "national origins" quota system in 1965, together with an amendment making family reunification a cornerstone policy (specifically family ties to U.S. residents), substantially altered the immigrant flow. Not only did the number of immigrants rise significantly, the proportion of immigrants from Europe and Canada fell from two-thirds to one-eighth, and the proportion originating in Asia rose from 6 percent to 37 percent. Current U.S. immigration law limits employment-related immigrants to 140,000 annually, while granting over 600,000 visas to family members and other immigrants.

Should U.S. immigration be restricted to the "best and brightest" and their families? This is hotly debated. Some favor the Canadian and Australian system where immigrant applicants are evaluated on the basis of their specific training and job qualifications, with points awarded for desirable characteristics in the areas of youth, schooling, apprenticeship or vocational training, technical skills and English language proficiency. Applicants whose points exceed a legislated threshold are admitted, together with their families. It has even been argued that extra points be awarded for family members with human capital skills and for applicants with successful U.S. relatives who are willing to accept financial responsibility for the new entrants.[17] A natural bonus would be that low-skilled immigrants would be kept out, which many would expect to increase wages for low-skilled U.S. workers.

Most legislators have been unwilling to be so crass as to slam the door on workers with less training. But they have been raising the cap on temporary (H1-B) visas, responding to the high demand for such high technology occupations as software engineers. They have also succumbed to political pressure in specific instances such as the Cuban Readjustment Act of 1966 that allows any Cuban who reaches American soil the right to stay but sends Haitians and others back to their countries of origin. Similarly, Chinese who say they have been victimized by Beijing's strict one-child population rules can enter and remain in the United States. There also have been cries in Congress and from the governors of the six states most affected by current immigration patterns for federal aid to help offset the full costs of social services for immigrants and refugees.

Prior to the September 11, 2001, terrorist attacks, the government had also increased spending on border patrols, with more agents, infrared night-vision scopes, low-light TV cameras, ground sensors, helicopters and all-terrain vehicles. There is no evidence that this increased level of spending reduced illegal immigration. It was, however, very politically popular and gave the appearance that "measures are being taken" and the United States is "tough" on illegal immigration. As mentioned above, illegal immigration has continued to flow at an annual rate of 200,000 to 300,000. By increasing the risk and cost of crossing the border, the increased border patrols actually just reduced the amount of commuting by aliens, specifically Mexicans. Instead of moving back and forth seasonally, these immigrants just extended their stay in the United States.[18] With NAFTA expected to displace approximately 1.4 million rural Mexicans due to lower-priced U.S. corn and beans, pressure on the border and illegal immigration are expected to rise.

The Christian Perspective

In Catholic social teaching, immigration is a right that the state cannot abridge.[19] From the standpoint of the state, this is a shocking non-utilitarian viewpoint. Doesn't the church realize that national interests are at stake? A country can't let itself be overrun by anyone who wants to move there. What about wages? What about resources? What about standard of living? You can imagine the protests of government officials over that stance.

But from a biblical perspective, is it really that shocking? Are we not the spiritual children of Abraham, who was called by God to emigrate from his country to a land that God would show him (Gen 12:1)? Are we not descended from a people who were strangers in a strange land? Didn't God lay down specific rules for the neighborly treatment of foreigners? "[God] loves the alien, giving him food and clothing. And you are to love those who are aliens, for you yourselves were aliens in Egypt" (Deut 10:18-19). Are we not called to show the same justice to the stranger as to our own? " 'You are to have the same law for the alien and the native-born. I am the LORD your God' " (Lev 24:22).

Old Testament law was supposed to be applied equally to the native and the stranger. Scripture includes immigrants in its call for the sabbath rest, the sabbatical, the Jubilee and gleaning. Immigrants were specifically entitled to own property and share in the inheritance of the land.

In Matthew 25 Jesus makes it clear that we are to invite strangers in, feeding them, clothing them, ministering to their physical ills and even visiting them in prison. When we do this for the least of the strangers and aliens among us, we do it for Christ. The parable of the Good Samaritan (Lk 10) confirms that nationality should be no obstacle. Jesus loves strangers and commands us to love them as well. Immigrants are created in the image of God and their immense value is to be upheld and respected in the political, social, cultural and economic spheres. Whether they are fleeing from persecution or from systemic deprivation of their basic rights (including subsistence), or are simply seeking a brighter economic future for themselves and their children, they deserve welcome from us. From a Christian ethical standpoint, we can conclude that countries should not close their doors to immigrants and that churches are to be advocates for strangers.

As Christians we are all temporal immigrants, joined to the great cloud of witnesses who were still living by faith when they died. They lived as aliens and strangers on earth. They were not thinking of the country they had left, instead they were longing for a better country—a heavenly one. "Therefore God is not ashamed to be called their God, for he has prepared a city for them" (Heb 11:16). How can we not open our hearts to the immigrant?

Conclusion

There is, then, a strong Christian argument that immigration is a right that the state cannot abridge. This position would support the dismantling of the cumbersome, often arbitrary, almost always frustrating, immigration bureaucracy in the United States. The doors would be open to those with the courage and initiative to leave their native cultures, extended families and familiar surroundings. They would not be supported by government social welfare services, but would work hard and pay their own way. This is what America has always been about and what our Christian roots support.

Discussion Questions

1. Respond to the charge that immigrants flood the labor market and drive down wages.

2. How does immigration contribute to economic growth?

3. What does Scripture say about the policy of limiting immigrants to persons by their level of education?

4. How should immigration laws respond to the threat of terrorism?

16

THE MALTHUSIAN BLUES
The Ethics & Economics
of Population Control

God blessed them and said to them:
"Be fruitful and increase in number; fill the earth and subdue it."

GENESIS 1:28

Proof of this crowding is the density of human beings.
We weigh upon the world; its resources hardly suffice to support us.
As our needs grow larger, so do our protests,
that already nature does not sustain us.

TERTULLIAN, A.D. 200

SYNOPSIS
Dire predictions that population growth would outstrip the earth's food supply and resources have existed for almost three centuries. They are no closer to happening today then they were in the 1700s. Population pressures are most severe in Less Developed Countries (LDCs), especially Southern Africa, where modern medicine has lowered the death rate but birth rates have not fallen substantially. Births rates will not fall until there is an improvement in the status of women (especially access to education) and there are increased economic opportunities for both men and women. Christians should actively support such policies as a means of fighting rising LDC rates of abortion and infanticide.

As Chicken Little demonstrated in the old children's story, you can get the attention of most folks by predicting that the sky is falling. Newspapers realize that bad news seems to sell better than good news. It is a quirk of our human nature. And just such a sentiment seems to underlie much of the concern over population control. Economist Thomas Malthus warned in the late 1700s in his essay on the British Poor Laws, population increases geometrically while food production increases arithmetically. In other words, sooner or later, without intervention the population would outstrip the food supply and millions would die of starvation.

Made famous by his essay and his dismal outlook, Malthus embarked on a speaking tour of Europe where he quickly discovered that his dire predictions generally had no merit. He concluded that population growth was held in check by two fundamental laws of society, the security of private property and the institution of marriage, which served to constrain selfishness and profligation. Subsequent centuries have proven Malthus's revised views correct but for slightly different reasons. First, in economies where private property is secure and where prices are allowed to rise and fall in response to relative levels of scarcity, individual entrepreneurs are highly motivated to provide more food. In the short term, they respond to rising prices by increasing supply and offering more substitutes and complements. In the long-run, they seek innovation and technology that raises productivity as well as providing new supplies of substitutes. Second, in economies where inflation-adjusted income rises, families with more income have fewer children.

In 1972 a group calling themselves the Club of Rome published a Malthusian update entitled *Limits to Growth.*[1] The book predicted that, barring major discoveries or, more importantly, change in government policy, the earth was likely to run out of most major resources by the middle of the twenty-first century, resulting in global depression and massive starvation. And that was its most optimistic scenario. *Limits to Growth* built upon work by biologist Paul Ehrlich and his Malthusian book *The Population Bomb* which predicted that resource scarcity would lead to widespread starvation by 1990.[2] J. W. Forrester, using more sophisticated computer dynamics but the same basic assumptions, similarly predicted the decline of America's cities in his book *Urban Dynamics.*[3]

However, there's a flaw in all these predictions. Their analysis excludes prices and the subsequent market reaction to rising prices as a result of increased scarcity. Seeing this, economist Julian Simon could not resist a rejoinder. According to Simon, "Just about every important long-run measure of human welfare shows improvement over the decades and the centuries, in the United States as well as in the rest of the world."[4] Based on prices, Simon realized that natural resources have been becoming *more* available rather than less. Consequently, in 1981 Simon issued a challenge to the Club of Rome doomsayers. They could pick any five exhaustible natural resources and if their average price, adjusted for inflation, rose over the next decade Simon would pay $1,000. If their price fell, Simon would receive $1,000. Only Paul Ehrlich accepted the bet and, based on the inflation-adjusted prices of chromium, copper, nickel, tin and tungsten, paid Mr. Simon $1,000 in 1991.

The market has a "magic" to it—simply the rational and imaginative responses of individuals to changing conditions. Examples abound. When the Black Death cut the European labor by more than a third, producers began to use waterpower technology that, in many instances, had been known since the time of the Romans but not widely used. When prices of sperm whale oil soared before the Civil War due to over-fishing, petroleum oil suddenly developed as a substitute for lubrication and lighting, and sperm whale oil prices fell to levels not seen since the early 1800s. As railroads spread rapidly across the United States, the demand for wood for bridges and railroad ties rose dramatically, as did demand for wood for residential and nonresidential construction. The U.S. Forestry Service was instituted in response. Although the Forestry Service has become the major seller of wood in the nation (at below-market prices), the demand for wood in the late 1800s eased as iron and steel was substituted for bridge construction and some nonresidential construction, and cement railroad ties came into use.

Consequently, researchers are now generally finding that, given competitive market conditions, rapid population growth can have a positive and statistically significant relationship to per capita income and economic development. In fact, over the past three decades as world population has soared, both food and mineral prices fell and food production per person rose steadily. This does not, however, reduce the potential damages of population expansion on unpriced resources such as clean air and water[5] (see chapter ten).

Similarly, as competitive markets resulted in rising incomes and improved medical care, the contribution of children became less important to maintaining the economic condition of the family, and falling infant and child mortality rates meant that fewer births were necessary to produce the same number of children who survived to adulthood. More of the average child's time could be devoted to education, thus enhancing the child's potential future productivity and economic well-being.

The world's population recently passed the 6 billion mark. Is the world's population exceeding its economic and environmental carrying capacity? In this chapter we will consider current world population trends and the factors behind those trends, the potential consequences of those trends and what might be the appropriate response of Christians to those trends.

World Population Trends

It took from the beginning of time until the year 1830 for the world's population to reach the 1 billion mark. The second billion took just a century. We reached that mark in 1930. Within just 30 years the third billion arrived, the fifth billion within just 15 years and the sixth billion within another 15 years.

For those concerned about overpopulation, that might seem alarming. Economist David Colander observes in his introductory textbook, "Population among low-income countries has grown an average of 2.3 percent a year since 1980, compared to 0.7 percent for high-income countries. High population growth presents a problem for economic growth (because) it makes providing sufficient capital and education for everyone difficult."[6]

But there's good news too. The runaway train of population growth seems to be slowing down a bit. The worldwide rate of annual population growth has dropped from a high of 2.2 percent in 1970 to less than 1.6 percent today.[7] The most recent World Bank forecast is a growth rate of less than 1.0 percent, resulting in a projected world population of just over 8 billion by the year 2030.[8]

What is behind this drop in the world population growth rate? Putting aside net migration, the rate of a nation's population growth is simply determined by its birth rate minus its death rate. Beginning in the mid-nineteenth century, a demographic transition occurred in the industrialized nations. There was a precipitous drop in the death rate that produced fast growth in population and was subsequently followed by a delayed and gradual drop in the birth rate. The causes, which have been well researched, include the following:

☐ Improved medical technology and medical care, including immunization of infants and children, and increased access to professional medical care raised life expectancy and meant fewer births were required for a particular number of children to survive to adulthood.

☐ Rising inflation-adjusted income and savings, and programs such as social security, unemployment compensation and worker's compensation, meant children were less important as a financial "safety net." This started a trend toward higher quality of life for fewer children among middle and upper income families (a trade-off between child quantity and perceived quality of life).

☐ A tremendous increase in agricultural productivity and a decrease in food prices resulted in better nutrition for prenatal mothers and for children.

☐ As women were given the opportunity for more formal education, they correspondingly provided better health care to their children.

☐ Increased labor force opportunities for and participation by women contributed to a rise in the age of first marriage, a delay in the birth of the first child and a reduction in the number of births per mother.

☐ Improved sanitation and treatment of drinking water, particularly in urban areas, reduced the spread of infectious disease.

☐ Advances in contraception technology and legalization of abortion lowered the live birth rate.

Just over a century ago, the industrialized nations had family sizes and population growth rates almost equal to those in today's less-developed countries
(LDCs). Now those industrialized nations have annual rates of natural increase of
less than one percent, with five nations having negative rates of population
change. Over the next two decades, 23 industrialized nations are expected to
move to negative population rates of change, including Austria, Germany,
Greece, Italy, Japan, the Russian Federation, Sweden and Switzerland.[9] Observes
Susan Power Bratton, "High per capita rates of resource consumption and pollution production," rather than exploding population, "would thus seem to be the
most critical population issue for the industrial democracies to address."[10] And,
given the tremendous disparities in wealth between the industrialized nations and
the LDCs, there is a significant role for industrialized nations to play in the institution of distributive justice (chapter fourteen).

The demographic transition began in the LDCs with a fall in the death rates in
the late nineteenth century as immunization, antibiotics and other medical technology began to become available. The most precipitous decline occurred after
WWII as the World Health Organization and other major nonprofit agencies began
to bring both medical and nutritional programs to LDCs. The LDC birth rate only
began to fall noticeably in the late 1950s and, as shown in table 16.1, the gap
between the industrialized and LDC birth rates is much greater than the gap in
their death rates. While there are many reasons for this, including cultural pressures and religious customs, the majority of reasons parallel the experience of the
industrialized nations. As seen in table 16.2, the income per capita remains
extremely low in most LDCs, access to health care is poor (as measured in health
expenditures per capita, physicians per 1,000 people and the proportion of population living in rural areas), the child mortality rate is high (over half of child mortality in LDCs can be linked to malnutrition) and the female literacy rate is low.

What policies are needed to encourage further decreases in the birth rates in
LDCs? Examples of the necessary conditions include:

☐ Improved status of women, including increased access to education. Statistically, female education has one of the strongest and most consistent negative
relationships to fertility in LDCs. Increased female education is associated with
delayed marriage, improved health care for children, improved efficiency in contraceptive use and increased labor force participation (raising the opportunity
cost of child care if the mother has to leave the labor force).

☐ Increased economic opportunities for men and women. This includes distributive justice with respect to land tenure (in part a legacy of colonialism), access to
capital and access to education.

Table 16.1

	Death Rate Per 1,000 People		Birth Rate Per 1,000 People	
	(1980)	(1998)	(1980)	(1998)
South Asia	14	9	37	28
Sub-Saharan Africa	18	15	47	40
Middle East & North Africa	12	7	41	27
Europe & Central Asia	10	11	19	12
Latin America & Carib.	8	6	31	23
Europe (EMU)	10	10	13	10
U.S.	9	9	16	14

Source: World Bank, 2000 World Development Indicators, Table 2.2, 44.

Table 16.2

	GNP Per Capita (1998)	Health Expenditure Per Capita (most recent 1990-98)	Physicians Per 1,000 People (most recent 1990-98)
South Asia	430	17	0.4
Sub-Saharan Africa	510	33	0.1
Middle East & North Africa	2,030	117	1.2
Europe & Central Asia	2,200	138	3.3
Latin America & Carib.	3,860	284	1.5
Europe (EMU)	22,350	1,974	3.7
U.S.	29,240	4,080	2.6

	Percent Rural (1998)	Infant Mortality Rate per 1,000 Live Births (1998)	Adult Female Illiteracy Rate (1998)
South Asia	72	75	59
Sub-Saharan Africa	67	92	49
Middle East & North Africa	43	45	48
Europe & Central Asia	34	22	5
Latin America & Carib.	25	31	13
Europe (EMU)	22	5	—
U.S.	23	7	—

Source: World Bank, 2000 World Development Indicators, Tables 1.1, 12; 2.2, 44; 2.14, 92; 3.10 152; 2.18, 108; 2.12, 84.

☐ Rising inflation-adjusted income with an increase in the equality of the income distribution. Death rates are relatively low when per capita GDP is over $1,000. With respect to equality, for example, currently in seven LDCs (Brazil, Chile, Guatemala, Lesotho, Sierra Leone, South Africa and Zimbabwe) the top 20 percent of the income distribution receives over 60 percent of all the annual income. Poor families have more children than middle- and upper-income families, but due to lack of resources experience high rates of infant and child mortality.

☐ Increased access to contraceptive technology and education, for both women and men, and especially among the poor.

☐ Changed cultural attitudes toward fertility limitation practices, including the decoupling of the value of a woman from her fertility.

☐ Establishment of social security systems and more secure capital markets (where savings are insured).

☐ Improved food security through increased access to food in the short term and access to income or the means to produce food in the medium term.

☐ Increased agricultural productivity through competitive markets (i.e., eliminate government price ceilings on agricultural goods), together with investment in infrastructure for transportation, storage and marketing of agricultural products.

Obviously, family planning and economic development are complements, not substitutes. Thus, issues in other chapters such as the determinants of economic growth (chapter five), the importance of private property rights to productivity (chapter four), the environmental impacts of economic activity (chapter ten), free trade and the extraordinary external debt of LDCs (chapter fourteen) are all relevant. Nevertheless, all other things being equal, aggressive family planning policies can have a significant impact. For example, Singapore, where per capita income is rising and women have liberal access to education and the labor force, has reached zero population growth rate through widely promoted free contraception, abortion and sterilization, increased medical costs for each birth, a sterilization benefit equal to one year's salary after the second child, and no paid maternity leave or tax exemptions after two children. China has even gone so far as coercing abortion after the second child in a family. At the least, the Chinese "one child per family" policy may encourage abortion or infanticide of females. The custom of dowries (although officially illegal), together with the availability of sonograms, has increased the rate of abortion of female fetuses in India.

What is the most biblical approach to stewardship in the area of population growth?

A Christian Perspective

For centuries Christian doctrine was ambivalent or even antagonistic toward birth control. From Justin, Clement and Augustine through the Middle Ages, the church opposed not only infanticide and abortion, but sterilization and most available natural forms of contraception as well. The biblical basis for opposition to infanticide and abortion are obvious. In Jeremiah 1:5 and Psalm 139:13-16 God makes it clear that he knows us even before we are formed in our mother's womb, has set us apart and has ordained all our days before one of them came to be. Throughout the laws of the Old Testament and in Jesus' ministry it is also made clear that children are a blessing from God, are to be highly valued and have a special place in the kingdom. Jesus says, "Let the little children come to me, and do not hinder them, for the kingdom of heaven belongs to such as these" (Mt 19:14). And taking a little child in his arms, Jesus says, "Whoever welcomes one of these little children in my name welcomes me; and whoever welcomes me does not welcome me but the one who sent me" (Mk 9:36-37).

But our position as Christians on abortion and infanticide should not lead us to be judgmental. Instead we should provide support to mothers before and after pregnancy, adequate food and care for the child after delivery, adoption services and shelter for abandoned children. Mother Teresa has expressed it succinctly: "If you hear of someone who does not want to have her child, who wants to have an abortion, try to convince her to bring the child to me. I will love that child, who is a sign of God's love."[11] In the United States alone approximately 1.3 million abortions are performed each year. Since abortion was legalized in the early 1970s over 38 million legal abortions have been performed. As Christians continue their efforts to restrict the legal limits under which abortion can be performed (e.g., to cases of rape, incest), we also need to provide health care as well as emotional and financial support to pregnant women; hospital care and post-birth support to mothers; child care and adoption services; and counseling for women who have experienced abortion.

The biblical basis for doctrinal opposition to contraception begins with Genesis 1:28 where, after creating man and woman in his own image, "God blessed them and said to them, 'Be fruitful and increase in number; fill the earth and subdue it.'" This appears on the surface to be a strong mandate for reproduction. However, read in the full context of the creation narrative that includes all living organisms, God's blessing is to be seen as integrated with the full realm of creation. Comments Susan Power Bratton, "Fruitfulness and increase were never intended to be relentless marching orders but were a call to living organisms to grace the earth with the beauty of God's handiwork. Human population growth has no mandate to damage or desecrate the cosmos."[12] And, in fact, in the Hebrew the word for "fill" *(male')* refers to filling but not overflowing. (It can also mean "to consecrate.")

And although a large family could be a blessing in the primitive agricultural economy of Old Testament times, because children then could make an early and direct contribution to a family's economic output, the greater blessing was to have a "child of promise"—as we see with Abraham and Isaac. Efforts to produce additional children through multiple wives or concubines led to strife, immorality and even bloodshed. Examples include Abraham and Hagar, the turmoil within the family of King David, and the excesses of Solomon that laid the groundwork for the fall of the nation of Israel.

We find no clear commands against contraception in Scripture. There is the odd story of Onan practicing *coitus interruptus* rather than impregnating his brother's widow. But he was judged for his greedy disregard of family customs, not for birth control in general. In fact, in the New Testament Paul says of the unmarried and widows, "It is good for them to stay unmarried" (1 Cor 7:8) unless their natural passions would lead to immorality. He explains that family obligations can keep people from serving the Lord fully. In general, the New Testament takes no position as to whether having children does or does not serve the Lord. And Jesus makes it clear that under the New Covenant the kingdom is to grow through the spreading of the Gospel, baptizing, teaching, personal witness and direct expressions of God's love—not through birthing.

Because of our abhorrence of abortion and infanticide, and our concerns over the sexual promiscuity facilitated by artificial birth control methods, many Christians have been ambivalent toward the development and implementation of contraception technologies. But as we view the population situation in LDCs, there are Christians who want us to reexamine our position. Throughout the world, the poorest of the poor endure disproportionate hardships from high birth rates and infant mortality rates. The rampant spread of AIDs is causing a health crisis in many LDCs. And we must also consider the environmental damage associated with low-income persons and nations placing short-term economic survival ahead of long-term environmental consequences. Based on all this, it would seem responsible for Christians to construct a "contraceptive ethos"[13] to complement the other policies listed above (and cited in other chapters of this book) and implement programs through churches and other Christian organizations.[14]

As we have seen, societies are creative enough to adjust to meet the challenges of exploding populations, as long as there are competitive markets, secure property rights, individual liberty and the regulatory authority of government to curb externalities and concentrations of power. Under such conditions, the scenario of massive starvation and environmental Armageddon is remote. But significant distribution challenges remain.

In sub-Saharan Africa, for example, some 3 million children under age five suffer blindness caused by lack of vitamin A. Two-thirds of the children who do not meet their requirements for vitamin A die from increased vulnerability to infection. That is one of many challenges we need to address with empathy and innovation. And in this case, help is on the way. Programs that distribute vitamin A capsules and fortify food have already reduced the number of children suffering blindness related to vitamin A deficiency by two-thirds over the past 20 years. To reach children in more remote rural areas, development workers are trying to extend the growing of high beta-carotene sweet potatoes that will provide sufficient vitamin A to meet the nutritional requirements of children.[15]

Conclusion

As Christians, we have a unique challenge: to work with the multitude of secular and governmental organizations seeking (1) to facilitate economic and social conditions that naturally lead to a decline in birth rate and (2) to ease the distribution effects of population growth, while maintaining the God-mandated dignity for the value of all life and upholding the sanctity of sexual relations within marriage.

Discussion Questions

1. Explain why competitive market economies don't have to fear the Malthusian blues.

2. What are the three most effective policies a developing country can adopt in order to decrease birth rates?

3. Are birth control pills just another form of abortion?

4. How should Christians be involved in sex education?

Appendix: Interactions Between This Book and Standard Economics Texts

Bulls, Bears & Golden Calves	Gwartney, Stroup, Sobel	Mankiw	Mansfield & Behravesh	McConnell & Brue	Miller	Samuelson & Nordhaus	Stiglitz
2. "Me, Myself & Why?"	chap. 1	chap. 1, 2, 7	chap. 1	chap. 1, 2	chap. 1, 2	chap. 2, 23	chap. 1, 2, 7
3. "Waste Not?"	chap. 3, 5, 16	chap. 7	chap. 1, 24	chap. 1, 2	chap. 2	chap. 2, 18, 23, 31, 34	chap. 1, 2, 13
4. "It's Mine!"	chap. 2	chap. 11, 24	chap. 4, 21	chap. 4	chap. 5, 6, 9	chap. 3	chap. 2
5. "How Does Your Garden Grow?"	chap. 16	chap. 24	chap. 1, 2, 11, 25	chap. 2, 7, 9, 18	chap. 2, 9, 11, 35	chap. 2, 10, 36	chap. 24, 26, 36
6. "Render unto Caesar"	chap. 5, 6, 11, 12, 15	chap. 6, 8, 11, 12, 30, 32	chap. 2, 5, 6, 12, 20, 24, 26	chap. 5, 10, 12, 19, 30, 31	chap. 5, 6, 13, 14, 32	chap. 2, 3, 9, 17, 32, 33, 35	chap. 1, 7, 16, 22, 23, 32, 39
7. "Overemployment"	chap. 2, 25	chap. 18, 19	chap. 4, 22	chap. 5, 7, 8	chap. 7, 27, 28	chap. 13, 15, 28, 29	chap. 9, 19, 25, 27, 34, 35
8. "Catching Your Interest"	chap. 9, 10, 14	chap. 21, 23, 32	chap. 8, 13, 23	chap. 8, 11, 14, 29	chap. 7, 11, 15, 17, 29	chap. 7, 11, 12, 30	chap. 6, 29, 30, 31
9. "A Clarion Call"	chap. 25, appen. 1, 7	chap. 19, 20	chap. 2, 24, 26	chap. 5, 34	chap. 30, 35	chap. 34	chap. 22
10. "Tending the Garden"	chap. 5, appen. 9, 10	chap. 10	chap. 21	chap. 30	chap. 31	chap. 33, 37	chap. 21
11. "Who's Responsible?"	chap. 20	chap. 13	chap. 15	chap. 5, 32	chap. 5, 21	chap. 20	chap. 20
12. "False Hope"	chap. 23, appen. 6	chap. 16	chap. 20	chap. 25, 31	chap. 25, 26, 29	chap. 24, 25	chap. 15, 16
13. "The Naked Gorilla"	chap. 17, 18	chap. 17	chap. 20	chap. 23, 25, 31	chap. 25, 26	chap. 24, 25	chap. 14, 16
14. "A Matter of Life & Debt"	appen. 7	chap. 24, 29, 30	chap. 27, 28	chap. 38, 39	chap. 33, 34, 35	chap. 37, 38, 39, 40	chap. 38, 40
15. "Give Me Your Tired, Your Poor . . ."	chap. 3, appen. 4	chap. 29	chap. 25	chap. 36	chap. 9, 27	chap. 28	chap. 40
16. "The Malthusian Blues"		chap. 24	chap. 25	chap. 33, 39	chap. 9	chap. 37	chap. 40

Notes

Introduction
[1]Richard Ross, Easter sermon, April 2000.

Chapter 1: Grid Work
[1]The ethical framework presented in this chapter draws initially on work by British economist Donald Hay (*Economics Today: A Christian Critique* [Grand Rapids, Mich.: Eerdmans, 1989], chap. 2), supplemented (and reinforced) by the thinking of other scholars, most notably E. Calvin Beisner (*Prosperity and Poverty: The Compassionate Use of Resources in a World of Scarcity* [Wheaton, Ill.: Crossway, 1988)], Rebecca M. Blank (*Do Justice: Linking Christian Faith and Modern Economic Life* [Cleveland: United Church Press, 1992]), Gregory M. A. Gronbacher ("The Humane Economy: Neither Right nor Left: A Response to Daniel Rush Finn," *Journal of Markets and Morality* 2, no. 2 [1999]: 247-70), M. Douglas Meeks (*God the Economist: The Doctrine of God and Political Economy* [Minneapolis: Augsburg, 1989]), Richard John Neuhaus (*Doing Well and Doing Good* [New York: Doubleday, 1992]), Michael Novak (*The Spirit of Democratic Capitalism* [New York: Simon & Schuster, 1982]), Ronald J. Sider (*Just Generosity: A New Vision for Overcoming Poverty in America* [Grand Rapids, Mich.: Baker, 1999]), Douglas Vickers (*Economics and Man: Prelude to a Christian Critique* [Nutley, N.J.: Craig, 1976]), and J. Philip Wogaman (*The Great Economic Debate: An Ethical Analysis* [Philadelphia: Westminster Press, 1977]). It was significantly enriched by the Oxford Declaration on Christian Faith and Economics (Herbert Schlossberg, Vinay Samuel and Ronald J. Sider, eds., *Christianity and Economics in the Post-Cold War Era: The Oxford Declaration and Beyond* [Grand Rapids, Mich.: Eerdmans, 1994], esp. pp. 11-30) and the encyclical *Centesimus Annus* issued by Pope John Paul II to commemorate the one hundredth anniversary of the encyclical *Rerum Novarum* (1891) (Rupert J. Ederer, *Economics As if God Mattered: A Century of Papal Teaching Addressed to the Economic Order* [South Bend, Ind.: Fidelity, 1995], esp. chap. 7).
[2]Gronbacher, "Humane Economy," p. 252.
[3]John F. Sleeman, *Basic Economic Problems: A Christian Approach* (London: SCM Press, 1953), p. 15.
[4]Hay, *Economics Today,* p. 21.
[5]Ibid.
[6]David C. Colander, *Economics*, 4th ed. (Boston: McGraw-Hill, 2001), p. 5.
[7]Gregory M. A. Gronbacher, *Economic Thinking for the Theologically Minded* (Grand Rapids, Mich.: Center for Economic Personalism, 2000).
[8]Oskar Gruenwald, "Christian Political Economy: Fact or Value?" *Journal of Interdisciplinary Studies* 3 (1991): 4.

[9]See, e.g., Ex 21—23; Lev 1—8; 11—27; Deut 4—27.

[10]Blank, *Do Justice,* pp. 21, 46.

[11]Hay, *Economics Today,* p. 75

[12]Vickers, *Economics and Man,* p. 127.

[13]Lev 19:13; Deut 24:14; Mal 3:5; 1 Tim 5:18.

[14]Evangelical Lutheran Church in America, "Sufficient, Sustainable Livelihood for All," Sixth Biennial Churchwide Assembly, August 20, 1999, p. 5.

[15]Gronbacher, "Humane Economy," p. 262.

[16]E. Calvin Beisner, "Christian Economics: A System Whose Time Has Come?" in *Christian Perspectives on Economics,* ed. Robert N. Mateer (Lynchburg, Va.: CEBA, 1989), pp. 38-40.

[17]Craig L. Blomberg, *Neither Poverty nor Riches: A Biblical Theology of Material Possessions* (Downers Grove, Ill.: InterVarsity Press, 1999), p. 245.

[18]Timothy J. Gorringe, *Capitalism and the Kingdom: Theological Ethics and Economic Order* (Maryknoll, N.Y.: Orbis, 1994), pp. 25-26.

[19]Vickers, *Economics and Man,* pp. 44-45.

[20]John C. Bennett et al., *Christian Values and Economic Life* (Stratford, N.H.: Ayer, 1954), p. 210.

[21]H. Richard Niebuhr, *Christ and Culture* (New York: Harper & Row, 1951), pp. 238-39.

Chapter 2: Me, Myself and Why?

[1]Adam Smith, *An Inquiry into the Nature and Causes of the Wealth of Nations* (Chicago: University of Chicago Press, 1976), p. 475.

[2]Ibid., p. 478.

[3]In his earlier work *The Theory of Moral Sentiments* Smith does use the term "invisible hand" once, as well as in reference to the rich giving sustenance to the poor and "thus without intending it, without knowing it, advanc(ing) the interest of the society" (1759; reprint, *The Theory of Moral Sentiments,* ed. D. D. Raphael and A. L. Macfie Oxford: Oxford University Press, 1979], pp. 184-85).

[4]Smith, *Inquiry,* p. 144.

[5]Ibid., p. 75.

[6]Ibid., p. 474.

[7]Ibid., p. 67.

[8]Ibid., p. 232.

[9]Douglas Vickers, *Economics and Man: Prelude to a Christian Critique* (Nutley, N.J.: Craig, 1976), p. 61.

[10]Smith, *Theory of Moral Sentiments,* p. 9.

[11]Ibid., p. 85.

[12]Jeffrey T. Young, *Economics as a Moral Science: The Political Economy of Adam Smith* (Cheltenham, U.K.: Edward Elgar, 1997), p. 24.

[13]Smith, *Inquiry,* p. 69.

[14]Ibid., p. 144.

[15]Ibid., *Inquiry,* pp. 208-9.

[16]Young, *Economics as a Moral Science,* p. 155.

[17]Edwin Mansfield and Nariman Behravesh, *Economics U$A,* 5th ed. (New York: W. W. Norton, 1998), p. 15.

[18]This is not true in all cases. Andrew Schotter, for example, states that "our first psychological assumption is selfishness—that people are interested only in their own utility or satisfaction and make their choices with just that in mind. While this assumption does not rule out sympathy for other human beings, it tells us that sympathy does not influence the decisions that people make" (*Microeconomics: A Modern Approach* [New York: Addison-Wesley, 2001], p. 33). For a comprehensive review of the discussion of ethics in today's leading introductory economics textbooks see John E. Stapleford, "Christian Ethics and the Teaching of Introductory Economics," *Association of Christian Economists Journal,* August 1999, pp. 1-22.

[19]Roger LeRoy Miller, *Economics Today,* 9th ed. (New York: Addison-Wesley, 1997), p. 12.

[20]David C. Colander, *Economics,* 3rd ed. (Boston: Irwin/McGraw-Hill, 1998), pp. 10-20.

[21] Richard Titmuss, as cited in D. M Hausman and M. S. McPerson, *Economic Analysis and Moral Philosophy* (Cambridge: Cambridge University Press, 1996).

[22] R. C. Sproul. *Chosen by God* (Wheaton, Ill.: Tyndale House, 1986), p. 108.

[23] Virgil Vogt, *Treasure in Heaven: The Biblical Teaching About Money, Finances, and Possessions* (Ann Arbor, Mich.: Servant, 1982), p. 32.

[24] Ibid., p. 49.

[25] Ibid., p. 50-52.

[26] Michael Novak, *The Spirit of Democratic Capitalism* (New York: Simon & Schuster, 1982), p. 353.

[27] Ibid., p. 341.

[28] James Halteman, *The Clashing Worlds of Economics and Faith* (Scottdale, Penn.: Herald, 1988), p. 121.

[29] James Buchanan, *Ethics and Economic Progress* (Norman: University of Oklahoma Press, 1994), p. 85.

[30] Ronald H. Nash, *Poverty and Wealth: The Christian Debate over Capitalism* (Wheaton, Ill.: Crossway, 1986), pp. 72-74.

Chapter 3: Waste Not?

[1] This section of the chapter draws heavily on Eloise Meneses and John Stapleford, "Defeating the Baals: Balanced Christian Living in Different Cultural Systems," *Christian Scholars Review,* fall 2000, pp. 83-106.

[2] N. Gregory Mankiw, *Principles of Economics* (Fort Worth, Tex.: Dryden, 1998), pp. 145-46.

[3] Lewis B. Smedes. *Sex for Christians* (Grand Rapids, Mich.: Eerdmans, 1994), p. 36.

[4] Ron Sider, *Rich Christians in an Age of Hunger: Moving from Affluence to Generosity* (Dallas, Tex.: Word, 1997), pp. 95-99.

[5] E. Calvin Beisner. *Prosperity and Poverty: The Compassionate Use of Resources in a World of Scarcity* (Wheaton, Ill.: Crossway, 1988), pp. 49-51.

[6] Scripture clearly recognizes the differences in gifts among individuals (Rom 12; 1 Cor 12). These differences in gifts lead to an unequal distribution of income, wealth, power and prestige, regardless of injustice. So the focus of distributive justice, Beisner argues, should be equal application of God's law to all individuals, not equality of economic condition. See ibid., p. 73.

[7] John Bodley, *Victims of Progress* (Mountain View, Calif.: Mayfield, 1990).

[8] Ibid., p. 207.

[9] Foraging societies take women nearly as seriously as men and afford their opinions full status in critical group decisions. Horticultural and pastoral societies, on the other hand, count only male opinions, with women being given a heavily restricted and subordinated position.

[10] Again, a notable exception is in the treatment of women, who are not accorded full status and sometimes mercilessly abused.

[11] Marcel Mauss, *The Gift* (New York: W. W. Norton, 1990).

[12] North Americans are inclined to wonder why the material need be part of social relations at all. (Tribal and peasant peoples never question this.) Theologically, the centrality of material exchange in social relationships is a matter of our human physical existence: God created us material. At the outset we have material needs, most notably to eat. The most common gift around the world to establish relationships is food. So the gift's strongest symbolism is of feeding one another, or caring for one another's most basic needs. Material exchange, then, fosters community.

[13] Relationships, however, can be positive or negative. Certainly, some reciprocal exchange is negative in the sense that it promotes competition between the partners rather than cooperation. The extreme case here is the potlatch of the Kwakiutl, a feast in which aggressive gift giving amounted to war between rival chiefs. Even in relatively benign cases such as our own Christmas gift giving, fear of competition causes us to restrict the size of gifts and to hide price tags. The point is that expressions of love can be used as expressions of hatred, given the prestige that naturally occurs to gift givers.

[14] World Bank, *World Development Report 1998/99: Knowledge for Development* (New York: Oxford University Press, 1998), table 1.

[15] Sider, *Rich Christians,* p. 29.

[16]World Bank, *World Development Report,* table 5. As might be expected, income distribution data are available for barely more than half of all the nations tracked by the World Bank, and in some cases data is estimated using regression analysis. The data are also for different years, although this is less troublesome because the income distribution in a particular country shifts very slowly.

[17]This basic result is unchanged even when adjustments are made for the falling number of persons per family and for family age structure and economies of scale (Lynn A. Karoly, "The Trend in Inequality Among Families, Individuals, and Workers in the United States: A Twenty-Five Year Perspective," in *Uneven Tides: Rising Inequality in America,* ed. Sheldon Danziger and Peter Gottschalk [New York: Russell Sage Foundation, 1993], pp. 19-97).

[18]Peter Gottschalk, Sara McLanahan and Gary D. Sandefur, "The Dynamics and Intergenerational Transmission of Poverty and Welfare Participation," in *Confronting Poverty: Prescriptions for Change,* ed. Sheldon H. Danziger, Gary D. Sandefur and Daniel H. Weinberg (Cambridge, Mass.: Harvard University Press, 1994), pp. 88-99.

[19]John H. Hinderaker and Scott W. Johnson, "Inequality: Should We Worry?" *The American Enterprise*, July-August 1996, pp. 35-39.

[20]Bradley R. Schiller, *The Economics of Poverty and Discrimination*, 5th ed. (Englewood Cliffs, N.J.: Prentice-Hall, 1989), p. 9.

[21]William J. Bennett, *The Index of Leading Cultural Indicators* (Washington, D.C.: Heritage Foundation, 1993).

[22]Thomas C. Reeves, *The Empty Church: The Suicide of Liberal Christianity* (New York: Free Press, 1996), pp. 51, 56.

[23]Ibid., pp. 62, 64.

[24]Ibid., p. 63.

[25]Bill W., *Alcoholics Anonymous*, 3rd ed. (New York: Alcoholics Anonymous World Services, 1976), pp. 2, 13.

Chapter 4: It's Mine!

[1]Tom Bethell, *The Noblest Triumph* (New York: St. Martin's, 1999), pp. 63-64.

[2]Ibid.

[3]Campbell R. McConnell and Stanley L. Brue, *Economics: Principles, Problems, and Policy,* 14th ed. (Boston: McGraw-Hill, 1999), pp. 61-62.

[4]James D. Gwartney, Richard L. Stroup and Russell S. Sobel, *Macroeconomics: Private and Public Choice,* 9th ed. (Fort Worth, Tex.: Dryden, 2000), p. 413.

[5]Ron Sider, *Rich Christians in an Age of Hunger: Moving from Affluence to Generosity* (Dallas, Tex.: Word, 1997), p. 71.

[6]Doug Vickers, *Economics and Man: Prelude to a Christian Critique* (Nutley, N.J.: Craig, 1976), p. 127.

[7]Quoted in Guy Routh, *The Origin of Economic Ideas* (New York: Random House, 1977), p. 130.

[8]N. Gregory Mankiw, *Principles of Economics* (Fort Worth, Tex.: Dryden, 1998), p. 530.

[9]E. Calvin Beisner, *Prosperity and Poverty: The Compassionate Use of Resources in a World of Scarcity* (Wheaton, Ill.: Crossway, 1988), p. 53.

[10]Court cases centering around the Fourteenth and Fifteenth Amendments to the U.S. Constitution eventually shifted the focus of compensation from the use of the property by the owner to the exchange-value of the property. The difficulties of this shift are obvious. If I claim that my riverfront junkyard was under consideration for development into a luxury resort-office complex, the government should certainly offer me higher compensation than if it were just to take over the site's use as a junkyard.

Chapter 5: How Does Your Garden Grow?

[1]Karl E. Case and Ray C. Fair, *Principles of Economics,* 6th ed. (Upper Saddle River, N.J.: Prentice-Hall, 2002), p. 631.

[2]Robert H. Nelson, *Reaching for Heaven on Earth: The Theological Meaning of Economics* (Lanham, Md.: Littlefield Adams, 1991), p. 7.

[3]Jonathan Sacks, "Markets and Morals," *First Things*, August-September 2000, p. 25.

[4]John Boersema, *Political-Economic Activity to the Honor of God* (Winnipeg, Manitoba: Premier, 1999), pp. 25, 89.

[5]Peter Marshall and David Manuel, *The Light and the Glory: Did God Have a Plan for America?* (Old Tappan, N.J.: Revell, 1977), pp. 55-59.

[6]David S. Landes, *The Wealth and Poverty of Nations: Why Some Are So Rich and Some So Poor* (New York: W. W. Norton, 1998), pp. 99-109.

[7]Marshall and Manuel, *Light and the Glory*, chaps. 1-2.

[8]Mark Perlman and Charles R. McCann Jr., *The Pillars of Economic Understanding: Ideas and Tradition* (Ann Arbor: University of Michigan Press, 1998), pp. 73-133.

[9]Landes, *Wealth and Poverty*, pp. 68-70, 114-19.

[10]Charles Colson with Ellen Santilli Vaughn, *Kingdoms in Conflict* (Grand Rapids, Mich.: Zondervan, 1987), pp. 98-108.

[11]Landes, *Wealth and Poverty*, pp. 186-291.

[12]Allen C. Guelzo, *Abraham Lincoln: Redeemer President* (Grand Rapids, Mich.: Eerdmans, 1999), p. 46.

[13]Jeremy Atack and Peter Passell, *A New Economic View of American History* (New York: W. W. Norton, 1994), pp. 427-30, 523.

[14]Ben J. Wattenberg, *The Statistical History of the United States: From Colonial Times to the Present* (New York: Basic, 1976), pp. 11-12.

[15]Richard K. Vedder, *The American Economy in Historical Perspective* (Belmont, Calif.: Wadsworth, 1976), pp. 98, 106.

[16]Bill Bryson, *A Walk in the Woods: Rediscovering American on the Appalachian Trail* (New York: Random House, 1998), pp. 210-11.

[17]Adam Markham, *A Brief History of Pollution* (London: Earthscan, 1995), p. 19.

[18]Bryson, *Walk in the Woods*, p. 48.

[19]The information on the microprocessor revolution comes from W. Michael Cox and Richard Alm, "The New Paradigm," *Federal Reserve Bank of Dallas 1999 Annual Report*, pp. 3-25.

[20]Fernand Braudel, *The Structures of Everyday Life: The Limits of the Possible* (Berkeley: University of California Press, 1979), p. 197.

[21]W. Michael Cox and Richard Alm, "Time Well Spent: The Declining Real Cost of Living in America," *Federal Reserve Bank of Dallas 1997 Annual Report*, pp. 2-23.

[22]Leonard I. Nakamura, "The Retail Revolution and Food-Price Mismeasurement," *The Business Review*, Federal Reserve Bank of Philadelphia, May-June 1998, pp. 6-7.

[23]W. Michael Cox and Richard Alm, "The Right Stuff: America's Move to Mass Customization," *Federal Reserve Bank of Dallas 1998 Annual Report*, p. 6.

[24]Douglas E. Booth, *The Environmental Consequences of Growth: Steady-State Economics as an Alternative to Ecological Decline* (London: Routledge, 1998), pp. 107-9.

Chapter 6: Render unto Caesar

[1]World Bank, *2000 World Development Indicators* (New York: Oxford University Press, 2000), table 4-13.

[2]Adam Smith, *An Inquiry into the Nature and Causes of the Wealth of Nations* (Chicago: University of Chicago Press, 1976), pp. 208-9.

[3]James D. Gwartney, Richard L. Stroup and Russell S. Sobel, *Macroeconomics: Private and Public Choice*, 9th ed. (Fort Worth, Tex.: Dryden, 2000), pp. 416-18.

[4]James Gwartney, Robert Lawson and Walter Block, *Economic Freedom of the World: 1975-1995* (Vancouver, B.C.: Fraser Institute, 1996), pp. xvi-xvii.

[5]Charles Colson with Ellen Santilli Vaughn, *Kingdoms in Conflict* (Grand Rapids, Mich.: Zondervan, 1987), p. 83.

[6]Ibid., p. 91.

[7]John Paul II, *Centesimus Annus: The Economics of Human Freedom*, May 1991, p. 34.

[8]Michael Novak, *The Spirit of Democratic Capitalism* (New York: Simon & Schuster, 1982), pp. 32-33.

[9]James D. Gwartney and Richard L. Stroup, *What Everyone Should Know About Economics and Prosperity* (Vancouver, B.C.: Fraser Institute, 1993), pp. 83-84.

[10]Christoph Schonborn, "The Hope of Heaven, The Hope of Earth," *First Things*, April 1995, p. 34.

Chapter 7: Overemployment

[1]Luladey B. Tadesse, "Balancing Religion and Work," *The News Journal*, January 29, 2001, pp. D6-8.

[2]"Religion in the Workplace: The Growing Presence of Spirituality in Corporate America," *Business Week*, November, 1999, pp. 152-58.

[3]U.S. Department of Commerce, Bureau of the Census, "Who's Minding Our PreSchoolers?" *Current Population Reports*, fall 1994.

[4]Juliet B. Schor (*The Overworked American: The Unexpected Decline of Leisure* [New York: Basic-Books, 1992], p. 29 and appendix B) and recent survey data from the Families and Work Institute (cited in *Entrepreneur International*, April-May 2000, p. 2) both show a workweek increase. See John P. Robinson and Geoffrey Godbey, *Time for Life: The Surprising Ways Americans Use Their Time* (University Park: Pennsylvania State University Press, 1997), pp. 81-96, for a discussion of workweek estimates overtime based on diary data.

[5]Robinson and Godbey, *Time for Life,* pp. 230-38; Cheryl Russell, "Overwork? Overwhelmed," *American Demographics*, March 1995.

[6]U.S. Department of Commerce, Bureau of the Census, *Statistical Abstract of the United States, 1984*, p. 414; and *Statistical Abstract of the United States, 1999*, p. 421.

[7]U.S. Department of Commerce, Bureau of the Census, *Statistical Abstract of the United States, 1999*, p. 420.

[8]Robinson and Godbey, *Time for Life,* pp. 100-102, 334.

[9]Lynn A. Karoly, "The Trend in Inequality Among Families, Individuals, and Workers in the United States: A Twenty-Five Year Perspective," in *Uneven Tides: Rising Inequality in America*, ed. Sheldon Danziger and Peter Gottschalk (New York: Russell Sage Foundation, 1994), p. 77.

[10]U.S. Department of Commerce, Bureau of the Census, *Statistical Abstract of the United States, 1999*, p. 79; and *Statistical Abstract of the United States, 1995,* p. 77.

[11]Robert Rector and Kate Walsh O'Beirne, "Dispelling the Myth of Income Inequality," *Backgrounder* 710 (1989): 8.

[12]David Blankenhorn, *Fatherless America: Confronting Our Most Urgent Social Problem* (New York: BasicBooks, 1995), p. 17.

[13]Bradley R. Schiller, *The Economics of Poverty and Discrimination,* 7th ed. (Upper Saddle River, N.J.: Prentice-Hall, 1998), pp. 108-12.

[14]Greg J. Duncan and Saul D. Hoffman, "Welfare Benefits, Economic Opportunities, and Out-of-Wedlock Births Among Black Teenage Girls," *Demography* 27, no. 1 (1990): 519-35; Chong-Bum An, Robert Haveman and Barbara Wolfe, "Teen Out-of-Wedlock Births and Welfare Receipt: The Role of Childhood Events and Economic Circumstances," *Review of Economics and Statistics* 75, no. 2. (1993): 195-208. The rise in out-of-wedlock birth rates occurred during a period when the inflation-adjusted value of the social welfare package fell about 30 percent. Nearly all Western European countries have much more generous welfare programs for single mothers yet much lower teen birth rates.

[15]Ronald B. Mincy, "The Underclass: Concept, Controversy, and Evidence," in *Confronting Poverty: Prescriptions for Change*, ed. Sheldon H. Danziger, Gary D. Sandefur and Daniel H. Weinberg (Cambridge, Mass.: Harvard University Press, 1994), pp. 112-22. Besides reviewing the research on the topic, the author notes the legacy of discrimination in America: a body of evidence of differential enforcement of criminal law for young blacks; and differential treatment in housing markets that results in a spatial mismatch between the locale of jobs suitable to less-skilled candidates and the growing suburban services and manufacturing sectors.

[16]Blankenhorn, *Fatherless America,* p. 18.

[17]Ronald J. Sider, *Just Generosity: A New Vision for Overcoming Poverty in America* (Grand Rapids, Mich.: Baker, 1999), p. 122.

[18]U.S. Department of Commerce, Bureau of the Census, "Money Income in the United States: 1997," *Current Population Reports,* p. xvii.

[19]Sider, *Just Generosity,* p. 128.

[20]John Russo and Brian R. Corbin, "Labor and the Catholic Church: Opportunities for Coalitions," *WorkingUSA,* July-August 1999, p. 82.

[21]Quoted in Timothy J. Gorringe, *Capital and the Kingdom: Theological Ethics and Economic Order* (Maryknoll, N.Y.: Orbis, 1994), p. 66.

[22]Leland Ryken, *Redeeming the Time* (Grand Rapids, Mich.: Baker, 1995), p. 164.

[23]Arthur O'Sullivan and Steven M. Sheffrin, *Economics: Principles and Tools,* 2nd ed. (Upper Saddle River, N.J.: Prentice-Hall, 2001), p. 380.

[24]Larry Burkett, *Business by the Book: The Complete Guide of Biblical Principles for Business Men and Women* (Nashville: Thomas Nelson, 1990), p. 27.

[25]Lev 19:13; Deut 24:14; Mal 3:5; 1 Tim 5:18.

[26]E. Calvin Beisner, *Prosperity and Poverty: The Compassionate Use of Resources in a World of Scarcity* (Wheaton, Ill.: Crossway, 1988), pp. 33-39.

[27]Russo and Corbin, "Labor and the Catholic Church," p. 82.

[28]James Halteman, *The Clashing Worlds of Economics and Faith* (Scottdale, Penn.: Herald, 1995), p. 49.

[29]Pho Lian Lim, "Wonder and Wildness: On Sex and Freedom," in *Finding God at Harvard: Spiritual Journeys of Thinking Christians,* ed. Kelly Monroe (Grand Rapids, Mich.: Zondervan, 1996), p. 135.

[30]Occupational licensure blocks potential providers who can't afford to pay the licensing fee or receive the requisite training, depriving them of work and artificially raising the price for the service.

[31]Arlie Russell Hochschild, *The Time Bind: When Work Becomes Home and Home Becomes Work* (New York: Henry Holt, 1997), pp. 197-210.

[32]John Richard Bowen, *Religion in Culture and Society* (New York: Allyn & Bacon, 1997), pp. 88-89.

[33]Ryken, *Redeeming the Time,* pp. 278-79.

Chapter 8: Catching Your Interest

[1]David Chilton, *Productive Christians in an Age of Guilt-Manipulators: A Biblical Response to Ronald J. Sider* (Tyler, Tex.: Institute for Christian Economics, 1981), p. 58.

[2]E. Calvin Beisner, *Prosperity and Poverty: The Compassionate Use of Resources in a World of Scarcity* (Wheaton, Ill.: Crossway, 1988), p. 39.

[3]Ron Sider, *Rich Christians in an Age of Hunger: Moving from Affluence to Generosity* (Dallas, Tex.: Word, 1997), pp. 75-76.

[4]James Halteman, *The Clashing Worlds of Economics and Faith* (Scottdale, Penn.: Herald, 1988), pp. 57-60.

[5]Sider, *Rich Christians,* p. 76.

[6]Kershaw Burbank Jr., "A Christian Perspective on Micro-Enterprise Loans and the Payment of Loan Interest" (St. Davids, Penn.: Eastern College, 1999), p. 16.

[7]Benjamin N. Nelson, "On the Taking of Interest," in *On Moral Business: Classical and Contemporary Resources for Ethics in Economic Life,* ed. Max L. Stackhouse et al. (Grand Rapids, Mich.: Eerdmans, 1995), p. 266.

[8]Ibid., p. 267.

[9]Ibid., p. 268.

[10]Carolus Molinaeus, "A Treatise on Contracts and Usury," in *Economic Justice in Perspective: A Book of Readings,* ed. Jerry Combee and Edgar Norton (Englewood Cliffs, N.J.: Prentice-Hall, 1991), pp. 48-54.

[11]Quoted in Nelson, "Taking of Interest," pp. 269-71.

[12]Ronald H. Preston, *Religion and the Ambiguities of Capitalism* (Cleveland: Pilgrim, 1993), p. 138.

[13]Rupert J. Ederer, *Economics As if God Matters: A Century of Papal Teaching Addressed to the Economic Order* (South Bend, Ind.: Fidelity, 1995).

[14]Larry Burkett, *Business by the Book: The Complete Guide of Biblical Principles for Business Men and Women* (Nashville: Thomas Nelson, 1990), pp. 167-68.

[15]Joe Remenyi and Bill Taylor, "Credit-Based Income Generation for the Poor," in *Christianity and Economics in the Post-Cold War Era: The Oxford Declaration and Beyond*, ed. Herbert Schlossberg et al. (Grand Rapids, Mich.: Eerdmans, 1994), p. 48.

Chapter 9: A Clarion Call

[1]Joseph Dalaker and Bernadette D. Proctor, *Poverty in the United States: 1999,* U.S. Census Bureau, Current Population Reports, Series P60-210 (Washington, D.C.: Government Printing Office, 2000), p. vi.

[2]Bradley R. Schiller, *The Economics of Poverty and Discrimination,* 7th ed. (Upper Saddle River, N.J.: Prentice-Hall, 1998), pp. 34-35.

[3]Ibid., p. 35.

[4]Kathleen Short, Thesia Garner, David Johnson and Patricia Doyle, *Experimental Poverty Measures: 1990 to 1997,* U.S. Census Bureau, Current Population Reports, Consumer Income, Series P60-205 (Washington, D.C.: Government Printing Office, 1999), pp. 1-20.

[5]Dalaker and Proctor, *Poverty in the United States,* p. xi.

[6]Schiller, *Economics of Poverty,* pp. 56-57.

[7]Charles Murray, "In Search of the Working Poor," *The Public Interest,* fall 1987, pp. 3-19.

[8]Leonard I. Nakamura, "Economics and the New Economy: The Invisible Hand Meets Creative Destruction," *Business Review,* Federal Reserve Bank of Philadelphia, July-August 2000, p. 25.

[9]U.S. Bureau of the Census, *Statistical Abstract of the United States: 1999* (Washington, D.C.: Government Printing Office, 2000), p. 479.

[10]Ibid., p. 488.

[11]Arthur O' Sullivan, *Urban Economics,* 4th ed. (Boston: McGraw-Hill, 2000), pp. 354-56.

[12]Schiller, *Economics of Poverty,* p. 168.

[13]Ibid., p. 169.

[14]Ibid., p. 150.

[15]Ronald J. Sider, *Just Generosity: A New Vision for Overcoming Poverty in America* (Grand Rapids, Mich.: Baker, 1999), p. 157.

[16]Ibid., p. 155.

[17]Schiller, *Economics of Poverty,* p. 154.

[18]Ibid., p. 155.

[19]Ibid., p. 156.

[20]U.S. Bureau of the Census, *Statistical Abstract of the United States: 1999,* p. 79; and *Statistical Abstract of the United States: 1995,* 77.

[21]David Blankenhorn, *Fatherless America: Confronting Our Most Urgent Social Problem* (New York: BasicBooks, 1995), p. 18.

[22]Karl E. Case and Ray C. Fair, *Principles of Economics,* 6th ed. (Upper Saddle River, N.J.: Prentice-Hall, 2002), pp. 360-61.

[23]U.S. Bureau of the Census, *Statistical Abstract of the United States: 1999,* p. 387.

[24]Sheldon H. Danziger and Daniel H. Weinberg, "The Historical Record: Trends in Family Income, Inequality, and Poverty," in *Confronting Poverty: Prescriptions for Change,* ed. Sheldon H. Danziger, Gary D. Sandefur and Daniel H. Weinberg (Cambridge, Mass.: Harvard University Press, 1994), p. 46.

[25]Schiller, *Economics of Poverty,* p. 212.

[26]John E. Stapleford, "Welfare-to-Work: What Are the Prospects," working paper (Newark, Del.: Bureau of Economic Research, University of Delaware, 1996).

[27]Gary Burtless, "Public Spending on the Poor: Historical Trends and Economic Limits," in *Confronting Poverty: Prescriptions for Change,* ed. Sheldon H. Danziger, Gary D. Sandefur and Daniel H. Weinberg (Cambridge, Mass.: Harvard University Press, 1994), p. 74.

[28]Ibid., pp. 75-83.

[29]Lawrence Bobo and Ryan A. Smith, "Antipoverty Policy, Affirmative Action, and Racial Attitudes,"

in *Confronting Poverty: Prescriptions for Change*, ed. Sheldon H. Danziger, Gary D. Sandefur and Daniel H. Weinberg (Cambridge, Mass.: Harvard University Press, 1994), pp. 366-76.

[30]Ibid., pp. 383-84.

[31]Sider, *Just Generosity*, pp. 164-66.

[32]Robert C. Linthicum, *City of God, City of Satan: A Biblical Theology of the Urban Church* (Grand Rapids, Mich.: Zondervan, 1991), p. 102.

Chapter 10: Tending the Garden

[1]Lynn White Jr., "The Historical Roots of Our Ecologic Crisis," *Science* 155 (1967): 1203-7.

[2]Robert H. Nelson, "Judeo-Christian Tradition Best Basis for Environmentalism," *Religion & Liberty* 9, no. 2 (2000): 2.

[3]Andrew Greeley, "Religion and Attitudes Toward the Environment," *Journal for the Scientific Study of Religion* 32 (March 1993): 19-29.

[4]Bradley R. Schiller, *The Economy Today,* 8th ed. (Boston: McGraw-Hill, 2000), p. 576.

[5]Adam Markham, *A Brief History of Pollution* (London: Earthscan, 1995), p. 3.

[6]Leslie Jones Sauer, *The Once and Future Forest* (Washington, D.C.: Island, 1998), p. 13.

[7]Ronald J. Sider, *Rich Christians in an Age of Hunger: Moving from Affluence to Generosity* (Dallas, Tex.: Word, 1997), pp. 162-63.

[8]Edward O. Wilson, "Vanishing Before Our Eyes," *Time,* special ed., April 2000, p. 30.

[9]Eugene Linden, "Condition Critical," *Time,* special ed., April 2000, p. 19.

[10]Ibid., p. 18.

[11]Carl Safina, "Cry of the Ancient Mariner," *Time,* special ed., April 2000, pp. 40-41.

[12]Mark Van Putten, "Restoring America's Grasslands," *National Wildlife* 38, no. 5 (2000): 7.

[13]Sider, *Rich Christians*, p. 165.

[14]Wilson, "Vanishing," p. 31.

[15]Sider, *Rich Christians*, pp. 159-60.

[16]Ibid., p.161.

[17]Paul R. Portney, "Environmental Problems and Policy: 2000-2050," *Resources*, Winter 2000, p. 9.

[18]The underlying structure for this section is credited to the excellent presentation in Campbell McConnell and Stanley Brue, *Economics: Principles, Problems, and Policies,* 14th ed. (Boston: Irwin, 1999), chap. 30.

[19]Markham, *Brief History of Pollution*, p. 80.

[20]Annetta Miller and Susanna Laurenti, "Companies Find It Pays to Be Green," *National Wildlife* 39, no. 2 (2001): 70.

[21]The Cambodian experience is based on research and firsthand participation by Larry Groff, a former graduate student at Eastern College and an MCC staff person.

[22]Douglas E. Booth, *The Environmental Consequences of Growth: Steady-State Economics as an Alternative to Ecological Decline* (London: Routledge, 1998), pp. 138-40.

Chapter 11: Who's Responsible?

[1]Michael Parkin, *Economics*, 3rd ed. (Reading, Mass.: Addison-Wesley, 1996), p. 215.

[2]Adam Smith, *An Inquiry into the Nature and Causes of the Wealth of Nations* (Chicago: University of Chicago Press, 1976), p. 144.

[3]Ibid., p. 75.

[4]Ibid., p. 474.

[5]Ibid., p. 67.

[6]David Hume, *Political Essays,* ed. Knud Haakonssen (Cambridge: Cambridge University Press, 1994), p. 59.

[7]Charles Higham, *Trading with the Enemy: The Nazi-American Money Plot 1933-1949* (New York: Barnes & Noble, 1983), p. xv.

[8]Ibid., pp. 1-19.

[9]Gregg J. Rickman, *Swiss Banks and Jewish Souls* (New Brunswick, N.J.: Transaction, 1999), p. xiv.

[10]Ibid., p. 231.

[11]O. C. Ferrell, John Fraedrich and Linda Ferrell, *Business Ethics: Ethical Decision Making and Cases* (Boston: Houghton Mifflin, 1999), pp. 291-97.

[12]Richard K. Vedder, *The American Economy in Historical Perspective* (Belmont, Calif.: Wadsworth, 1976), p. 309.

[13]Bill Bryson, *A Walk in the Woods: Rediscovering America on the Appalachian Trail* (New York: Broadway, 1998), p. 180.

[14]Douglas A. Blackmon, "From Alabama's Past, Capitalism and Racism in a Cruel Partnership," *Wall Street Journal*, July 16, 2001, pp. A1, A10.

[15]*Commonwealth v. Hunt*, Supreme Court of Massachusetts, 1842.

[16]U.S. Bureau of the Census, *Statistical Abstract of the United States, 1999* (Washington, D.C.: Government Printing Office, 1999), p. 452.

[17]David S. Landes, *The Wealth and Poverty of Nations: Why Some Are So Rich and Some So Poor* (New York: W. W. Norton, 1998), pp. 473-74.

[18]James R. Tybout, "Manufacturing Firms in Developing Countries: How Well Do They Do, and Why?" *Journal of Economic Literature* 38 (March 2000): 33-39.

[19]Ferrell, Fraedrich and Ferrell, *Business Ethics*, pp. 282-90.

[20]Thomas Donaldson and Patricia H. Werhane, *Ethical Issues in Business: A Philosophical Approach*, 6th ed., (Upper Saddle, N.J.: Prentice-Hall, 1999), pp. 446-47.

[21]Milton Friedman, *Capitalism and Freedom* (Chicago: University of Chicago Press, 1962), p. 133; "The Social Responsibility of Business Is to Increase Its Profits," *New York Times Magazine*, September 13, 1970, pp. 122-26.

[22]Harry J. Van Buren III, "Religious Faith as a Source of Moral Norms in the Economic Arena: Is It Possible to Do More Than Obey the Law?" working paper (Rochester, N.Y.: Roberts Wesleyan College, 1999), p. 9.

[23]Hershey H. Friedman, "Biblical Foundations of Business Ethics," *Journal of Markets & Morality* 3, no. 1 (2000): 45.

[24]U.S. Bureau of the Census, *Statistical Abstract of the United States, 1999*, p. 405.

[25] Ferrell, Fraedrich and Ferrell, *Business Ethics*, pp. 226-37.

[26]Scott B. Rae and Kenman L. Wong, *Beyond Integrity: A Judeo-Christian Approach to Business Ethics* (Grand Rapids, Mich.: Zondervan, 1996), pp. 255-66.

[27]Thomas K. McCraw, *Prophets of Regulation* (Cambridge, Mass.: Harvard University Press, 1984), p. 300.

Chapter 12: False Hope

[1]Reuven Brenner with Gabrielle A. Brenner, *Gambling and Speculation: A Theory, a History, and a Future of Some Human Decisions* (Cambridge: Cambridge University Press, 1990), p. 7.

[2]Rex M. Rogers, *Seducing America: Is Gambling a Good Bet?* (Grand Rapids, Mich.: Baker, 1997), pp. 55-58.

[3]Brenner, *Gambling and Speculation*, p. 79.

[4]Rogers, *Seducing America*, p. 31.

[5]Brenner, *Gambling and Speculation*, p. 14.

[6]Rogers notes that shaved or crooked dice have been found buried with the pharaohs and loaded dice were found in the ruins of ancient Pompeii (ibid., pp. 29-30).

[7]Public Agenda, *Gambling: Is It a Problem? What Should We Do?* (New York: National Issues Forum, 1999), p. 3.

[8]Richard McGowan, "Legalized Gambling: A History," in *Legalized Gambling*, ed. David Bender (San Diego, Calif.: Greenhaven, 1999), pp. 12-16.

[9]National Gambling Impact Study Commission, *Final Report: 1999* (Washington, D.C.: Government Printing Office, 2000), p. 1.1.

[10]Robert Goodman, *The Luck Business: The Devastating Consequences and Broken Promises of America's Gambling Explosion* (New York: Free Press, 1995), p. 3.

[11]National Gambling Impact Study Commission, *Final Report*, p. 2.6.

[12]David Bender, ed., *Legalized Gambling* (San Diego, Calif.: Greenhaven, 1999), p. 99.

[13]Rogers, *Seducing America*, p. 50.

[14]Goodman, *Luck Business*, p. 1.

[15]National Gambling Impact Study Commission, *Final Report*, p. 2.1.

[16]Roger LeRoy Miller, *Economics Today: The Micro View,* 9th ed. (Reading, Mass.: Addison-Wesley, 1997), p. 649.

[17]Charles T. Clotfelter and Philip J. Cook, *Selling Hope: State Lotteries in America* (Cambridge, Mass.: Harvard University Press, 1989), p. 107.

[18]National Gambling Impact Study Commission, *Final Report*, p. 1.3.

[19]Charles T. Clotfelter and Philip J. Cook, "On the Economics of State Lotteries," *Journal of Economic Perspectives* 4, no. 4 (1990): 111.

[20]National Gambling Impact Study Commission, *Final Report*, pp. 2.4-5.

[21]Brenner, *Gambling and Speculation*, p. 114.

[22]National Gambling Impact Study Commission, *Final Report*, p. 2.3.

[23]Ibid., p. 1.3.

[24]Public Agenda, *Gambling*, p. 8.

[25]Rogers, *Seducing America*, p. 99.

[26]National Gambling Impact Study Commission, *Final Report*, p. 2.14.

[27]Public Agenda, *Gambling*, p. 9.

[28]Rogers, *Seducing America*, p. 74.

[29]Kevin Heubush, "Taking Chances on Casinos," in *Legalized Gambling,* ed. David Bender (San Diego, Calif.: Greenhaven, 1999), p. 23.

[30]National Gambling Impact Study Commission, *Final Report*, p. 2.6.

[31]Brenner, *Gambling and Speculation*, p. 38.

[32]National Gambling Impact Study Commission, *Final Report*, p. 7.5.

[33]Clotfelter and Cook, "Economics of State Lotteries," p. 112.

[34]National Gambling Impact Study Commission, *Final Report*, p. 7.10.

[35]Ibid., p. 7.10.

[36]Public Agenda, *Gambling*, p. 15.

[37]Goodman, *Luck Business*, p. 43.

[38]Jennifer Vogel, ed., *Crapped Out: How Gambling Ruins the Economy and Destroys Lives* (Monroe, Maine: Common Courage, 1997), pp. 5, 64-65.

[39]Hurst, "Legalized Gambling," p. 84.

[40]James Dobson. *Family News*, April 1999, p. 6.

[41]Goodman, *Luck Business*, p. 84.

[42]Public Agenda, *Gambling*, p. 10.

[43]Clotfelter and Cook, "Economics of State Lotteries," pp. 104-5.

[44]Public Agenda, *Gambling*, p. 12.

[45]Rogers, *Seducing America*, p. 75.

[46]Public Agenda, *Gambling*, p. 14.

[47]Brenner, *Gambling and Speculation*, p. 52-53.

[48]Rogers, *Seducing America*, p. 68.

Chapter 13: The Naked Gorilla

[1]*Webster's New Twentieth Century Dictionary of the English Language*, 2nd ed. (New York: World Publishing, 1970).

[2]Frederick S. Lane III, *Obscene Profits: The Entrepreneurs of Pornography in the Cyber Age* (New York: Routledge, 2000), p. 8.

[3]"Religious Leaders Craft Anti-Porn Plan," *Christianity Today,* March 6, 1995, p. 58.

[4]Diana E. Russell, *Dangerous Relationships: Pornography, Misogyny, and Rape* (Thousand Oaks, Calif.: Sage, 1998), pp. 28-29.

[5]Lane, *Obscene Profits*, p. 160.

[6]Ibid., p. 62.

[7]Ibid., p. 105.

[8]Arthur J. Mielke, *Christians, Feminists, and the Culture of Pornography* (Lanham, Md.: University Press of America, 1995), p. 5.

[9]Erin McClam, "Experts Believe Cybersex Damaging Relationships," *Wilmington News Journal,* May 7, 2000, p. A14.

[10]Judith A. Reisman, *"Soft Porn" Plays Hardball: Its Tragic Effects on Women, Children and the Family* (Lafayette, La.: Huntington House, 1991), p. 141-42.

[11]Russell, *Dangerous Relationships,* p. 128.

[12]Ibid., p. 127.

[13]T. Trent Gegax, "An Odd Fall from Grace: Computer Porn Undoes a Divinity-School Dean," *Newsweek,* May 31, 1999, p. 70.

[14]This is a summary of the results of at least thirty research articles.

[15]Research by anthropologist P. R. Sanday, "The Socio-Cultural Context of Rape: A Cross-Cultural Study," *Journal of Social Issues* 37, no. 4 (1981): 5-27, as cited in Larry Baron and Murray A. Straus, "Sexual Stratification, Pornography, and Rape in the United States," in *Pornography and Sexual Aggression,* ed. Neil M. Malamuth and Edward Donnerstein (Orlando, Fla.: Academic Press, 1984), p. 186.

[16]See, for example, Nadine Strossen, *Defending Pornography: Free Speech, Sex, and the Fight for Women's Rights* (New York: Doubleday, 1996).

Chapter 14: A Matter of Life and Debt

[1]Special credit and appreciation to Marvin Rees, graduate student at Eastern College, for his research contributions to this chapter.

[2]World Bank, *2000 World Development Indicators*, table 1.1, pp. 10-12.

[3]Joseph E. Stiglitz, *Economics,* 2nd ed. (New York: W. W. Norton, 1997), p. 982.

[4]Philippe Aghion, Eve Caroli and Cecilia Garcia-Penalosa, "Inequality and Economic Growth: The Perspectives of the New Growth Theories," *Journal of Economic Literature* 37 (December 1999): 1615-60.

[5]Robert Naiman and Neil Watkins, "A Survey of the Impacts of IMF Structural Adjustment in Africa: Growth, Social Spending, and Debt Relief," paper presented at the Preamble Center, April 1999.

[6]World Bank, "Overview of Poverty Reduction Strategies," <www.worldbank.org/poverty/strategies/overview.htm>.

[7]E. Calvin Beisner, *Prosperity and Poverty: The Compassionate Use of Resources in a World of Scarcity* (Wheaton, Ill.: Crossway, 1988), pp. 63-65.

[8]Larry Burkett, *Business by the Book: The Complete Guide of Biblical Principles for Business Men and Women* (Nashville: Thomas Nelson, 1990), pp. 167-68.

[9]Stephen L. S. Smith, "Christian Ethics and the Forgiveness of Third World Debt," *Faith and Economics,* spring 2000, p. 9.

[10]Roland Hoksbergen, "That the Work of God Might Be Displayed: Debt Forgiveness and Development," *Faith and Economics,* spring 2000, p. 18.

Chapter 15: Give Me Your Tired, Your Poor . . .

[1]Michael Howell-Moroney, former graduate student at Eastern College, provided valuable research assistance in the production of this chapter. The focus of this chapter is on legitimate immigrants, not terrorists. The ideas expressed are directed towards policy regarding persons desiring to live in a country, temporarily or permanently, in order to achieve a better life. It does not attempt to address defense measures necessary to protect against terrorist activities.

[2]George J. Borjas, "Introduction," in *Issues in the Economics of Immigration,* ed. George J. Borjas (Chicago: University of Chicago Press, 2000), p. 1.

[3]Thomas Sowell, *Migrations and Cultures: A World View* (New York: BasicBooks, 1996), p. 39.

[4]George Church, "Send Back Your Tired, Your Poor . . ." *Time,* June 21, 1993, pp. 26-27.

[5]Paul Glastris and Warren Cohen, "The Alien Payoff," *U.S. News and World Report,* May 26, 1997, pp. 20-22.

[6]Pia Orrenius and Alan D. Vivard, "The Second Great Migration: Economic and Policy Implica-

tions," *Southwest Economy*, May-June 2000, p. 4.

[7]Julian R. Betts and Magnus Lofstrom, "The Educational Attainment of Immigrants: Trends and Implications," in *Issues in the Economics of Immigration*, ed. George J. Borjas (Chicago: University of Chicago Press, 2000), pp. 109-10.

[8]George Borjas, "Know the Flow," *National Review*, April 17, 1995, pp. 44-50. The perspective on education is found in Vernon Briggs, "Immigration Policy and the U.S. Economy," *Journal of Economic Issues* 30, no. 2 (1996): 370-90.

[9]"The New Americans: Economic, Demographic and Fiscal Effects of Immigration," *Wilson Quarterly* 21, no. 3 (1997): 141-42.

[10]George Borjas, quoted in David Francis, "Shedding Light on Immigration," *Christian Science Monitor*, May 21, 1997, p. 8.

[11]Yeh Ling-Ling, "U.S. Can't Handle Today's Tide of Immigrants," *Christian Science Monitor*, March 23, 1995, p. 19.

[12]Roger LeRoy Miller, *Economics Today: The Micro View*, 9th ed. (Reading, Mass.: Addison-Wesley, 1997), p. 624.

[13]Guillermina Jasso, Mark R. Rosenzweig and James P. Smith, "The Changing Skill of New Immigrants to the United States," in *Issues in the Economics of Immigration*, ed. George J. Borjas (Chicago: University of Chicago Press, 2000), p. 222.

[14]Susan B. Carter and Richard Sutch, "Historical Perspectives on the Economic Consequences of Immigration into the United States," in *The Handbook of International Migration: The American Experience*, ed. Charles Hirschman, Philip Kasinitz and Josh DeWind (New York: Russell Sage Foundation, 1999), p. 319.

[15]David Card, John DiNardo and Eugena Estes, "The More Things Change," in *Issues in the Economics of Immigration*, ed. George J. Borjas (Chicago: University of Chicago Press, 2000), p. 264.

[16]Ronald D. Lee and Timothy W. Miller, "The Current Fiscal Impact of Immigrants and Their Descendants: Beyond the Immigrant Household," in *The Immigration Debate: Studies on the Economic, Demographic, and Fiscal Effects of Immigration*, ed. James P. Smith and Barry Edmonston (Washington, D.C.: National Academy Press, 1998), p. 200.

[17]Barry Chiswick, "Immigration Policy for a Post-Industrial Economy," *American Enterprise* 6, no. 2 (1995): 46-50.

[18]Peter Andreas, "Borderless Economy, Barricaded Border," NCLA *Report on the Americas* 33, no. 3 (1999): 14-25.

[19]Andrew M. Yuengert, "Catholic Social Teaching on the Economics of Immigration," *Journal of Markets and Morality* 3, no. 1 (2000): 88.

Chapter 16: The Malthusian Blues

[1]Donella Meadows and Dennis Meadows, eds., *The Limits to Growth: A Report for the Club of Rome's Project on the Predicament of Mankind* (Cambridge, Mass.: Wright-Allen, 1973).

[2]Paul R. Ehrlich, *The Population Bomb* (New York: Ballantine Books, 1968).

[3]J.W. Forrester, *Urban Dynamics* (Cambridge, Mass.: MIT Press, 1969).

[4]Julian Simon, "Apocalypse in Rio: The End of the World As We Know It?" *Cato Policy Report*, July 1998, p. 7.

[5]Gerald M. Meier and James E. Rauch, *Leading Issues in Economic Development*, 7th ed. (New York: Oxford University Press, 2000), p. 241.

[6]David C. Colander, *Economics*, 4th ed. (Boston: McGraw-Hill, 2001), p. 549.

[7]Ronald J. Sider, *Rich Christians in an Age of Hunger: Moving from Affluence to Generosity* (Dallas, Tex.: Word, 1997), pp. 14-17.

[8]World Bank, *2000 World Development Indicators*, table 2.2, p. 44.

[9]Ibid., table 2.1, pp. 38-40.

[10]Susan Power Bratton, *Six Billion and More: Human Population and Regulation & Christian Ethics* (Louisville, Ky.: Westminister John Knox, 1992), p. 136.

[11]Mother Teresa, *Loving Jesus* (Ann Arbor, Mich.: Servant, 1991), p. 29.

[12]Bratton, *Six Billion and More*, pp. 42-43.

[13]Ibid., p. 198.

[14]Some Christians make a sound case that, aside from natural family planning, just about all the procedures we call contraception are abortifacient most or some of the time, including the IUD, the morning-after pill and the birth control pill. Marriage is a sacrament that may lead to the creation of a new life made in the image of God. Such contraceptives thus subordinate the God-bestowed life-giving commitment of faithful marriage. This view of a "contraceptive ethos" otherwise encompasses abstinence outside of marriage, natural family planning and trust of God's will within marriage.

[15]"Preventing Childhood Blindness in Africa with Sweet Potatoes: Root Crop on a Mission to Remote Areas," *World Bank Issues and Viewpoints*, July 20, 2000.